OXFORD MODERN
AND LITERATURE MONOGRAPHS

THE POET AND
THE MYSTIC

*A Study of the Cántico
Espiritual of San
Juan de la Cruz*

BY

COLIN P. THOMPSON

OXFORD UNIVERSITY PRESS
1977

Oxford University Press, Walton Street, Oxford OX2 6DP

OXFORD LONDON GLASGOW NEW YORK
TORONTO MELBOURNE WELLINGTON CAPE TOWN
IBADAN NAIROBI DAR ES SALAAM LUSAKA ADDIS ABABA
KUALA LUMPUR SINGAPORE JAKARTA HONG KONG TOKYO
DELHI BOMBAY CALCUTTA MADRAS KARACHI

British Library Cataloguing in Publication Data

Thompson, Colin P
    The poet and the mystic. – (Oxford modern
    languages and literature monographs).
    1. John of the Cross, *Saint*. Cántico espiritual
    I. Title   II. Series
    861'.3   PQ6400.J8C/

ISBN 0-19-815531-X

*Set by Hope Services, Wantage
and printed in Great Britain by
Billing & Sons Ltd
Guildford, London and Worcester*

to
MY MOTHER AND FATHER

ACKNOWLEDGEMENTS

It is a pleasure to record, as this shortened and revised version of my doctoral thesis presented in the University of Oxford comes to be published, my deep appreciation of all those who have helped me over the years in which it has been developing. First, to Mr. E. H. Cunningham of the Royal Grammar School, Colchester, who introduced me to the literature of the Spanish Golden Age; and to my late and much missed tutor in Oxford, Cyril Jones, to whom I owe so much. I am especially grateful to those who have encouraged me in my studies in the Spanish mystics; for the help given to me by Dr. A. J. Kenny and the Revd. Dr. V. A. Demant in the philosophical and theological aspects of my quest; for the encouragement and advice of Dr. R. W. Truman and Professor E. M. Wilson; for the friends I have made in the Discalced Carmelite Order, and especially for the deep knowledge of its history and founders which Fr. Bede Edwards has so generously shared with me; and for the guidance and inspiration of Professor P. E. Russell, who supervised my thesis for most of the time, and whose enthusiasm for my work gave me energy to continue when my spirits were flagging. And I am also indebted to Christ Church, Oxford, for having given me the time and the environment for completing my revision.

It is my hope that this book will help its readers to appreciate a little more keenly the marvellous poetry and spirituality of San Juan de la Cruz. And, as a Protestant clergyman venturing into Roman Catholic history, I would like to think that it may also contribute to the ecumenical spirit which is allowing us to learn from one another's traditions and become aware of our fundamental unity.

Ash Wednesday, 1976   COLIN THOMPSON

CONTENTS

ABBREVIATIONS AND REFERENCES

I. PERIODICALS

BH	*Bulletin hispanique*
BHR	*Bibliothèque d'humanisme et renaissance*
BHS	*Bulletin of Hispanic Studies*
EC	*Ephemerides Carmeliticae*
HR	*Hispanic Review*
MC	*El Monte Carmelo*
MLR	*Modern Language Review*
NRFE	*Nueva revista de filología española*
RE	*Revista de espiritualidad*
RFE	*Revista de filología española*
RFH	*Revista de filología hispánica*
RL	*Revista de literatura*
VS	*La Vie spirituelle*

II. SERIES

BAC	Biblioteca de autores cristianos
BAE	Biblioteca de autores españoles
BMC	Biblioteca de mística carmelitana
CC	Clásicos castellanos
LCC	Library of Christian Classics
NBAE	Nueva biblioteca de autores españoles

III. WORKS OF SAN JUAN

CA	*Cántico espiritual* (first redaction)
CB	*Cántico espiritual* (second redaction)
L	*Llama de amor viva*
N	*Noche oscura*
S	*Subida del Monte Carmelo*

IV. OTHERS

BN	Bibliothèque Nationale de Paris
BNM	Biblioteca Nacional de Madrid
CUP	Cambridge University Press
IUP	Irish University Press
OUP	Oxford University Press
MUP	Manchester University Press
SCM	Student Christian Movement Press

Spelling of quotations from San Juan's poems and commentaries follows the BAC 6th edn. (Madrid, 1972), in which the spelling of CB is modernized but CA is not. This is not a satisfactory solution, but until the BAC editions adopt a consistent policy it must be followed. The non-Spanish-speaking reader is referred to the translations of E. Allison Peers, 3 vols. (London, 1953), where knowledge of the text is important for the argument; and to the English version of the *Cántico* in the Appendix, which, like the translations without acknowledgement in the text, is my own.

I

SAN JUAN AND THE MYSTICAL TRADITION

Men celebrated by later generations normally achieve fame through their contribution to a particular area of human endeavour. San Juan de la Cruz (1542–91) achieved greatness on two counts: in the realm of spirituality, as a mystic; and in literature, as a poet. He stands at a high peak in the mystical tradition of the Christian West, the Mystical Doctor of the Roman Catholic Church; and he is regarded as among the greatest lyrical poets Spain has ever produced. If we want to explore and to understand his work, then both sides of his achievement must be recognized and studied, however difficult this proves to be. Otherwise, the picture will be incomplete. With one or two exceptions, however, this has not been done, and men of letters have praised the poems while theologians have concentrated on the spiritual teaching of the prose works.[1] Such a division, though understandable, can only be acceptable if the two sides are unconnected. But the prose commentaries, in which San Juan concentrated on his task as a theologian of the spiritual life, grew for him out of the handful of poems which have impressed themselves so vividly upon generations of readers, and through which his gifts as a shaper of language so beautifully shine. It is the aim of this book to examine both areas of San Juan's contribution to Western civilization, in themselves and in relation to each other, in order to reach a truer measure of his stature; and if, in doing this, a rather different picture of San Juan the poet and theologian emerges from the one most commonly held, that aim will have been fulfilled.

San Juan the man eludes us. This is not the place to write his biography; such may easily be found elsewhere.[2] But there could scarcely be a stronger contrast than with the lively and forceful personality revealed by the other great representative of sixteenth-century Spanish mysticism, Santa Teresa de Avila (1515–82), in her works. She herself chose San Juan to assist her in the task of reforming the Carmelite Order,

---

[1] The most notable exception is Crisógono de Jesús, *San Juan de la Cruz, su obra científica y su obra literaria* (Ávila, 1929).
[2] e.g. Crisógono de Jesús, in *Vida y obras de San Juan de la Cruz*, 6th edn. (Madrid, BAC, 1972); and Gerald Brenan, *St. John of the Cross: His Life and Poetry* (Cambridge, 1973).

by returning to a strict observance of the long-mitigated primitive rule.[3] Perhaps it is just as well that he could not compete with her energy and vitality! Because of his self-effacing nature, it is sometimes hard to imagine San Juan as a child of his time, and when his work is compared with that of contemporary poets like Fray Luis de León (1527–91) and Fernando de Herrera (1534–97), the difficulty grows. He is so unlike them. And the temptation grows to treat him as a wholly exceptional being who, because of the loftiness of his experience, is quite unconnected with the world of theological debate and literary values around him.

While this could be true, it might equally be the case that we consider San Juan so exceptional because our understanding of the sixteenth century in Spain, particularly with regard to the religious literature then produced, is deficient. In order to correct any such deficiency, San Juan's indebtedness to the theological and mystical literature and tradition of the West must be considered; and he will then appear not as an isolated phenomenon but as a culminating point in an ancient and influential tradition which has left its mark on the literature of the Golden Age.

Little is known of the formative years of San Juan. From 1559 to 1563 the young Juan de Yepes studied at the Jesuit college in Medina del Campo, founded only eight years earlier. There he must have studied Greek, Latin and Rhetoric.[4] The texts used by Juan Bonifacio to illustrate his Latin and Rhetoric classes there are known and provide a useful insight into the kind of education Juan must have received:

Me presto sin dificultad . . . a leer a Valerio Máximo, a Suetonio, a Aliciato; declaro algunos pasajes de Amiano Marcelino, de Plinio, de Pomponio Mela; traduzco algunos trozos difíciles del Breviario y algunos himnos eclesiásticos, el Catecismo, las cartas de San Jerónimo y el Concilio Tridentino. A mis discípulos ordinarios les leo Cicerón, Virgilio y alguna vez las tragedias de Séneca; Horacio y Marcial expurgados, César, Salustio, Livio y Curcio, para que tengan ejemplos y modelos de todo: de oraciones, de poesía y de historia.[5]

P. Crisógono concludes:

En el Colegio de la Compañía se cursan humanidades con la perfección, amplitud y competencia que en las mejores universidades españolas . . . A estos años hay, pues, que referir, indudablemente, el primer contacto–el primero y quizá el más fuerte–del futuro autor del *Cántico espiritual* con los clásicos latinos y españoles y la iniciación en sus preferencias renacentistas.[6]

---

[3]   Santa Teresa herself writes at length of their work in her *Libro de las fundaciones*, in *Obras completas,* 2nd edn. (Madrid, 1967), pp. 516–628.

[4]   See Crisógono, *Vida*, pp. 38–40.

[5]   Olmedo, *Juan Bonifacio* (Santander, 1938), p. 54.

[6]   *Vida*, p. 40.

This sounds overstated; but these formative years must have left their mark on Juan, and they represent the only period of his life when he was open to various secular influences. From the time he left Medina for Salamanca, already a Carmelite novice, his life was one of self-discipline and renunciation, and one must suppose that his exposure to secular literature would have been minimal.

From 1564–1568 Suan Juan studied at the Colegio de San Andrés, the Carmelite college in Salamanca, and at the university received a thorough grounding in philosophy and theology. Salamanca was reaching the height of its fame as the prime university of Spain and could boast of a glittering array of scholars. Bound by the discipline of his Order, San Juan can scarcely have plunged into the rough-and-tumble of student life or have been an active participant in the lively and some-times violent debates; though he must have seen something of the rivalry between the Orders, and especially the Dominicans and Augustinians. As Jedin has observed, during and after the Council of Trent a regener-ated scholasticism took the lead in Spanish theology, under such men as Domingo Soto, Melchor Cano, and Francisco de Vitoria.[7] At the Colegio de San Andrés, the dominant theology was scholastic but not pure Thomism. Instead, it was a Thomism interpreted through the fourteenth-century Carmelite Doctors, Baconthorpe and Bologna. The Chapter General of the Order had prescribed them for study in 1548, so that when San Juan arrived in Salamanca there was already a school of Carmelite Thomism. P. Crisógono isolated seven theological principles in San Juan, and in only one does he depart from Aquinas, by following Augustine and making memory into a third faculty, alongside under-standing and will.[8]

Apart from the evidence that can be gleaned from references in his works, we have very little further indication of the intellectual formation of San Juan. Fray Juan Evangelista, his secretary for many years, testified:

Era muy amigo de leer en la Sagrada Escritura, y así nunca jamás le vide leer otro libro sino la Biblia (la cual sabía casi toda de memoria), y en un S. Agustín *contra haereses*, y en el *Flos sanctorum*; y cuando predicaba alguna vez, que fueron pocas, o hacía pláticas, que era de ordinario, nunca leía otro libro sino la Biblia.[9]

[7] Jedin, *A History of the Council of Trent*, 2 vols. (London, 1957–), i, 399–400.

[8] See, e.g., Augustine's *De Trinitate* x.17, xiv.13–15 (LCC VIII. 87, 112–14). The threefold pattern dictates San Juan's scheme in the *Subida*, Book 3, where chs. 1–15 deal with memory, 16–45 with will, and the rest, had they been written, would have involved the understanding. For the seven principles, see Crisógono, *San Juan*, I.iii; and for studies of San Juan's teaching on memory and hope, Efrén de la Madre de Dios, 'La esperanza según San Juan de la Cruz', *RE* 1 (1941–2), 255–81; and André Bord, *Mémoire et espérance chez Jean de la Croix* (Paris, 1971).

[9] In his 'Relación acerca de la vida del santo' (BMC XIII.386).

Since, with the exception of one or two juvenile works long vanished, the writings of San Juan belong to the late 1570s and the 1580s, when he had been following the way of withdrawal and renunciation for many years, his literary activity coincides with this rather restricted diet of reading. This is perhaps one of the reasons why San Juan is so unlike contemporary writers, who, even when they are friars, like Luis de León, draw on considerable sources of learning, sacred and secular.

We are thus forced to look elsewhere for clues towards understanding the environment which helped to shape the outlook and techniques of San Juan. Fortunately, we do not have to look far. In the prologue to the *Cántico* which San Juan addressed to M. Ana de Jesús, prioress of the Discalced nuns in Granada, is this statement:

y así espero que, aunque se escriban aquí algunos [puntos] de teología escolástica cerca de el trato interior del alma con su Dios, no será en vano haber hablado algo a lo puro de el espíritu en tal manera, pues, aunque a V. R. le falte el ejercicio de teología escolástica con que se entienden las verdades divinas, no le falta el de la mística, que se sabe por amor en que, no solamente se saben, mas juntamente se gustan.[10]

Although M. Ana is ignorant of scholastic theology, she is none the less well versed in mystical theology, in which divine truths are not only understood but experienced through love.

The contrast between scholastic and mystical theology, between a theology accessible only to the specialist and a theology which could be learnt through religious experience by anyone, was nothing new. It is very much present in the Erasmian writers of the earlier sixteenth century—in Erasmus himself, Alfonso de Valdés, the *Viaje de Turquía*. It crops up later in Luis de León, who speaks in the *Nombres de Cristo* with contempt of those who 'con un pequeño gusto de ciertas cuestiones contentos e hinchados, tienen títulos de maestros teólogos y no tienen la teología', because of their disregard for Scripture. 'Mystical theology' is not the theological analysis of mysticism but experience of the mystical encounter itself. When Juan de Valdés makes a distinction between 'ciencia' and 'sabiduría', he claims the former is given to preachers and teachers whereas the latter, 'que es sciencia sabrosa, es para conoscer, gustar y sentir a Dios' and may be given 'a una viejezica y a un idiota y niégala a un letradazo'.[11] San Juan uses the same expression in CA 18: 'Allí me enseñó sciencia muy sabrosa', and links this in the commentary specifically to mystical theology.

[10] Prologue, 1.3.
[11] *Diálogo de doctrina christiana*, ed. Ricart (Mexico, 1964). Other references in this paragraph are to *Colloquios de Erasmo*, NBAE, *Orígenes de la Novela* iv (Madrid, 1915), 156; A. de Valdés, *Diálogo de Mercurio y Carón*, CC (Madrid, 1965), pp. 125, 208; *Viaje de Turquía*, attrib. Villalón, ed. Solalinde (Madrid, 1942), pp. 115, 161–3; Luis de León, *De los nombres de Cristo*, 3 vols., CC (Madrid, 1948), i.9.

This is not to make an Erasmian of San Juan, though in the third book of the *Subida* (chs. 27–45) he clearly attacks those who depend too much on exterior forms and ceremonies—fasting, pilgrimages, images—and states that 'la persona devota de veras, en lo interior pone su devoción . . . porque la viva imagen busca dentro de sí, que es Cristo crucificado' (35.5). The introspection taught by San Juan is of a very different kind from the interior religion praised by Erasmus. But the underlying protest is perhaps the same: a protest against a religion which ties itself up in dogmatic niceties or external observances, and has nothing to offer to the deeper, inner needs of man. Mysticism, in seeking to supply those needs, is also a protest against a sterile religion.[12] But this is a constant of Christian experience and not simply a sixteenth-century phenomenon, as we shall see. The thread of the authentic spiritual protest against a mechanical or over-institutional religion is already present in the New Testament; in the later Middle Ages it can be traced in Hus, Wyclif, and the Lollards, Geert Groote and the Brethren of the Common Life, the *devotio moderna,* the Rhineland mystics, even the esoteric neo-Platonism of Ficino and Pico. And in the sixteenth century the thread can likewise be traced in a variety of forms—Erasmus, Luther, Calvin and the more radical forms of Protestantism, and within Spain in the reforming work of Cardinal Cisneros, the puzzling phenomenon of illuminism, the enthusiasm for Erasmian spirituality, and in the growing numbers of works of a more definitely mystical bent.[13]

Thus the tension between scholastic and mystical theology which we have begun to discern belongs to a much wider tension characteristic of the Christian religion over the centuries. It may further be seen in the works of two influential writers on spirituality who belonged to the generation before Santa Teresa and San Juan: Francisco de Osuna and Bernardino de Laredo. Osuna states that mystical theology, 'aunque sea suprema y perfectísima noticia puede empero ser habido de cualquier fiel, aunque sea mugercila e idiota'; while Laredo writes of it: 'Y hase de notar que no hay ningún pobrecito, ni varón, ni mujercita si quisiere ser su discípulo, que no la pueda aprender.' He also refers to 'las letras interiores, las cuales declaren muy bien los muy simples pobrecitos

[12] This idea will be taken up in Ch. 7. It has been noted by Tillich (see p. 149 below) and by H. R. Trevor-Roper, *Historical Essays* (London, 1957), p. 37; while Ozment, *Mysticism and Dissent* (New Haven and London, 1973), demonstrates the influence of the medieval Catholic mystics on the most revolutionary of the Protestant groups.

[13] The illuminists (*alumbrados*) are relatively little understood but seem to have consisted of groups with little in common except the suspicion of the orthodox. See Fr. Román de la Inmaculada, 'El fenómeno de los alumbrados y su interpretación', *EC* 9 (1958), 49–80; and Márquez, *Los alumbrados: orígenes y filosofía 1525–1559* (Madrid, 1972).

cebados en la experiencia de mística teología'.[14] Both seem anxious to stress that whatever intellectual skills are needed for formal, systematic theology, mystical theology is open to the uneducated, the poor, even women!

But this is no new theme. Rather it is the recovery of a current of Christian experience which had rarely been absent from the Western Church, though equally rarely predominant. Richard Rolle (c. 1300–49), in his *Fire of Love*, makes the same points. In his prologue he writes: 'I offer this book for the attention, not of the philosophers and sages of this world, not of the great theologians bogged down in their interminable questionings, but of the simple and unlearned, who are seeking rather to love God than amass knowledge'; and, later: 'An old woman can be more expert in the love of God ... than your theologian with his useless studying.'[15] Rolle may be more anti-intellectual than other medieval mystics, but the link with later writers is unmistakable. Set against this background, San Juan's remarks in his prologue are very illuminating and acquire an unsuspected significance. He is echoing, as are Osuna and Laredo, an idea deep-rooted in the mystical tradition of the Western Church. And it is to that tradition that we must look before anything else if we are to understand the sources of the fountain from which he sprang.

Dom Cuthbert Butler has outlined the characteristics of Western mysticism as expressed by Augustine, Cassian, Gregory, and Bernard.[16] The large body of literature deriving from them and their followers stressed light and fulness, not darkness and emptiness; it is pre-scholastic, in that it presents no systematic teaching; it is largely unconcerned with visions, locutions, and revelations and gives rise to few psychosomatic phenomena; and it lays no emphasis on the intervention of the Devil. Butler terms it 'a mysticism purely and solely religious and empirical'.[17] At first sight, San Juan seems to represent something different, for he writes of darkness, emptiness, visions and other phenomena, the ruses of the devil, and uses scholastic terminology. But, as Butler himself indicates, new currents of spirituality after Bernard marked the tradition profoundly, and it is the tradition as it developed during the Middle Ages which provides a rich digging-ground for the origins of many aspects of San Juan's literature and teaching.

Two problems arise at once. First, San Juan inherited a different attitude towards the past from ours. The past did not merely provide source material, but authority. As Aumann points out, 'the canonized

---

[14] Osuna, *Tercer Abecedario*, 12.5; Laredo, *Subida del Monte Sión*, 3.15, 41.
[15] Rolle, *The Fire of Love*, trans. Wolters (Penguin Classics), pp. 46, 61.
[16] Butler, *Western Mysticism*, 3rd edn., with 'Afterthoughts' (London, 1967).
[17] Op. cit., p. 128.

texts of some author ruled the approach to given problems.'[18] The
Church acknowledged certain writers as authoritative and they could
be appealed to in order to test new ideas or questionable claims. They
were the established bearers of truth, because, as San Juan himself
implies in his prologues, experience needed to be interpreted by wisdom
beyond that of the individual. Thus he submits all he writes to the
judgement of the Church, and especially to the authority of Scripture
as interpreted by the Church. Second, San Juan's world scarcely shared
the modern insistence on accurate texts and critical scholarship. When
San Juan quotes from Boethius or Gregory he has not necessarily read
them in the original, but rather in medieval compilations or selections
of their works, inaccurate by modern standards; or he may be quoting
from memory. He accepts as authentic works now held as spurious,
like the *Soliloquia* attributed to Augustine, the opuscule *de Beatitudine*
to Aquinas, and the works of Dionysius, then believed to be the disciple
of Paul mentioned in Acts 17:34 and hence with an immense authority,
closer to the teaching of Jesus than any of the Fathers.[19] So instead of
historical scholarship, textual accuracy, and a healthy scepticism with
regard to the received wisdom, we find a world which sets high store by
a tradition handed down through the centuries and mediated through
corrupt texts. San Juan accepted the authorities of his age as readily as
most people of ours accept the verdicts of experts.

The roots of the Western mystical tradition go very deep. Its great
figures drew freely from older sources—Plotinus, Aristotle, Plato—and
thus it has some claim to be regarded as a link in the unbroken chain of
Western civilization which Curtius has revealed.[20] But it was constantly
being modified, as new authors acquired an authoritative status. The
discovery of Dionysius in the West profoundly altered the direction of
this tradition.[21] From the Lateran Council of 649 he had been regarded
as an authority, though his work remained unknown in the West long
after. Around 830 Hilduin, Abbot of St. Denis, made a Latin translation
of Dionysius at the behest of the Byzantine Emperor; but it was not till
some forty years later, when Charles the Bald ordered a retranslation,
undertaken by John Scotus Erigena, that his influence began to be felt.
Aquinas knew him through this translation, and 'through the mediating
influence of such men as Hilduin, John Scotus . . . and Hugh of St.

---

[18] *St. Thomas Aquinas: Summa Theologiae,* ed. Gilby and O'Brien, 60 vols.
(London and New York, 1964–); in vol. 46, 'Action and Contemplation', ed.
Aumann, p. 4, fn. 7. All references to the *Summa* are from this edition.

[19] See S 1.5.1, N 1.12.5, CB 1.6, 4.1; CB 38.4; S 2.8.6, N 2.5.3, CB 14–15.16
for the appropriate references. For the reverence in which Dionysius (often called
the pseudo-Dionysius) was held, see the last two lines of the quotation in Ch. 2,
p. 24.

[20] Curtius, *European Literature and the Latin Middle Ages* (London, 1953).

[21] The most convenient text is de Gandillac, *Oeuvres complètes* (Paris, 1943).

Victor, he entered the mystical tradition of the later Victorines, Bonaventure, the Rhenish mystics, Cusa, Ruysbroeck, and the *German Theology*'.[22] To the positive way, approaching the light and fulness of God through his attributes, Dionysius added the *via negativa*, maintaining that no human words or concepts could adequately describe God, and that the closer man approached him, the deeper the darkness he encountered: 'Unto this Darkness which is beyond light we pray that we may come, and may attain unto vision through loss of sight and knowledge, and that in ceasing thus to see or to know we may learn to know that which is beyond all perception and understanding (for this emptying of our faculties is true sight and knowledge).'[23] The influence of this 'mystical theology' in its concepts and its language of paradox was to be crucial in determining the future course of the tradition. Famous examples may be seen in the anonymous English work, *The Cloud of Unknowing*,[24] Nicholas of Cusa's paradoxical 'docta ignorantia',[25] and Walter Hilton's 'luminous darkness' and 'fruitful nothing'.[26] The discovery of Dionysius brought from the East a dark and mysterious language for the mystic to explore in his search for words to describe the ineffable.

When San Juan quotes Dionysius he does little more than reiterate the expression 'mística teología' or speak of the 'tinieblas'.[27] But behind his fundamental idea that a man must negate his desires, will and intellect in order to approach God, and travel instead a road of darkness, lies the unmistakable substratum of Dionysian theology. To him may therefore ultimately be traced San Juan's central symbol, the 'noche oscura', though San Juan develops it further. His dark night is an intimate personal experience compounded of many features, whereas Dionysius is concerned primarily with the metaphysical gulf which lies between the human and the divine.

Writers on San Juan's background have pointed to a whole host of authors said to have influenced him apart from Dionysius. Simeón de la Sagrada Familia has listed no fewer than fifty-four.[28] Among these are Augustine, Gregory, Bernard, the Victorines, the Rhineland mystics, Aquinas, and the Carmelite Doctors Baconthorpe and Bologna, Bonaventure, Llull, Osuna, Laredo, Santa Teresa, Luis de León. It is an impressive list—but it needs to be treated with caution. It is usually impossible to locate his sources precisely, because he is indebted to the

---

[22] *Late Medieval Mysticism*, ed. Petry, LCC XIII.33.
[23] Quoted by Payne, *The Holy Fire* (London, 1958), p. 276.
[24] Trans. Wolters, Penguin Classics (Harmondsworth, 1961).
[25] See LCC XIII. 354, 363.
[26] Hilton, *The Scale of Perfection*, trans. Sitwell (London, 1953), pp. 203–9.
[27] S 2.8.6, N 2.5.3, CB 14–15.16, L 3.49.
[28] In 'Fuentes doctrinales y literarias de San Juan de la Cruz', *MC* 69 (1961), 103–9.

accumulated tradition rather than to specific authors. Robert Ricard, discussing the alleged influence of Laredo on San Juan's 'Fonte' poem, writes: 'Plus on pratique les écrits spirituels, plus on s'aperçoit que cette immense littérature repose sur des traditions diffuses dont les éléments, parfois très anciens, sont d'autant plus difficiles à isoler et à suivre dans leur destinée historique que leur transmission s'est faite en très grande partie de façon orale.'[29] And Ruíz Salvador repeats the warning: 'Los autores más ponderados o sus críticos terminan siempre reduciendo los hallazgos a proporciones de conjetura y probabilidad; semejanza, pero no sabemos si dependencia; dependencia, pero no sabemos si directa, o a través de fuentes intermedias, o a través de la mentalidad corriente.'[30]

This is borne out by the way in which San Juan uses the tradition. He does quote specific authors (Boethius, Dionysius, Gregory, Augustine, Francis, Bernard, Aquinas), but only in isolated phrases, giving a tag as an authority. More often he refers to 'los filósofos' or 'los teólogos', that is, to the authoritative tradition in general. Chasing after exact sources may thus be counter-productive.

It is such considerations which prompt the method of this chapter. It is the developing tradition, rather than individual authors, which needs to be appreciated. And the best way of doing this is to look at the main themes of medieval mysticism which San Juan inherits, as they are contained in a representative selection of its literature. Some of these works we have already encountered; others will be added. The themes to be examined are fundamental to the tradition and to San Juan. An exhaustive list of examples would be pointless, because there are far too many; but anyone can add to the few given here by further reading of the authors mentioned.

The division of the spiritual life into three ways, made in the 'argumento' added to the second redaction of the Cántico, is a very ancient one, already present in Origen and Dionysius.[31] 'This classification antedates Christian contemplation. It is often suggested, and sometimes explicitly stated, in Platonic and neo-Platonic thought . . . It is well to be forewarned, however, that an infinite variety of gradations are interlocked with such relatively simple classifications of the mystic ascent or development', writes Petry.[32] The ways of purgation, illumination, and union, for beginners, proficients, and the perfect, were standard divisions which San Juan could hardly have ignored. He uses some of the other gradations, not in opposition to the threefold way, but seeing the mystical journey from another perspective. Such are the seven

---

[29] 'La Fonte de Saint Jean de la Croix et un chapître de Laredo', BH 58 (1956), 271.

[30] Introducción a San Juan de la Cruz (Madrid, 1968), p. 90.

[31] For Origen's important contributions to the growth of the mystical tradition see Daniélou, Origen, trans. Mitchell (London and New York, 1955), pp. 293–314.

[32] LCC XIII. 21.

degrees of love (CB 26.3), used by Augustine, Bernard, and the Victorines, and 'los diez grados de la escala mística de amor divino según San Bernardo y Santo Tomás' (N 2.19–20).[33] To these he adds his own analysis through the dark nights, active and passive, of sense and spirit, original, though with many traditional elements. Always, it is the same fund of experience being studied, only from different viewpoints. Ancient, too, is the distinction between active and contemplative lives. Time after time mystical writers stress the superiority of the latter, usually under the types of Mary, who chose the better part over Martha, and Rachel, for whom Jacob served seven years, having already served seven for the less comely Leah. Origen, Augustine, Gregory, and Bernard allegorize the stories in this way and it is repeated in medieval treatises and occurs in Osuna and Laredo. The argument is followed by San Juan: the contemplative life is superior because it concentrates undistractedly on God.

One of the most insistent calls echoing through the whole tradition is the renunciation of self and every created thing for God. Its roots lie in pre-Christian antiquity and it occurs in other faiths.[34] There are endless variations on the theme, but the principle behind it is unchanging. God is All, the creatures nothing; and only God can satisfy man's hunger for his Creator. Bonaventure links this with the Dionysian paradox: 'Forgetting all created things and liberated from them thou shalt rise above thyself and beyond all creation to find thyself within the shaft of light that flashes out from the divine, mysterious darkness.'[35] The Imitation of Christ sums up the idea: 'A man must rise above all created things, and perfectly forsaking himself, see clearly that nothing in creation can compare with the Creator. But unless a man is freed from dependence on creatures, he cannot turn freely to the things of God.'[36]

Several things are associated with this renunciation and reappear in San Juan. The flesh is a prison in which the soul is bound, and must be subjugated to the spirit.[37] Pride must be conquered, humility won: medieval treatises consistently praise humility as the highest of the virtues. To practise detachment, the soul must seek quiet and solitude, withdrawing not only from the commerce of men but also from physical and mental activity. Ruysbroeck speaks of the need for 'true peace, inward silence, and loving adherence if a man would have fruition of

---

[33] In his edition of St. Bernard on the Love of God (London etc., 1915), Gardner says the ten degrees are wrongly attributed to Bernard (p. 21).

[34] See Zaehner, Mysticism Sacred and Profane (Oxford, 1961), p. 149, quoting the same idea from the Sufis.

[35] LCC XIII. 141.

[36] Trans. Sherley Price, Penguin Classics, 3.31.

[37] Fire of Love, pp. 154–8; LCC XIII. 88 (Hugh of St. Victor).

God';[38] Chapter Five of *De institutione primorum monachorum* urges the monk to 'flee from familiarity with crowds' and 'mourn in solitude for your own sins and the sins of others'.[39]

Though the soul may be criticized now for inactivity, the mystic knows he is not 'doing nothing' and must not be hindered from progress by useless activity.[40] For contemplation is a gift infused by God, and the soul must wait passively until he deigns to grant it. 'It is not within man's power to achieve it, and however great his efforts they will be inadequate. But God is generous, and it is granted to those who truly love him.'[41] Meister Eckhart explains the reason by linking the need for quiet to the gift of contemplation: 'If a person is quite unoccupied, and his mind is stilled, God undertakes its work.'[42]

As the soul draws nearer to God, she becomes more aware of the darkness which surrounds him. At this point the Dionysian language comes into its own. Because God transcends the light of human understanding man must tread the path of faith through the darkness to him. But from time to time, rays of light and sudden raptures will flash upon the soul: 'He may . . . send out a shaft of spiritual light, which pierces this cloud of unknowing between you, and shows you some of his secrets.'[43] At other times, the soul feels oppressed, as though God has abandoned her. Hilton suggests that it seems as if grace is partially withdrawn. Then the soul must persevere till God grants her renewed contemplation. The Devil may also attack the soul's defences.[44] What is required above all is a 'simple, single gaze', 'loving adherence', and a 'naked intention': terms very reminiscent of San Juan's 'advertencia amorosa' and 'desnudez'.[45] Thus ideas which seemed alien to the characteristics of Western mysticism as outlined by Butler—particularly the language of darkness and the stress on demonic interference—are introduced into the tradition and received and used by San Juan.

The experience of union with God is the end of the mystical journey. Zaehner has shown that there are many kinds of such union, not always religious, though the two main forms are monistic and theistic. In monistic union the self is merged into the One and loses its identity; in theistic union, personal identity is retained, but the soul is transformed

[38] LCC XIII. 318.

[39] I am indebted to Fr. Bede Edwards for use of his unpublished translation of this work, which first appeared in 1370 and was studied by every Carmelite novice from that date till beyond the time of Santa Teresa and San Juan.

[40] Zaehner notes the danger of quietism in such attitudes and shows how Ruysbroeck and Suso both attacked its extreme exponents (op. cit., pp. 170–4).

[41] *Fire*, p. 153. 'Contemplation' is the old word for the specifically mystical encounter, which can only be God-given.

[42] LCC XIII. 180.

[43] *Cloud*, p. 87.

[44] Ibid., pp. 105–6, 114–17.

[45] LCC XIII. 317–18; *Cloud*, pp. 61, 84.

in union with God. Orthodox Christian mysticism must be theistic, so that the metaphysical distinction between creature and Creator is maintained, however intimate the union. Clement of Alexandria (2nd century) and Origen (3rd century) are both early witnesses to the Christian tradition, with roots in Greek philosophy but under the discipline of Christian revelation. Origen was the first writer to interpret the union symbolized in the Song of Songs between Bride and Bridegroom as between the Word of God (the Logos) and the individual soul— an interpretation which was to become immensely influential.[46] 'Transformation' is the commonest description of what happens in union. The term is open to monistic misinterpretation, but the tradition makes it clear that transformation does not involve the dissolution of the individual's identity, and San Juan is to be understood in the context of the tradition. Zaehner demonstrates this clearly, quoting a passage from Suso's *Little Book of Truth* which concludes: 'If anything remained in man, and was not entirely poured out of him, then the Scripture could not be true that says: God is to become all things to all things. Nevertheless, his [the faithful servant's] being remains, though in a different form, in a different glory, and in a different power.' After issuing forth from God, each creature has its own separate essence which it will retain: 'the stone is not God, and God is not the stone, although the stone and all creatures are what they are through Him.'[47] Suso is a valuable witness, because he was a pupil of the near-monist Meister Eckhart, yet also a *beatus* of the Roman Catholic Church.[48] Here, then, is a clear example of how lack of awareness of the medieval mystical tradition can lead to an erroneous interpretation of San Juan's language of union and make him into a monist.

Another element in the description of divine union is that no height reached in this life can compare with the bliss of the beatific vision after death. 'There is a great difference between the brightness of the saints and the highest brightness . . . to which we may attain in this life', writes Ruysbroeck.[49] Beyond this life, therefore, lies a realm of experience unreached by the soul in the mortal body. The last five stanzas of CB relate to this final vision of God, so that the author of CB is only including in his teaching another element from the tradition.[50] This also stresses the ineffability of union, which William James has seen as

---

[46] Philo of Alexandria had identified the Bridegroom with God and the Bride with his chosen people, Israel. Early Christian exegetes tended to see Christ as the Bridegroom and the new people of God, the Church, as the Bride, following Revelation 21–2.

[47] Zaehner, op. cit., pp. 21, 190.

[48] Twenty-eight propositions from Meister Eckart's writings were condemned soon after his death, by Pope John XXII in 1329.

[49] LCC XIII. 314.

[50] For the implications of this for the authenticity of CB, see Ch. 3, pp. 43–5.

a characteristic of mystical experience, present in Christian writers from Paul onwards (II Corinthians 13:4).[51] Even if secret knowledge is vouchsafed in union, it cannot be reduced to language and communicated to others. 'So mysterious and sublime is this experience', writes Bonaventure, 'that none save he to whom it has been given knows anything of it.'[52]

We have already remarked on the way in which the mystical tradition of the Middle Ages took into itself elements which were unknown to its earlier elaborators. Most of the examples quoted so far have raised theological problems. It is quite clear from any reading of San Juan's prose that for him these are to be envisaged in a primarily Thomistic way. The mysticism of Augustine and Bernard belongs to a period before the rise of the great theological system known as scholasticism. But San Juan, like many of his more recent predecessors, was trained to analyse problems through scholastic eyes, and so it is that the rigorous methods of Aquinas are introduced into the analysis of mystical theology, which provided the alternative form of religious experience for those who could not cope with the scholastic approach. It is one of the small ironies of the subject that San Juan, for all his commendation of mystical, experiential theology in the prologue to the *Cántico,* could not but study it in the way he had been trained—using the tools of Aquinas and his followers. Because the influence of Aquinas or the Carmelite Doctors on San Juan is so large a subject, we shall look at one aspect as an example—the way in which he uses Thomist epistemology, for this is fundamental to any philosophy or theology.

Durbin writes: 'St. Thomas offers for the first time in the history of cognitional thinking a genuinely comprehensive, internally coherent, realistic theory of knowledge', which he characterizes as 'a succinct and precise summary of the Aristotelian *via media* between Platonism and pre-Socratic sensism'.[53] The soul is a *tabula rasa* on which knowledge is written, gained by man through his sense perceptions and abstracted by the mind from the data they provide. If the senses are impaired, so too is intellectual discernment, as it will be based on faulty information. The intellect understands this information through acts of the imagination and is itself divided into active (agent) or passive (possible). The latter stores the abstractions, the former enables the soul to dematerialize things by abstracting their essence from their conditions of material individuality. Although knowledge begins with the senses, therefore, it has to be received and interpreted. Thus Aquinas brings into a unified scheme all knowledge from sense perception to understanding of universals, which the intellect perceives existing in the particular things the senses experience.

[51] This is more fully discussed in Ch. 7, p. 148.
[52] LCC XIII. 140.   [53] *Summa* vol. 12 (1a. 84–9), xxi.

This is far removed from the Platonic scheme, with its Ideas or Forms, and its doctrine of anamnesis, innate ideas remembered by the soul, providing it with true knowledge.[54] One might expect a mystic to incline more naturally to this teaching, which lends itself better to a Christian interpretation: deep in the soul lies awareness of man's divine creation, but this awareness is masked by original and personal sin. San Juan, it is true, occasionally uses expressions like 'la cárcel del cuerpo', which imply a more Platonic theory of the body-soul relationship and are closer to Luis de León.[55] But one should not make too much of a sixteenth-century writer possessing an Aristotelian-Thomist epistemology with Platonic overtones. The two ancient philosophies had been influencing each other for many centuries by then.

Like Aquinas, San Juan begins with the traditional picture of the 'tabula rasa': 'como dicen los filósofos, el alma, luego que Dios la infunde en el cuerpo, está como una tabla rasa y lisa en que no está pintado nada, y, si no es lo que por los sentidos va conociendo, de otra parte naturalmente no se le comunica nada.'[56] In S 2.3 he describes how natural knowledge comes via the senses and how the soul understands by means of phantasms and figures. You cannot know what you have never seen: an animal the likeness of which is unknown to you, or the colours yellow and white if you are blind. The imagination can only imagine things presented to it through the five exterior senses, that is, only created things; and he also makes use of the distinction between active and passive intellects.[57] Here the problem of supernatural knowledge arises. The soul has to negate her natural knowledge as she progresses and to wait for God to infuse in its place supernatural knowledge. Such knowledge, Aquinas taught, could not be acquired in the normal way. The soul may rise to a limited knowledge of immaterial things from the material, but not to a perfect knowledge, because there is not sufficient proportion between material and immaterial realities. Seeing the creatures, we do not know the whole power or essence of God, but are helped to be persuaded that he exists and is first cause of all things. It is grace which provides that more perfect knowledge—a gift, beyond our natural capacity.[58] San Juan often uses the term 'proportion' when explaining how the creatures cannot be a means of union with God, because they have no proportion with his being.[59] But he is more thoroughgoing than Aquinas and insists that even the partial knowledge of things immaterial gained through contemplation of the creation must be negated in the dark nights.

[54] See la 2ae 84.3–4.
[55] e.g. in Luis de León's poem 'A Felipe Ruiz'.
[56] S 1.3.3.   [57] S 2.12; CB 39.12.
[58] la 88.2; la 12.12–13.   [59] S 2.8, 3.12.

Supernatural knowledge, given through grace, is experienced in, for example, the supernatural gifts known as the theological virtues (derived from Paul's faith, hope, and love in 1 Cor. 13). Following Aristotle, Aquinas and San Juan describe the intellectual, moral, and cardinal virtues, but the theological virtues move sharply away from the Aristotelian system into Christian revelation. Man is given faith, added to his natural intellect, so that he may be adapted to his end, which is God. 'In things beyond our powers' the theological virtues 'surpass all virtue that is in proportion to human nature.'[60] This introduces a passive element into man's experience of God, a point beyond which a man cannot pass until first God acts in him, fundamental to San Juan and integral to Christian theology.[61] Man cannot reach God unaided; nature must be perfected by grace. Through baptism in the Triune name the Trinity dwells within the soul, which may then seek God in the depths of her being. So there is present within him the object of man's ultimate concern, hidden, to be searched for, in a sense innate, as the Platonists might have said, but only because of grace. Hence the first line of the *Cántico*: '¿Adónde te escondiste, Amado?' The soul is directed to search within herself for the hidden Beloved—perhaps the final christianization of the Socratic 'know thyself' and the Platonic innate knowledge, with God himself dwelling in the soul, only hidden by the distractions of all that the dark nights must purge away.

For the modern reader this whole area is hard to appreciate, both in the concepts it uses and the language it expresses them in. Yet it is surely important to recognize the philosophical and theological debt of San Juan to Thomist thinkers, for it dictated the way in which he set about analysing the experiences referred to in his prose commentaries and related him firmly to the intellectual outlook of Spanish Catholicism in the second half of the sixteenth century.

Another area bristling with similar difficulties is San Juan's use of a mystical exegesis of Scripture. He is careful to cite Scripture as his chief authority for the doctrine expounded in the commentaries and he constantly has recourse to the Biblical text. But he has inherited a tradition of exegesis with which today's historical, critical scholarship is almost entirely out of sympathy. It was not until the eighteenth century that the old tradition began to break down; until then, the generally accepted view was that the Bible could be interpreted in different, mutually complementary ways. First came literal or historical exegesis, then the moral sense, the allegorical and finally the anagogical or mystical. It should be stressed that texts did not have to be expounded in each of these ways,

---

[60] 1a 2ae 62.3.
[61] A useful discussion of this subject may be found in *Summa*, vol. 23, appendx. 3 (pp. 247–8).

for sometimes one or more of them would not be applicable. But the three non-literal forms of exposition, and especially the allegorical and mystical, allowed for great imaginative scope in explaining the meaning, and it this movement away from the obvious meaning into subjective and frequently eccentric interpretations that most disconcerts the modern reader. San Juan does make some use of the literal way, but he has inherited the accepted view that hidden under Scriptural figures lay many clues to the spiritual life which he, either following previous exegetes or using his own insight, was able to uncover.[62] His use of the Song of Songs must be understood in the light of some fifteen hundred years of Jewish and Christian exegetical practice. We have already noted the main interpretations of the Lover and Beloved in the Song: the Church and Christ, the Soul and the Word. Bernard's eighty-six sermons on the Song mark an influential shift in the latter direction, and San Juan generally adheres to this, though there are traces of the older view.[63] From the Song came many of the images used by the mystical tradition to describe the spiritual life: bride and bridegroom, lover and beloved, betrothal and marriage, wound, spark, wine, and so on; and from it too comes that mixing of love sacred and profane so characteristic of the language of mysticism.

It may seem strange that San Juan uses the Bible so thoroughly when, as the sixteenth century progressed, there had been a move away from it as the inspiration for Christian discipleship in countries where the Reformation was being opposed. Yet he is in fact reflecting the climate of the Tridentine Church. Erasmus and even more so the Reformers had insisted on the authority of the Bible over any other claim; but Trent also debated its position, and drew important conclusions about Scripture and Tradition. Christian people ought to be better acquainted with the Bible, which needed to be interpreted by the Church. Bishops were to ensure that the Latin Bible was taught to the clergy in the Cathedral or corresponding place. Allgeier claims that the Tridentine decrees were already foreshadowed by Erasmus, while critical scholarship and Patristic studies can be traced well back into the fifteenth century. [64] San Juan's generation would have been the first to benefit

[62] The historical exegesis in S 2.19–22 studied by Nieto, 'Mystical theology and "salvation-history" in John of the Cross: two conflicting methods of Biblical interpretation', *BHR* 36 (1974), 17–32, is the exception rather than the rule. On the history of Biblical exegesis see Grant, *The Bible in the Church* (New York, 1960), and Hanson, *Allegory and Event* (London, 1959), a study of Origen.

[63] As in CB 30.7: 'Este versillo se entiende harto propiamente de la Iglesia y de Cristo.' See St. Bernard of Clairvaux, *On the Songs of Songs*, trans. Walsh (Shannon, 1971).

[64] Lorenzo Valla is the obvious example; see Jedin, i. 156. He also gives a long list of early sixteenth-century critical editions of the Fathers, other than those of Erasmus.

directly from the new seriousness with which Biblical study was taken after Trent. But it was the Latin Bible, not the vernacular. That problem had not been resolved at Trent, and sharp differences of opinion had been revealed, with the Spanish Bishops leading the attack against the vernacular Bible.[65] Though San Juan often gives his texts in the vernacular, it must be remembered that he was not writing for publication but privately for nuns who knew no Latin. He would no doubt have extended his occasional practice of giving the Latin text first had publication been envisaged.

We do not, unfortunately, know which Latin Bible San Juan used, nor which breviary. Though Trent had called for the publication of a corrected text of the Vulgate, in the light of criticisms by Valla, Erasmus, and others, no official version appeared till the Clementine Bible of 1590. Most versions before that were based on the 1452–5 Gutenburg Bible.[66] With regard to the breviary, the evidence is more confused. No fewer than fifteen' Carmelite breviaries appeared during the sixteenth century, though in 1585 the Discalced changed to the Roman breviary because of extensive alterations in the Carmelite one. Which of the earlier ones San Juan used is not known.[67]

Linked with concern for study of the Scriptures was the Tridentine debate on preaching and teaching. No record survives of San Juan's sermons or homilies, but his chapter on preaching (S 3.45) well reflects the concern that the faith should be better communicated. The actual decree of 17 June 1546 Jedin describes as 'the first, and we may add at once, the only successful attempt to combine church reform with whatever was sound in Christian humanism.'[68] Doubtless inspired by this decree, a considerable number of manuals of sacred rhetoric were published in the later sixteenth century.[69] San Juan must have studied the art of sacred rhetoric during his training, and in S 3.45 refers to 'retórica', 'estilo', 'lenguaje', and 'término', while the prologue to the *Cántico* also mentions 'figuras', 'comparaciones', and 'semejanzas'. The significance of this training will become evident when we study the

[65] Allgeier, 'Erasmus und Kardinal Ximenes in den Verhandlungen des Konzils von Trient', *Spanische Forschungen der Görresgesellschaft* (1933), 193–205; and Jedin, ii. 75–6.

[66] The Vulgate text used in this book is BAC, 4th edn. (Madrid, 1965), based on the Clementine Bible. Comparison of San Juan's quotations with this text show that he is very close to it, even if he was quoting from memory: see one of his longest Latin quotations, Job 4: 12–16 (CB 14–15.17), identical with the BAC text.

[67] See Fr. Pancratius Lenferink, *Bibliography of the printed Carmelite breviaries and missals* (unpublished).

[68] ii. 122.

[69] See Martí, 'La retórica sacra en el siglo de oro', *HR* 38 (1970), 264–98; and his book *La preceptiva retórica espanola en el siglo de oro* (Madrid, 1972).

poetic technique of San Juan, for he handles a large number of rhetorical devices with great assurance, for which his early training in sacred rhetoric must have been invaluable.

Already we have passed from the thematic to the more distinctly literary aspects of San Juan's inheritance. The place of the Bible and the importance of sacred rhetoric are connected with the post-Tridentine Roman Church yet they are not exclusive to it. The kind of Scriptural exegesis to which we briefly alluded belongs to the mystical tradition which San Juan inherited; while the tradition already unites poetry and prose in the endeavour to communicate the mystical experience. Without realizing this, we shall fail to appreciate how natural it was for San Juan to use both poetry and prose in his own attempt to do this. Already the exegetical history of the Song had given rise to many commentaries in prose on its poetry. The dialogue form San Juan uses stems ultimately from it, though there are prose dialogues in many medieval writers, like Hugh of St. Victor, Suso, and in the *Imitation of Christ*. Llull, Ruysbroeck, and Rolle each managed to combine prose and poetry. Llull writes a very poetic, heightened prose, while the others interrupt their prose by breaking into poetry from time to time. None of these examples has the formal perfection or lyrical beauty of San Juan's *liras*, but they should be remembered as we try to assess the literary characteristics of the Western mystical tradition. The following example from the *Fire of Love* will show how Rolle turns to poetry as he longs for the Beloved, and introduces the same themes as those at the beginning of the *Cántico*:

> If only you would send me a companion for my journey
> so that the longing could be lightened by his encouragement,
> and the chain of my sighings loosed!
> for if that lovely vision of yourself
> does not come quickly and release me,
> it will press so heavily on your lover
> as to force him to leave this prison of flesh . . .
> My love, my honey, my harp,
> My psalter and song the whole day long!
> When are you going to heal my grief?
> You, the root of my heart,
> When are you coming to receive my spirit
> which is always looking for you?
> I am wounded to the quick by your fair beauty.[70]

We do not know that San Juan ever read Rolle, and most of the pictures in any case come from traditional exegesis of the Song; but the dialogue form, the emotionally charged language, with interrogation and exclamation, the interplay of Biblical images with the writer's own

[70] *Fire*, pp. 154–5.

words, belong to the tradition inherited by San Juan and help us to understand the kind of literature mysticism was likely to produce.

But a more contemporary joining of poetry and prose occurs in Laredo's *Subida del Monte Sión*.[71] Chapter 40 of Part III contains twenty-four poetic epigrams, beginning 'El que con amor trabaja, holgando gana ventura'. Laredo expounds each of these briefly in a prose commentary, and concludes his chapter with further 'entrañables aforismos' in the same style. In the drawing San Juan made for his own *Subida*, he included a number of similar aphorisms, discussed briefly in S 1.13.11. Not only are they like Laredo's in form and content, but like his they are connected with the ascent of a mountain—Carmel in his case, Zion in Laredo's.[72] Laredo prefaces his chapter: 'De la declaración de los versos del amor que fueron puestos en el capítulo 21 de aquesta tercera parte en la primera impresión, porque esta declaración me ha sido muy demandada en el nombre de Jesús.' The parallel with San Juan is again close: mystical verses, expounded in prose because such an exposition has been requested. That was the sequence of events which led to the *Cántico*. Earlier examples of mystical literature showed not poetry being expounded in prose but a heightened prose leading naturally into poetry. Only in the Song is there a tradition of poetry being expounded in treatises on the mystical life. This example from Laredo, which San Juan certainly knew, brings us much closer in time and method to the *Cántico*. The difference is that San Juan's poems are not simply collections of spiritual aphorisms but great works of literature in their own right.[73]

It ought also to be noted that many of the images and similes used by San Juan belong to the literary traditions of Western mysticism. His favourite is that of the sun shining through glass either revealing the specks of dust which cannot otherwise be seen, or as a demonstration of the same light that is in the sun streaming from it in rays without diminishing it. The analogy of the river flowing into the sea is not confined to Christian writers,[74] and the bird pining for her mate, and the nightingale, have centuries of use behind them. The analogy of fire burning and consuming the wood appears to come from Hugh of St. Victor, though San Juan may have found it elsewhere, and a very

---

[71] Cuevas García, in his 'La prosa métrica en Fray Bernardino de Laredo', *RL* 35 (1969), 5–51, has suggested that much of Laredo's *Subida* is in fact written in metrical prose.

[72] The drawing can be seen in *Vida y obras completas*, p. 436. More recently, San Juan's verses have been borrowed and restated by T. S. Eliot in *Four Ouartets*, 'East Coker', lines 135–46.

[73] Emblem books use a similar technique: Latin verse, followed by prose expositions of the moral. However, the main period of emblematic culture in Spain in 1580–1630, rather late to consider as an influence on San Juan.

[74] Zaehner, op. cit., p. 145, gives an example from the Bhagavad-Gita.

beautiful example of it occurs in Luis de León.[75] Paradox and antithesis also played an important part in the language of mysticism, full of notions of light and darkness, living and dying, pain that is pleasure, suffering that is joy.

The aim of this introduction has not been to provide a complete understanding of the background to San Juan's work. It has attempted to sketch out a rather different approach to his theological and literary inheritance from the one normally taken. Many of the points made here with brevity deserve a much fuller treatment; some of them will be taken up later in this book. But all the examples point to the same conclusion. San Juan has drawn on a vein of inherited wisdom running rich and deep for some fifteen hundred years. New authorities were constantly being added to the old ones, so that new insights and ideas came to replenish the tradition. Where we might see different schools of theology or mystical teaching, and note many changes and developments, San Juan and his contemporaries saw one body of authoritative literature guarding the truth from contamination. Individual authors were important as contributing members of this distinguished tradition. The broad outlines of the mystical journey had been drawn, and many details were already in place. This had given rise to a recognizable form of literature, using the kind of techniques we have looked at. These are all present in San Juan, not because he created a new kind of literature, but because he worked within a defined tradition. To them he added what he himself had acquired from his Jesuit education and his training at Salamanca, notably scholastic theology, a grounding in rhetoric, and a profound love of the Bible. His last and most intimate source was his own extraordinary mystical experience. What he could never have known was that with the blending of all these ingredients he too in time would become one of the greatest of all the authorities for those who followed his footsteps in the soul's ascent to God.

[75] For Hugh's text, see LCC XIII. 91; for Luis de León's, *Nombres de Cristo*, ed. Onís, CC (Madrid, 1948), 'Esposo', ii. 250.

2

THE ORIGINS OF THE CÁNTICO

The unsuspecting reader who opens a modern edition of the works of San Juan sees only the end of a long and involved process of textual history. In a study of the origins and growth of the *Cántico* problems arise at every turn, concerning the genesis of the poem itself, the different forms of the poem and the prose commentaries in various manuscripts, and the vexed question of which version most accurately represents the intentions of San Juan. Because of their complexity, and their repercussions on anything that is to be established about the *Cántico*, these problems cannot be ignored. The textual problem is the first of four problems stemming from the poetry of San Juan isolated by Dámaso Alonso and described as 'los más dificultosos de la literatura española'.[1] In this chapter we shall be concerned to establish from the available historical evidence how the poem and commentaries reached the forms in which they are now known and published, so that the question of the authenticity of the so-called second redaction may then be tackled.

There is a very substantial body of historical evidence from which information about San Juan and his works may be drawn. It is found primarily in the documents relating to his beatification cause, covering 1600–30; much comes from people who had known him, and some from his closest associates in the Carmelite Reform. It is therefore a prime source for all biographical and literary studies of the saint. Most of it has been published by P. Silverio.[2]

Santa Teresa had been beatified on 24 April 1614 and San Juan, who had been so closely associated with her in the Reform, must have been a natural candidate for this honour. Silverio writes: 'Se hablaba de él, según

---

[1] In *La poesía de San Juan de la Cruz*, 4th edn. (Madrid, 1966), p. 18.
[2] Noteworthy among the early biographers of San Juan are Alonso de la Madre de Dios, *Vida, virtudes y milagros del santo padre fray Juan de la Cruz* (BNM MS. 13460); José de Jesús María (Quiroga), *Historia de la vida y virtudes del venerable P. F. Juan de la Cruz* (Brussels, 1628); and Jerónimo de San José, *Historia del venerable padre Fr. Juan de la Cruz* (Madrid, 1641). They used these documents and also obtained information privately. For the documents, see P. Silverio de Sta Teresa, *Obras de San Juan de la Cruz*, 5 vols. (Burgos, 1930), BMC 10–14.

luego depusieron testigos de la época, "como de santo canonizado".[3] On 29 November 1613 the Father General of the Spanish Congregation of the Discalced inaugurated the official process of investigation into the life, sanctity, and miracles of San Juan. In the examination before the Ordinaries, depositions were taken in many places between November 1614 and April 1618, where he had resided or was known to people. Once collected, official copies were sent for examination to Rome, and when a favourable response was forthcoming, the apostolic examination was started, and information gathered in a similar fashion between June 1627 and November 1628. Many witnesses from the early examination reappeared to corroborate their testimonies, and once more, authorized copies were sent to Rome.[4]

It is important to note that the tribunals which examined this evidence were not haphazard affairs. Every step was taken to impress upon witnesses the solemnity of the occasion and the need for accuracy. The examinations proceeded under canon law, with an ecclesiastical tribunal hearing the evidence submitted by the witnesses according to a prepared document of questions.[5] The Procurator of the Order was present, and notaries took copies of the proceedings. We are not therefore dealing with a body of information collected under conditions which encouraged any unconfirmed rumour to be accepted as the truth. The point was to establish certain facts about San Juan, on the basis of which the beatification cause would succeed or fail. The evidence must thus be taken seriously.

That is not to say it must all be accepted without question. The witnesses do not always agree with one another, and in such cases the testimonies of those closest to San Juan must be given priority. The discrepancies are well illustrated by comparing the various accounts of San Juan's escape from prison. The further away from the original, the greater the tendency towards the miraculous. Fortunately, the evidence of Fr. Juan de Santa María, San Juan's gaoler at the time, has been preserved. In his deposition (23 June 1616) he describes the prison conditions in considerable detail, and then provides a dramatic reconstruction of the escape, not without its elements of miracle, but

---

[3]   BMC 14. vii.

[4]   Places and dates of the examination before the Ordinaries are as follows: Medina del Campo (Nov. 1614–Jan. 1615), Caravaca (July 1615), Segovia (Apr.– July 1616), Ávila (June–July 1616), Jaén (Dec. 1616–Mar. 1618), Baeza (Feb. 1617–Jan. 1618), Úbeda (Mar. 1617–Jan. 1618), Málaga (Nov. 1617–Feb. 1618), Alcaudete (Feb. 1618) and Beas (Mar.–Apr. 1618). Of the apostolic examination: Medina del Campo (June 1627–Nov. 1628), Jaén (Aug.–Sept. 1627), Granada (Sept.–Oct. 1627), Baeza (Sept. 1627–Jan. 1628), Segovia (Sept. 1627–Apr. 1628), Málaga (Sept. 1627–Jan. 1628) and Úbeda (Nov. 1627–Apr. 1628).

[5]   The documents for the two examinations, containing thirty-six and thirty questions respectively, are in BMC 14. 1–10 and 306–15.

far more factual than accounts of the same event given by those who only heard about it.[6] So the evidence cannot all be treated with the same respect. Nevertheless, both examinations contain eye-witness accounts, and as Silverio remarks, 'sus dichos constituyen un tesoro riquísimo y seguro de información.'[7] Other information, less in bulk but equal in interest, comes from information gathered privately by those interested in the life of San Juan or officially appointed to write his biography. While they draw freely from the beatification documents, they possess other material, both earlier and later than these; for example, the valuable letters of Isabel de Jesús María and M. Ana de San Alberto, dated 1614, the letters and 'Relación de la vida del S. Juan de la Cruz' of M. Magdalena del Espíritu Santo, and the letters of Juan Evangelista, all dating from 1630.[8]

It would have surprised these people, concerned with honouring San Juan in the Church, to discover that their statements would be used, over 350 years later, to provide information about incidental matters like the saint's poems. So a rider must be added to this evidence. The seventeenth-century investigators were scarcely concerned with San Juan's status as a poet, much more with his potential sanctity. References to his written works only occur because of the effect they produced on the devotional lives of the men and women of the Carmelite Reform. It would be wrong to use them as though they had been written for our concerns. The investigators make it quite clear what they are doing. First, there is the Father General's letter to all the Provincials of the Discalced in Spain, asking for information about San Juan, 'porque el tiempo no sepulte cosas tan maravillosas.'[9] The Instruction to the Provincials sets out clearly the manner and scope of the investigation:

Ante todas cosas, envíe V.R. un precepto formal a cada uno de los conventos de su provincia, así de frailes como de monjas . . . en que mande a cada prior o vicario o religiosas de ellos, que digan y declaren todo lo que supieren que sea de substancia y consideración acerca de la santidad, virtudes y milagros de este santo varón y de las cosas admirables que Nuestro Señor hubiere hecho por su medio e intercesión, así en vida como en muerte; y también lo que acerca de esto hubieren oído o sabido de otras personas, así de dentro como de fuera de la Religión, especificando quién son y los lugares donde están.[10]

The first ten questions in the 'interrogatorio' for the investigation before the Ordinaries deal with San Juan's birth, education, entrance

---

[6] BMC 14. 290–1; compare the account of Francisca de la Madre de Dios, ibid. 173–4.
[7] Ibid. xiv.
[8] BMC 13. 371–2; 400–3; BMC 10. 319–39; 340–6.
[9] BMC 10. 313. The letter is signed Fr. Joseph de Jesús María and dated at Alcalá, 14 Mar. 1614.
[10] Ibid. 315.

into Carmel, and founding of convents. The rest concern his saintly qualities as reflected in his dealings with others, his particular gifts, and miracles associated with him before and after his death. The twenty-fifth concerns his imprisonment and escape. Only the penultimate question deals with his literary achievements, and it is loaded. The witnesses are asked:

Si saben que los libros que dejó escritos de Teología mística están llenos de sabiduría del cielo, y muestran bien la grande luz y levantado espíritu que tuvo su autor . . . Por lo cual estos libros son muy estimados de personas doctas y espirituales, y se han sacado innumerables traslados de ellos, que andan por estos Reinos de España, y se han llevado a las Indias, Italia, Flandes y otros Reinos remotos; y es común concepto de las personas que los leen que resplandece en ellos la doctrina y espíritu que el apóstol San Pablo comunicó a San Dionisio, su discípulo, para toda la Iglesia.[11]

Although the earliest depositions date from twenty-six years after San Juan's death, the evidence they provide is reliable enough to give considerable insight into the origins and growth of the *Cántico*. The first fact that can be established from them is that the poem originated during San Juan's confinement in the conventual prison at Toledo between 2 December 1577 and August 1578, where he was detained in solitary confinement by Carmelites who followed the mitigated rule, for persisting to further the cause of the Reform against the wishes of his superiors. The evidence here is overwhelming, though it begins to show divergences when dealing with how much of the poem was composed there, and whether any of it was written down. But it is as well to state firmly that the often repeated view that San Juan began the *Cántico* during his imprisonment is not a pious legend but an accurate reflection of historical fact.[12] Isabel de Jesús María was living in the Toledo convent when San Juan escaped to it from prison. In a letter from Cuerva (where she had moved in 1586), dated 2 November 1614, she writes:[13]

Acuérdome también, que en aquel rato que le tuvimos escondido en la iglesia, dijo unos romances que traía de cabeza—y una religiosa los iba escribiendo—, que había él mismo hecho. Son tres, y todos de la Santísima Trinidad, tan altos y devotos, que parece pegan fuego; y en esta casa de Cuerva los tenemos que empiezan: 'En el principio moraba el Verbo, y en Dios vivía'. Esto pasó estando yo novicia en Toledo.
. . . Son tan estimadas sus obras, que no parece tener tanto trato de espíritu, que

[11] BMC 14. 10.
[12] Witnesses describe a number of other poems also written in prison, as their testimonies show. P. Eulogio, *San Juan de la Cruz y sus escritos* (Madrid, 1969), states that these were 'el breve poema rotulado *Cantar del alma que se huelga de conocer a Dios por fe* y los romances sobre *el Evangelio "in principio erat Verbum"* . . . y sobre el Salmo *Super flumina Babylonis*' (pp. 112–13).
[13] BMC 13. 371–2.

como un precioso tesoro las tienen y guardan, sin que basten ruegos ningunos de personas que las piden para sacarlas. Y de éstas, y con esta estima, tiene el conde de Arcos unas liras o líricos, con su glosa o declaración a cada copla, cosa muy delicada y espiritual, que comienzan: 'Adónde te escondiste'.

It is not clear from this whether or not she includes the *Cántico* among the works inspired by his imprisonment, but it certainly suggests that he was engaged in composing poetry, remembered rather than written down, during those lonely months.

Further evidence comes from the investigation before the Ordinaries. Francisca de la Madre de Dios, one of the nuns at Beas and an important witness for the origin of the last five stanzas, testified:[14]

En la dicha prisión había estado como nueve meses, y que era mucho el consuelo que tenía en aquella estrecha cárcel, porque le parecía estaba en el cielo, y que la visitaba Nuestro Señor, y que particularmente había comenzado a cantar aquella canción que dice: 'A donde te escondiste, Amado,–y me dejaste con gemido! etc.'

Her insistence on 'había *comenzado* a cantar' agrees with her later statement, which will be examined shortly, and with that of Ana de San Alberto, who was prioress of Caravaca while San Juan was at El Calvario. In a letter written from Caravaca on 4 November 1614 she says with reference to his imprisonment:[15]

Allí hizo aquellas canciones que comienzan: 'A donde te escondiste', y también la otra canción, que comienza: 'Por cima de las corrientes que en Babilonia hallaba'. Todas estas canciones están en los libricos que yo envié al P. Fr. José de Jesús María.[16] Díjome que con estas canciones se entretenía y las guardaba en la memoria para escribirlas.

And in the investigation at Caravaca she confirms this: 'Estando en aquella prisión había hecho las *Canciones,* sobre que después escribió un libro, el cual esta testigo lo ha tenido en su poder, escrito de mano, que se lo dio el mismo padre Fr. Juan de la Cruz', likewise sent to Madrid.[17]

Magdalena del Espíritu Santo, another of the Beas nuns, gives an important account of the origins of the *Cántico* in her 'Relación de la vida del S. Juan de la Cruz', addressed in 1630 the historian of the Discalced, Fr. Jerónimo de San José:[18]

Sacó el santo Padre, cuando salió de la cárcel, un cuaderno que estando en ella había escrito de unos romances sobre el Evangelio *In principio erat Verbum,* y unas coplas que dicen: 'Que bien sé yo la fonte que mana y corre, aunques de noche', y las canciones o liras que dicen: 'Adónde te ascondiste', hasta la que dice; 'Oh ninfas de Judea'. Lo demás compuso el Santo estando después por Rector del Colegio de Baeza, y las *Declaraciones,* algunas hizo en Beas respondiendo a preguntas que las religiosas le hacían, y otras estando en Granada.

---

[14] BMC 14. 173–4.   [15] BMC 13. 40.
[16] This refers to the Father General's letter requesting information.
[17] BMC 14. 201.   [18] BMC 13. 325.

Este cuaderno que el Santo escribió en la cárcel, le dejó en el Convento de Beas, y a mí me mandaron trasladarle algunas veces. Después me le llevaron de la celda, y no supe quién. Causándome admiración la viveza de las palabras y su hermosura y sutileza, le pregunté un día si le daba Dios aquellas palabras que tanto comprendían y adornaban, y me respondió: 'Hija, unas veces me las daba Dios, y otras las buscaba yo.'

This remarkable testimony indicates that San Juan actually wrote down in prison the first thirty or thirty-one stanzas of the *Cántico* as well as other poems, and brought the book with him to the convent, where it was copied out several times. In view of the fact that Magdalena quotes the first line of stanza 31, it seems natural to interpret 'hasta' inclusively, 'up till and including' rather than 'as far as the one that begins'.[19] There is some manuscript evidence for this proto-Cántico, which may reflect the versions of the poem copied out by Magdalena and others after San Juan's escape. The best manuscripts in this tradition are those associated with Ana de San Bartolomé, secretary to Santa Teresa, and according to Fr. Simeón de la Sagrada Familia one of them (the Antwerp Cathedral version) 'nos lleva seguramente hasta lecturas muy primitivas del *Cántico*.'[20] Magdalena's testimony is therefore strengthened by this manuscript evidence, and the tradition of a thirty-one-stanza *Cántico* disseminated by copies made before 1584, when the Sanlúcar manuscript gave the familiar thirty-nine-stanza version of CA, is generally accepted today, even though little can be established about it with any certainty. But as the process of dissemination continued, the text of the poem no doubt became distorted, and the end product is the kind of corrupt text generally found in manuscripts with thirty-one stanzas. Her evidence further suggests that the expositions of the *Cántico* were made over several years, at Beas (1578–9), Baeza (1579–82) and Granada (after 1582), and were started in the first instance at the request of nuns who were moved by the poem but unable—not surprisingly—to grasp its meaning.

All this strongly suggests a dynamic *Cántico*; not a single work written

[19] For discussion of this point, see P. Eulogio, op. cit., pp. 139–40. Some scholars (among them P. Crisógono and P. Silverio) reckoned that San Juan composed only the first seventeen stanzas in prison, but this error is due to their following the CB order of verses, in which CA 31 = CB 18. It is highly unlikely that Magdalena is herself referring to the CB enumeration, as she specifically states that the poem was the one brought out of prison.

[20] In 'Tríptico Sanjuanista', *EC* 11 (1960), 197–233 (p. 213). BNM MS. 868 shows a thirty-one-stanza poem but is a seventeenth-century manuscript and part of a miscellany for private devotion. This and the Valladolid MS. 83 P. Eulogio describes as a case of 'degeneración textual, no de ordenación primitiva'. For his study of the problem, op. cit., pp. 142–50. The most exhaustive survey of this difficult issue has been undertaken by Duvivier, *La Genèse du "Cantique spirituel" de saint Jean de la Croix* (Paris, 1971), pp. 24–78, though the arguments are very complex and the results bound to be dependent at least in part on conjecture.

at one specific time, but a poem and a prose exposition which developed and grew beyond its genesis during San Juan's imprisonment. The work continued to mature in his mind from 1578 to 1584, and beyond that date, the evidence, as we shall see, points to a further expansion in the commentaries. But there are difficulties in pin-pointing the exact moments at which any development took place. Magdalena's evidence insists that San Juan actually wrote down what he had composed in prison, and conflicts with that of Ana de San Alberto. It is, however, corroborated by Juan Evangelista, in a letter to P. Jerónimo de San José, dated 1 January 1630: [21]

En lo que toca al haber visto escribir a nuestro venerable Padre los libros, se los vi escribir todos, porque, como he dicho, era el que andaba a su lado. La *Subida del Monte Carmelo* y *Noche Oscura* escribió aquí en esta casa de Granada, poco a poco, que no lo continuó sino con muchas quiebras; la *Llama de Amor viva* escribió siendo Vicario Provincial, también en esta casa, a petición de Da. Ana de Peñalosa, y lo escribió en quince días que estuvo aquí con hartas ocupaciones. 'A dónde te escondiste' fue el primero que escribió y fue también aquí, y estas canciones escribió en la cárcel que tuvo en Toledo.

In a second letter (18 February) he repeats this information, though not without some obscurity of meaning, because he has already stated that the *Canciones* were begun in prison: 'En lo que toca al haber escrito nuestro Santo Padre sus libros en esta casa, diré lo que es sin duda, y es que *Las Canciones* de "A dónde te escondiste" y la *Llama de amor viva* los escribió aquí, porque en mi tiempo los comenzó y acabó.' [22] Presumably he is referring to the composition of the prose expositions, and not of the poem, at Granada. So although he agrees with Magdalena that the *Cántico* poem was written down in prison, he conflicts with her in locating all the prose expositions at Granada.

P. Eulogio has noted further evidence for a written poem emerging from prison. He claims San Juan may have begun to write down his poems when he was given writing materials by his new gaoler, Fr. Juan de Santa María, to whose evidence we referred earlier. There is only one source for this information: the deposition of Inocencio de San Andrés, in a sworn statement of 8 March 1608, described by P. Eulogio as probably 'la mejor historia de los meses de encarcelamiento'. [23] In BNM MS. 8568, f. 544, Inocencio states: 'Al religioso que tenía cuidado del padre fray Juan le fue pareciendo bien su paciencia y modestia, como no le oía quejarse de nadie. Y un día le pidió el padre fray Juan que le hiciese caridad de un poco de papel y tinta, porque quería hacer algunas cosas de devoción para entretenerse. Y se las trajo.' It is true that Fr. Juan had compassion on his prisoner when he took charge of him in May 1578, and allowed him out of his cell from time to time; but of the

---

[21] BMC 10. 343.   [22] Ibid.
[23] Op. cit., p. 103, fn. 6. The evidence is given on pp. 108, 133–7.

provision of writing materials there is no mention in his own detailed testimony. First hand evidence is therefore lacking. His gaoler may have forgotten San Juan's small request; Inocencio knew San Juan well and for a time was his vice-rector at Baeza. On the other hand, Magdalena may have been mistaken, and supposed that a copy made of the poems composed mentally in prison and made almost as soon as San Juan reached safety had in fact been brought with him out of prison.

Confusion is understandable when trying to establish when the prose commentaries were written. A final fair copy may well have been written wholly at Granada, as Fr. Juan Evangelista states; but this does not rule out the possibility that sketches of expositions for particular stanzas were made at Beas when the nuns there requested explanations, as Magdalena indicates. It was not until some time later that San Juan decided to expound the whole poem, by which time it had grown into thirty-nine stanzas. These testimonies may therefore not conflict, but reflect different stages in the production of the commentaries: first, isolated expositions, undertaken after specific requests from the nuns, and only later a commentary on the complete poem.

In the end it hardly matters whether San Juan emerged from prison with the thirty-one stanzas written down or in his head. They were quickly enough copied out at Toledo. His capacity for remembering is well attested: he evidently knew long passages from the Bible by heart.[24] The picture of a deeply sensitive man in prison filling the long hours by composing poems around the passages of Scripture he loved so well, without needing to commit them to paper, is a convincing one to those who sense the kind of man San Juan was. But it is only a picture. Certainly he brought the major part of the *Cántico* poem out of his dark and narrow prison cell. Its images of beauty, freedom, and space—fields, flowers, rivers, mountains, wild beasts, blowing winds—bear eloquent testimony to the power of a man's mind to create a world vibrant with life, light, and colour, even in the deadness of a prison cell. The composition of the *Cántico* cannot as a matter of historical fact be divorced from San Juan's bitter prison experience. We are bound to carry that fact in the back of our mind. Poetry is not written in isolation from human experience and feeling, at least, not poetry like this.[25]

While at Granada, San Juan paid regular visits to the nuns at Beas, to preach and hear confessions. It was during one of these visits that, according to Francisca de la Madre de Dios, he was inspired to write what we know as CA 35–9:[26]

[24] See the quotation from Juan Evangelista in Ch. 1 p. 3.
[25] This is not meant to imply, however, that poetry is to be *evaluated* solely or primarily in terms of the depth or sincerity of feeling it may convey. It is merely a point to be made about the historical origins of the *Cántico*.
[26] BMC 14. 170.

Y asimismo, preguntándole un día a esta testigo en qué traía la oración, le dijo que en mirar la hermosura de Dios y holgarse de que la tuviese; y el Santo se alegró tanto de esto, que por algunos días decía cosas muy levantadas, que admiraban, de la hermosura de Dios: y así, llevado de este amor, hizo unas cinco canciones a este tiempo sobre esto, que comienzan: 'Gocémonos, Amado' y 'Vámonos a ver en tu hermosura' etc.

There is no reason to doubt this eye-witness glimpse into a private conversation, and the composition of these final stanzas can therefore be placed between early 1582, when San Juan left Baeza for Granada, and 1584, when they appear in the Sanlúcar manuscript. If Magdalena was right in thinking that the prose commentaries had been begun, however sketchily, at Beas, then the last five stanzas of the poem would have been composed with the idea of developing them into prose expositions for spiritual teaching already established in the mind of San Juan. So the notion that the poem was finished before the prose expositions were started probably has to be discarded. At least for a time, both aspects of the *Cántico* were developing alongside one another.

There still remain four stanzas (CA 32—4 and CB 11) which have not been accounted for. What is known about the origin of these? There is some evidence suggesting that the origin of the diminutive 'Carillo' in CA 32 lies in a song San Juan heard a boy singing outside the prison walls:[27]

> Muérome de amores,
> Carillo, ¿qué haré?
> Que te mueres, ¡Alahé!

This information comes from P. Jerónimo de San José, via an unknown source. However, if San Juan did use this snatch of popular poetry in CA 32, he cannot have written the stanza until after escaping from prison, in view of the tradition of the thirty-one-stanza *Cántico* which in one form or another he brought out of prison. Copies of this must have been in circulation before CA 32 was written, if Magdalena's testimony is accepted. P. Eulogio cites various pieces of evidence which add up to the hypothesis that CA 32—4 were written together, at Granada. San Juan was preoccupied with solitude and hiddenness at this time. A homely anecdote tells how Catalina de la Cruz, the convent cook at Beas, asked San Juan on one of his visits why all the frogs in the pond disappeared whenever anyone approached. He replied that 'Aquel era el lugar y centro donde tenían seguridad para no ser ofendidas y conservarse; y que así había de hacer ella, huir las criaturas e irse y zambullirse a lo hondo y centro que es Dios, escondiéndose en El.' At the end of 1582 he wrote to the nuns from Granada 'convidándolas a lo escondido y retirado de la soledad, donde comunica Dios su verdadero

---

[27] BNM MS. 12378, f. 693. See P. Eulogio, op. cit., pp. 128–33.

espíritu y luz'.[28] The theme of the soul fleeing to the hidden depths of God is particularly dear to San Juan, and it is brought out in the exposition (CA 32.2). Duvivier, on the other hand, is inclined to discount this admittedly tenuous evidence as a likely source for CA 32—4. He suggests that the theme of 'amour caché et solitude' belongs properly to the whole of CA 32—9: 'Pour moi, j'élargirais volontiers cette constatation à la totalité des huit derniers strophes du Cantique.'[29] San Juan could have been inspired by his interview with Francisca to complete what he already had in mind—these last eight stanzas.

It is probably unrealistic to imagine San Juan suddenly seized to write eight more stanzas for his prison *Cántico* after an interview with a nun or because of a preoccupation with solitude, which is in any case present throughout his work. 'Hermosura' only occurs in CA 35, but notions of hiddenness and solitude are not much to the fore either, except in CA 32 and 37. The emphasis is on the fruition of love in full security. CA 32 is quite different from 33—4, in which the traditional secular imagery of the solitary dove who finds her mate is joined to the Biblical image of the dove sent forth from Noah's ark. In any case, the argument that stanzas showing a common theme must belong together in their composition is not a sound way of approaching the poem, because there is little thematic linking between any of the stanzas, even those composed in prison, as we shall later discover. It is therefore impossible to know anything for certain about the composition of CA 32—4, except that they must have been written after the thirty-one-stanza poem had begun to circulate and probably a little while before the last five stanzas were added. There is no manuscript evidence for a thirty-four-stanza *Cántico*, except BNM MS 868, which gives CA 33, 32, and 34 as a sonnet of rather unusual form in a corrupt text. So this interim stage between thirty-one and thirty-nine stanzas is not well enough attested except to be noted with interest. At some point probably in 1582—3 CA 35—9 were added to a poem which San Juan had already expanded to include CA 32—4. But when the time came to make a fair copy of this longer poem and the prose commentaries which now accompanied it, the eight additional stanzas seem to have been included together.

Confirmation of the fact that the *Cántico* was a dynamic rather than a static creation is found in the history of the one stanza added to the poem of the second redaction—CB 11. Moreoever, this is as far as is known the only stanza introduced into the body of the poem rather than attached to the end. It is always found with its commentary, and

---

[28] P. Eulogio, op. cit., pp. 188—98. The story comes from P. Alonso's *Vida*, BNM MS. 13460, ff. 114ʳ—116ᵛ.

[29] Duvivier, op. cit., p. 113.

is an important witness in resolving the problem of the authenticity of this second redaction. There is no evidence to suggest that anyone other than San Juan wrote it, and even those who have opposed the authenticity of CB are prepared to admit that stanza and commentary alike may be authentic.[30] It is true that CB 11 did not appear in print until the Italian translation (Rome, 1627) and then the edition of Madrid, 1630. But the first printed edition of CA did not appear until 1622, and then only in Gaultier's French translation. This time lapse cannot be an argument against CB 11's authenticity: it is part of the general mystery surrounding the delay in publishing any version of the *Cántico*.[31] In any case, the existence of this stanza is attested before its publication. In 1614, Francisca de Jesús, a Discalced nun from Medina, recited two stanzas of the *Cántico* 'que esta testigo sabe de memoria'. One was CA 8, the other, 'Descubre tu presencia', which is CB 11. This means that a forty-stanza poem was already known there.[32] The date of the composition of CB 11 and its insertion into the poem cannot be ascertained, and its history is closely bound up with the problem of CB, to be tackled in the next chapter.

It is interesting to note that these early editions of the *Cántico* with CB 11 (Rome, 1627, and Madrid, 1630) also print its commentary as it is found in other CB redactions, yet leave the rest of the text largely untouched save for minor revisions. It looks as if considerable confusion was caused early in the seventeenth century by the existence of both a thirty-nine and a forty-stanza poem. The early editors compromised by taking the outstanding addition from the longer version, and simply inserted it into the otherwise CA text. Why they did this must remain a mystery. It may have been that they were genuinely puzzled by the discrepancies in the manuscripts before them; or they may have been unaware that other parts of the *Cántico* had been significantly changed at all. References to the number of stanzas the poem had are not decisive. Alonso de la Madre de Dios refers to 'las treinta y nueve *Canciones* con su explicación', but in his *Vida* writes of 'el libro de las cuarenta *Canciones*'.[33] Other testimonies show the same vacillation. The problem is simply to know whether forty is merely being used as a round number for thirty-nine, or as an accurate description of a *Cántico* which included CB 11, and perhaps other CB material also.

[30] e.g. Chevallier, 'Le "Cantique spirituel" de saint Jean de la Croix a-t-il été interpolé?', *BH* 24 (1922), 307–42 (p. 330).
[31] See P. Eulogio, 'Primeras ediciones del *Cántico espiritual*', *EC* 18 (1967), 3–48.
[32] The testimony is found in Vatican MS. 2838 (S25), f. 29; quoted by P. Eulogio, *San Juan de la Cruz y sus escritos*, pp. 336–7. For further study of CB 11, see Duvivier, *Le Dynamisme existentiel dans la poésie de Jean de la Croix* (Paris, 1973), pp. 39–42.
[33] BMC 14. 397 (22 Dec. 1627); cf. BNM MS. 13460, f. 79ᵛ.

But already this introduces the whole problem of CB. Before passing on to it, it would be useful to summarize what has been learned about the origins of the *Cántico*. San Juan began the poem while in the conventual prison at Toledo between December 1577 and his escape in August 1578. It was not the only poem he composed there; and from May 1578 he may have had the opportunity to write his compositions down. The original nucleus of the poem consisted of CA 1–31, and copies were made and began to circulate very soon after his escape. Some manuscripts appear to stem from this nucleus. The prose expositions were begun without any thought of writing a complete treatise, later in 1578 or 1579, and were continued over several years. There is no reason to suppose that they began with the first stanza and proceeded systematically; it is much more likely that they were sketched out to meet requests from nuns to explain particular passages they could not understand. CA 32–4 and 35–9 were added in 1582–3, perhaps stimulated by events and San Juan's preoccupations during that period. But CB 11 was composed independently, at an undetermined time, after 1584, when the Sanlúcar manuscript gave the definitive CA text; and it was added to the *Cántico* in its present position either by San Juan or his editors. It was recognized as part of the forty-stanza tradition before the first printed edition of the *Cántico* appeared. There is some confusion in the evidence as to whether the poem had thirty-nine or forty stanzas, which is hardly surprising, as many copies seem to have been made, and distortions inevitably crept into the manuscripts the further removed they were from the original. No witness shows awareness of two distinct stages in the life of the poem and commentary, which we recognize as CA and CB. But it is certain that even in its first redaction, the *Cántico* developed over a period of years, and San Juan added a great deal to his original prison poem. The first prose commentaries pre-date the final stanzas, which would have been written, unlike the rest, in the knowledge that they were going to receive such expositions. No evidence suggests that San Juan ever intended to publish this work, or any other. It was for a very limited readership, and for devotional and didactic purposes. All these things must be borne in mind because they bear directly on the most intractable textual problem of all in San Juan: who was responsible for the second redaction of the *Cántico*? We can go no further until that has been solved.

3

THE QUESTION OF *CÁNTICO* B

The main textual problem of the *Cántico* arises from the existence of
two distinct redactions of the poem and commentary. Is the second
redaction (CB), based on the Jaén manuscript, an authentic revision by
San Juan of the first (CA), based on the manuscript of Sanlúcar de
Barrameda?

The text of the poem is almost identical in both redactions, apart
from one major addition and a few small alterations. The addition is
CB 11:

> Descubre tu presencia,
> y máteme tu vista y hermosura;
> mira que la dolencia
> de amor, que no se cura
> sino con la presencia y la figura.

This is inserted between CA 10 and 11. Otherwise, textual changes
are minimal: CA 25 'Cogednos' becomes CB 16 'Cazadnos'; CA 21
'florecidas', CB 30 'floridas';[1] CA 12 'tu buelo', CB 13 'su vuelo';[2]
CA 26 'sus olores', CB 17 'tus olores'; and CA 32 'las campañas', CB 19
'las compañas'. Elsewhere, the two manuscripts agree on the text of the
poem. But the order of stanzas offers considerable dislocation in CB.
Only the first ten and last seven stanzas retain their original position.
CA 15–24 are transposed to become CB 24–33, a large block of ten
stanzas thus assuming a radically different place in the body of the
poem. There are four other transpositions, each affecting two stanzas:
CA 25–6 become CB 16–17; CA 27–8, CB 22–3; CA 29–30, CB 20–1;
and CA 31–2, CB 18–19.

The problem is acuter in the commentary to CB, which betrays signs
of an extensive reworking. CB inserts an 'argumento' between the prologue and the text of the poem, and adds annotations, sometimes of
considerable length, before the exposition of each verse, a procedure
which is restricted in the first redaction to CA 13–14. And although

---

[1] This alteration reduces the fourth line of the *lira* to six syllables, unless a
hiatus is intended between 'tu' and 'amor'.
[2] In the Jaén MS., the copyist has omitted the possessive adjective altogether,
and has had to insert it later above the line of text.

somewhere over half the paragraphs of CA have passed more or less unchanged into CB, many others have undergone a thorough process of revision, and particularly of amplification; while a few have been suppressed. The CB commentary thus incorporates a lot of new material, with the result that CA is only about three-quarters the length of the second redaction. In the following list these alterations are set out according to the paragraphs in which they occur (numbered according to CB except where they occur only in CA), and the extent to which they affect the CA original. Brackets indicate that the additions or omissions in any given paragraph affect only part of it. Small, significant changes have generally been given more weight than frequent, insigificant ones. Some of the changes are due to additions and omissions of Biblical quotations in Latin and Spanish, a related problem which will be considered later.

1. *Paragraphs identical or scarcely altered in both redactions*:
Prologue; 1.1–3, 16–18, 22; 2.1–2, 4, 8; 3.5–10; 4–8 (complete); 9.2–3; 10.4–7; 12.3–8; 13; 14–15.2–28; 16.8–9; 17.6–7; 18.3–4, 6, 11; 19.3–4; 20–1.5–10; 22.4–5, 8; 23.3–5; 24.6; 25.2–10; 26.2–12, 18–19; 27.3–7; 28.2–3, 5–6, 9–10; 29.5–9, 11; 30.2–9; 31.3–5, 9; 32.2–6; 33.3; 34.2; 35.3–6; 36.3–4, 9–10; 37.3, 5; 39.5, 7.

2. *Paragraphs showing some alterations from CA in CB*:
1.4–5, 15, 20–1; 2.3, 5, 7; 3.4; 9.5–7; 10.9; 16.11; 17.3–5, (8), 9, 11; 18.7; 19.7; 20–1.11, 15; 22.2, 6; 24.3–5; 25.11; 28.4; 31.8; 32.8; 35.7; 36.5, 7, 11; 37.8; 39.3, 6, 9, 12; 40.2, 5–6.

3. *Paragraphs showing considerable and important alterations*:
1.6, 13, 14; 2.6; 3.1; 12.2; 16.1, 4, 10; 17.2; 19.5–6; 20–1.4, 16, 18; 22.3, 7; 23.1–2; 24.2; 28.7–8; 32.7; 33.5, 9; 34.4–6; 35.2; 36.6; 37.2, 4; 38.3–4; 39.2, 8, 11; 40.3–4.

4. *Paragraphs added by CB*:
Argumento; 1.7–12, (14); (2.3); 3.2–3; 9.1; 10.1–3, (8); 11 (complete); 12.1, 9; 13.1; 14–15.1, 29–30; 16.2–3, (5), 6–(7); 17.1; 18.1–2, (5); 19.1; 20–1.1–3, 12–14, (19); 22.1, (6); 23.6; 24.1, (7–9); 25.1; 26.1, (13–17); 27.1–2, 8; 28.1, (7); 29.1–4, (10); 30.1, 10–11; 31.1–2, 6–7, (10); 32.1, 9; 33.1–2, 4, (6–7), 8; 34.1, (3); 35.(1)–2; 36.1–2, (5–6), (8), (12–13); 37.1, (6–7); 38.1, (3–4), 5–9; 39.1, (4), 10, 13, (14)–15; (40.1, 4, 7).

5. *Paragraphs in CA suppressed by CB*:
(1.19); 31.(8)–9; (32.2); (36.6); 37.(2–3), 6; 38.1, (11), 13–(14), 15; (39.1, 4).

Was San Juan responsible for all these alterations to the poem and commentary, or was it the work of someone else? In either case, why were they made? And what is their effect on our understanding and appreciation of the *Cántico*? Since there are two distinctive versions of it, this issue has to be raised in order to establish which of the two, if not both, it is proper to examine for interpreting and evaluating the work. If CB is not the work of San Juan, then clearly no findings can be based upon its version of the text. If it is, then some account must be given of the relationship between the two. That is the extent of the problem now to be tackled.

The Sanlúcar manuscript bears the date 1584, and is the starting-point for any discussion of this complicated issue. It gives the CA text in its earliest and best form and was obviously copied with great care.[3] Its prime position has never been disputed, and it must represent the *Cántico* as it was soon after the last eight stanzas had been added and the commentaries completed, but before the addition of CB 11. Throughout the seventeenth century, *Cántico* editions followed the text of the first editions (Rome, 1627, and Madrid, 1630), which was a modified form of CA, generally designated CA', with the inclusion of CB 11. The earliest edition (Paris, 1622) had not included this latter. CA is reflected in six manuscripts as well as in the Paris and Brussels (1627) editions; CA' in twelve, as well as the editions above. The differences between CA and CA' are in no way like those between CA and CB, and consist of a general tightening up of language and a different method of quoting from Scripture. CA' stops giving the Latin texts in CA 13, line 4, whereas in CA (Sanlúcar) these are given throughout. The alterations may be scribal, or they may be the work of San Juan. P. Eulogio states that 'los retoques respetan los módulos de la prosa sanjuanista'.[4] It is important to note that CA' was the normal seventeenth-century version, and that there is no manuscript witness for the combination of CA' and CB 11 characteristic of these early editions. This suggests that the combination was in fact editorial.

No edition of CB appeared until 1703, when P. Andrés de Jesús María produced his edition of the *Cántico* at Seville. This was based on a manuscript which will become very important in this argument: the Jaén manuscript of the forty-stanza poem and heavily revised commentary.

---

[3] This manuscript is described in the BAC *Obras*, p. 998. It also contains San Juan's shorter poems. P. Silverio produced a photocopy of the manuscript, and references in this chapter are to his edition (Burgos, 1928).

[4] P. Eulogio, *San Juan de la Cruz y sus escritos*, p. 301. He gives a useful summary of the characteristics of CA and CA', pp. 281–304. In the discussion which follows on the arguments about CB, it is impossible to analyse in detail every article or point of view which has been offered. The bibliography of this particular issue is enormous, and, one may venture to say, the results it has produced are not in proportion to the number of words that have been written. Here, therefore, only the major articles will be cited, and their arguments outlined. A more complete list of references will be found in the bibliography.

This was to become the dominant version of the text until its authenticity as representing San Juan's intentions was challenged in a famous article by Dom Philippe Chevallier in 1922.[5] The CB text is given by ten other manuscripts. The early editors of CB give the impression that the Jaén manuscript contained the only authentic text. There is no suggestion that San Juan himself revised CA to produce CB until the middle of the eighteenth century, when P. Andrés de la Encarnación first noted the distinctiveness of the two redactions, and modern critical scholarship of San Juan's texts begins with him. All the early editors, of CA and CB alike, believe they are dealing with the work of San Juan, and in the case of the latter, take the view that the older versions are corrupt.

There is no manuscript of the *Cántico* in the hand of San Juan, and it is certain that some manuscripts have been lost over the centuries. These facts, together with the lack of any critical approach to the problem before P. Andrés, mean that the evidence on which any argument can be based is somewhat fragmentary. Hypothesis rather than fact has to be used, though in the course of the long argument about the authenticity of CB some of the more obvious facts have been overlooked. Chevallier attempted to demonstrate that CB could not possibly represent the intentions of San Juan. His first article sparked off a controversy which lasted for forty years and is still being conducted, though in a muted form. He was followed by other writers, though the direction of their attack gradually changed. But Chevallier began by casting doubt on CB from the evidence of manuscript transmission; and so it is there we must begin.

He argued that if San Juan had revised his work between 1584 and his death, he would surely have given a copy of this revision to M. Ana de Jesús, to whom CA has been dedicated.[6] M. Ana left for the Low Countries in 1604, taking with her only the CA text, which was the foundation for the 1622 French translation. Moreover, the Rome and Madrid editions could not have taken CB 11 from a CB manuscript, because CB quotes Biblical texts in Spanish only, whereas the editions give both Latin and Spanish, as promised in the prologue. CB must therefore have taken stanza 11 from these editions, and not vice versa. The CB text also contains some faulty readings, wrong references and contradictions, and therefore cannot stem from San Juan. In a later series of articles, Chevallier divided *Cántico* manuscript history into six different states, which he called a, A, A′, B, R, and R′. The last two had to be inferred, because they were not represented by manuscripts, but were the hypothetical original texts on which the Italian translation of

---

[5] See p. 31 below.
[6] See *Life of the Venerable Anne of Jesus*, by a Sister of Notre Dame de Namur (Sister Anne Hardman, London, 1932).

1627 and other translations during that century were based.[7] Needless to say, it is hard to accept an argument which relies so heavily on the existence of hypothetical manuscripts and appears to take no account of the fact that the work of the Italian translators, where it differs from other manuscripts, may owe more to translators' whims than to supposed new families of manuscripts. Nor is it a sound method to divide manuscripts into families whenever there is a change in the text. According to normal canons of study, there must be clearly defined features present throughout groups of manuscripts before it becomes possible to treat them as separate families. The only such features present among the extant manuscripts lead to the conclusion that there are only two main families of the *Cántico,* CA and CB, and within CA, the groups CA and CA', which are not distinctive enough to be classed separately.

Unfortunately, Chevallier did not remain consistent in his attack on CB. Though from start to finish he refused to admit its authenticity, he changed the grounds of his objection to it on several occasions. For example, it was not long before he believed that the Rome and Madrid editions must, after all, have taken CB 11 from a CB manuscript, which he had denied in 1922.[8] Until 1930 he maintained that CA was the only authentic version of the *Cántico*; but from that date, he abandoned this position, and, because of a CA' manuscript which came into his possession at Solesmes, accepted and published CA' as the definitive text.[9] Such a procedure does not inspire scholarly confidence.

Nevertheless, there must have been good reason for his doubting the authenticity of CB in the first place, a position which others were not slow to adopt. So the facts which can be established about the relationship of the Sanlúcar and Jaén manuscripts must be rehearsed, to see where there are embarrassing gaps in the traditional explanation of their history. This claims that San Juan himself revised the *Cántico,* and several copies were made of the new redaction. There is enough evidence for a forty-stanza poem in the beatification depositions; and there are also a number of CB manuscripts. The reason for the long delay in publishing a CB text is straightforward. Seventeenth-century editors were confused by the different manuscript traditions, and the Jaén manuscript, as it bears witness itself, was not available. There are strong textual links between Sanlúcar and Jaén, while the former bears a

---

[7] Chevallier, 'Le "Cantique Spirituel" interpolé', *VS* supplements (1926–31); see especially July–Aug. 1926, 109–62.

[8] Op. cit., pp. 146–7. His inconsistency has been exposed by P. Eulogio, op. cit., pp. 314–15.

[9] See his 1930 edition, *Le "Cantique spirituel"*; and *Le Texte définitif* (Solesmes, 1950). The best study of his general inconsistency was written after his last intervention in the debate, Fr. Juan de Jesús María, 'La última palabra de dom Chevallier sobre el "Cántico espiritual" ', *MC* 60 (1952), 309–402.

number of marginal annotations in the hand of San Juan which are only developed in Jaén and subsequent CB manuscripts. One or more of these claims has to be demonstrated unsound if the authenticity of CB is to be undermined.

At first sight, the late appearance of a printed CB text seems to justify doubts about its validity. But the tradition of CB can be traced back long before 1703.[10] The Jaén manuscript contains a long note inserted at the front by P. Salvador de la Cruz, and dated 1670. In it he traces the history of the manuscript, giving it pre-eminence over other, corrupt versions of the text circulating till that date.[11] P. Salvador begins by stating that the 'book' deserves great veneration because it is written by San Juan himself, not only by comparison with his handwriting elsewhere,

como porque lo certificó así la Venerable Madre Ana de Jesús Lobera, a la Venerable Madre Isabel de la Encarnación, Priora que fue del Convento de nuestras Religiosas descalzas Carmelitas de la ciudad de Jaén, a quien, siendo novicia en el Convento de . . . Granada y Priora de él la Venerable Madre Ana de Jesús, le dio la misma Venerable Madre Ana . . . este libro en cuadernos sueltos, certificándole eran escritos de mano y letra propia de nuestro Venerable Padre frai Juan de la Cruz de quien lo avía recebido. Y la misma Venerable Madre Isabel . . . siendo Priora del Convento de . . . Jaén, estando para morir, dio estos quadernos ya unidos y enquadernados como están a la Madre Clara de la Cruz, Religiosa en el mismo convento de Jaén y Priora que después ha sido de él, certificándole lo mismo.

In this way he seeks to establish the historical pedigree of the manuscript. Later he comments on the differences between this *Cántico* and those previously published. Because, he says, of the multiplicity of manuscripts of the works of San Juan which were circulating all over Spain and consequently becoming corrupted, the Order had decided to counter the risk of further mutilation by causing to be published

. . . el año de 1618 en Alcalá y el siguiente de 1619 en Barcelona la primera y segunda impresión de las obras que se pudieron haller entonces de Nuestro Venerable Padre, ajustadas ambas impresiones, no con los originales que entonces no se hallaron, sino con los más fieles manuscritos que se pudieron haller. Faltando en ambas impresiones, como en ellas se vee, este Cántico, quizá porque a la ocasión no se halló traslado de él. Aviendo después hallado la Religión algunos de los originales de Nuestro Venerable Padre, hizo nueva impresión de sus obras . . . en Madrid, año de 1630 . . . añadiendo en esta impresión este Cántico y su explicación, aunque viciado y corrupto . . ., por no haberle ajustado con este original, que siempre a estado oculto sucesivamente en poder de las tres Religiosas arriba dichas, sin tener noticia de él la Religión.

He goes on to describe in great detail the differences between this *Cántico* and the earlier editions, including all the textual variants and

[10]   See above p. 31.
[11]   Entitled 'Noticia cierta de quién escribió este libro', and found in BMC 13. 422–8.

changes in stanza position in the poem. He cannot do the same for the commentary, but outlines the chief distinctions between the two versions, and concludes by remarking that other poems of San Juan have suffered a similar fate.

P. Salvador is not concerned with critical questions. He wants to establish the most accurate texts so that the truths taught by San Juan may be passed on uncorrupted. Jaén, he claims, is such a text, and must therefore be venerated. Apart from the assurance that the manuscript is in San Juan's hand (and one must remember that the seventeenth century was much less particular than ours in such matters), P. Salvador's information, where it can be tested, is remarkably accurate. That such a manuscript could have been hidden away in the convent and treated doubtless as a precious relic is quite probable—indeed, it is still brought out on public display in Jaén![12] But the most interesting part of his note is the pedigree he establishes for it, right back to M. Ana, to whom the first *Cántico* had been dedicated. If this is true, it means that she did receive a copy of CB, though she left it behind in Spain when she went to the Low Countries, taking with her, presumably, only CA. The handwriting of the manuscript is not conclusive, as it is in an italic script consequently less easy to date; but it certainly could belong to a date around 1600.[13]

But the significance of the Jaén manuscript can be more firmly demonstrated another way. It gives a very pure text of the poem, purer than many of the later CA versions. Its text is nearly always closer to Sanlúcar than the early seventeenth-century editions based on CA/CA' texts. This becomes clear from the comparative readings P. Salvador gives in his 'Noticia cierta'. He compares his manuscript with a number of printed editions of the poem, those in P. Jerónimo's *Vida*; Madrid, 1630; and Cologne, 1639 (Latin); as well as pointing to certain features of their respective commentaries. For example, where CA 1 in the *Vida* has 'Ya eras ido', Madrid, Cologne, Jaén and Sanlúcar all have 'Y eras ido'. In CA 2, Cologne has 'los que fueredes', while all the others agree on 'los que fuerdes'. In Jaén, the extra 'e' has deliberately been crossed out (and in the rhyming 'vierdes'). In CA 8 Madrid and *Vida* read 'O

---

[12] See Lowe, *The South of Spain* (London, 1973), pp. 397–8. It is in the Convent of the Carmelitas Descalzas.

[13] The closest likeness to the Jaén hand I have been able to find is fig. 52 (between pp. 46–7) of Millares Carlo and Mantecón, *Album de Paleografía Hispanoamericana*, 3 vols. (Mexico, 1955), vol. i. The figure shows a passage from Bartolomé de las Casas, *De unico vocationis modo* (16th century). The italic of Jaén is inclined to join the letters a little more frequently than this example; and numerals for the stanzas are given in Arabic, not Roman form. Although the latter predominated till the end of the seventeenth century, the former sometimes occurs at the beginning. If it were possible to examine the manuscript itself, the paper might provide more conclusive evidence for dating.

alma no viviendo donde vives', whereas Cologne, Jaén, and Sanlúcar (in one of the marginal annotations shortly to be discussed) read 'O vida, no viviendo donde vives'. Sometimes Sanlúcar and Jaén agree against all three editions, having 'del Amado', 'de hermosura', 'en púrpura tendido', and 'de mil escudos' for 'de mi Amado', 'de su hermosura', 'en púrpura tenido', and 'con mil escudos' in CA 4, 5, and CA 15/CB 24 respectively. Only on four occasions does Jaén disagree with Sanlúcar (apart, of course, from the inclusion of CB 11, and also one uncertain reading where the copyist has been at fault[14]), and these are precisely the four examples given at the beginning of this chapter as characterizing the text of the poem in its second redaction.

This is an impressive piece of evidence, which opponents of CB's authenticity have to explain away. Obviously, there is a close affinity between the texts of the poem in the two manuscripts, and this strongly suggests that whatever the origins of Jaén are, they are closely linked with Sanlúcar. Thus there is an historical link between CA and Jaén, described by P. Salvador, and a textual one, at least for the poem, because Jaén gives a text closer to Sanlúcar than any of the other CA' versions. But the connection between the two manuscripts is further strengthened by the presence on the Sanlúcar manuscript itself of a number of marginal and interlinear annotations, which have been developed and incorporated into the CB redaction alone. The provenance of these annotations has occasioned much debate in the arguments about CB, and it is important to discover what evidence they provide.

At the foot of the title-page, a hand other than that of the copyist has written: 'Este libro es el borrador de q̄ ya se saco en limpio—fr. Ju.° de la +'. Taken at face value, the note claims that Sanlúcar is the rough copy from which San Juan himself made a fair version. In the same hand, in the margins and between the lines, are a number of notes, of varying length. Some are corrections, others sketch out additional material. Examination of these annotations demonstrates that they form the basis of ideas included only in the CB redaction. Some of them are very small: CB follows the Sanlúcar note and adds 'y san Pablo' at 19.10. CB 20—21.19 expands the annotation 'por qué dice la flor de la viña y no el fruto', explaining how the one refers to this life, the other to the next. Others are longer: CB 26.16 has a lengthy addition based on a marginal note concerning the perfecting of natural knowledge by supernatural; while CB 38.3 adds the involved theological annotation about the soul loving in the Spirit and with the Spirit, not as his instrument but together with him, her lack of love supplied through transformation in the Spirit. These, then, are some of the typical treatments of the annotations given by CB. It becomes immediately clear why

---

[14] The insertion of 'su' above the line in CB 13.

Sanlúcar was described as the 'borrador' from which a fair copy was taken.

But is the statement on the title-page, and are the annotations in the text, in the hand of San Juan? It might seem simple to determine this, as there are know autographs of his hand.[15] But it is wellnigh impossible to examine these and the Sanlúcar manuscript in the original and in the same place. Moreover, the handwriting of the annotations is affected by the fact that it is squeezed in between lines or into margins, and so more susceptible to distortion than in a carefully written document. A number of disinterested experts have examined the evidence, and with one exception, their findings support the traditional and obvious conclusion, that inscription and annotations alike are the work of San Juan.

For his edition of the *Obras,* P. Silverio sought the opinions of Pedro Longas and Matías Martínez Burgos, from the Cuerpo de Archivos, Bibliotecas y Museos del Estado; and he publishes the latter's conclusions, accepting that the annotations are in the hand of San Juan.[16] In 1946 Fr. Juan de Jesús María consulted a leading Jesuit expert, P. Dionisio Fernández Zapico, who knew nothing of the CB controversy.[17] He concluded: 'La letra de las anotaciones y añadiduras marginales que están en el "Cántico espiritual . . . Sanlúcar" según mi parecer son de la misma mano que escribió los "Avisos y sentencias espirituales" ', these being among the known autographs of San Juan, published by P. Gerardo. Later, Fernández Zapico made it clear that the inscription on the title-page was also included in this judgement. Duvivier has recently added another expert view, from M. Jacques Stiennon, professor of palaeography at Liège. He examined photocopies of the annotations, P. Gerardo's collection of autographs, and the copy of the life of Catalina de Cristo, edited by the Carmel of Begona and generally held to be in the hand of San Juan. His conclusions, though rightly guarded because he could not examine the originals together, tend to support the authenticity of the annotations. The Catalina manuscript, he says, is unlike the others, and in a different hand; the inscription and annotations in Sanlúcar are probably in the same hand, though the former is written more carefully (understandably, since there is more room for it). The annotations and the autograph of the 'Avisos' are so close that 'on peut envisager l'œuvre d'un seul et même scribe.'[18]

---

[15] Photocopies of these have been published by P. Gerardo de San Juan de la Cruz, *Los autógrafos que se conservan del Místico Doctor San Juan de la Cruz* (Toledo, 1913).

[16] BMC 13. 427—41.

[17] In '¿Las anotaciones del códice de Sanlúcar, son de s. Juan de la Cruz?', *EC* 1 (1947), 154—62.

[18] Duvivier, *La Genèse,* intro., p. xxxii.

Only once has evidence been presented against the view that the annotations are in San Juan's hand, and that was by Dom Chevallier.[19] His attack was based on the conclusions of an anonymous expert. Though asked to name him, he never did, and in later years preferred to forget the matter. Today it is commonly supposed that the anonymous expert was none other than Chevallier himself. In any case, he changed his mind once more, because in 1922 he had thought that the annotations were the work of San Juan but developed by a disciple of his into CB around 1626. When it became clear that the annotations had to be proved to be in another hand if CB were to be thoroughly discredited, he managed to alter course and thereby show up his inconsistency.

To deny the authenticity of the Sanlúcar annotations involves more than Chevallier seems to have realized. In the first place, the links between the two manuscripts have to be discounted, both in the text of the poem and in the development of the annotations, and some other explanation found for them. Also, the other CB manuscripts have to be ignored, even though some of them seem firmly anchored in the circle of San Juan. A good example is the Segovia manuscript.[20] It contains a note dated 1636, which reads: 'es original de su misma mano, que le dio a una persona de esta ciudad de Segovia muy devota suya. Está impreso con las demás obras del V. P. en Madrid año 1630, y en Barcelona año 1635.' It is signed 'Diego de Colmenares'. It is not in fact a holograph, nor is it the manuscript on which the editions named are based—again, we note the seventeenth-century lack of awareness of the problems which concern us. But the middle statement, that it was given by San Juan to someone in Segovia, still demands explanation if CB is not admitted as the work of the saint. Then again, if such a position is adopted, an alternative explanation has to be found for the fact that the handwriting of the annotations appears to be that of San Juan; and it has to be assumed that any reference to a forty-stanza *Cántico* in the beatification documents and elsewhere is no more than CA described by a convenient round figure.

In the course of the controversy many hypotheses have been offered, and the profusion of theories is due at least in part to the gaps in the manuscript tradition. The historical processes governing the origins of certain important manuscripts are shrouded in mystery. It is not surprising, therefore, that critics on both sides have tended more recently to argue that the manuscript evidence cannot by itself determine the

---

[19] In his series of articles in the *VS* supplements.

[20] For its description, see BAC *Obras*, pp. 999–1000. P. Eulogio summarizes the various CB MSS., op. cit., pp. 326–47. He concludes; 'En Castilla son Segovia, Alba, Salamanca, Medina del Campo y Burgos los centros carmelitanos que conocen y difunden las 40 Canciones. En Andalucía las lee y propaga desde Granada, Baeza, Úbeda y Jaén' (p. 347).

problem of CB, and that attention must be paid to the changes in doctrinal exposition between the two redactions, to see if CB is doctrinally compatible with its predecessor. At the same time, little work has been done on assessing the internal evidence the two redactions provide in comparison with each other and other authentic works of San Juan, to discover whether or not CB as literature is consonant with the rest of the saint's output.

From 1927 Chevallier began to claim that the doctrine expounded in CB was different from that in CA, and as San Juan could not have been so inconsistent, CB could not be his work. There are, of course, many changes made in the CB commentary, but they cannot all be termed doctrinal in substance, and one must avoid the temptation of regarding changes of emphasis as contradictions of earlier teaching. The only safe method is to admit as contradictions only those passages in CB which are quite incompatible with the teaching of CA. If any can be found, they will be valuable aids in concluding that CB is the work of another mind. A good example of failure to observe this method occurs in the attitude of Chevallier to the exposition of the last five stanzas of CB. Whereas in CA San Juan had referred them to the highest state possible in this life, CB sets them in the context of the beatific vision, beyond death: 'Sólo le queda una cosa que desear, que es gozarle perfectamente en la vida eterna; y así, en la siguiente canción y en las demás que se siguen se emplea en pedir al Amado este beatífico pasto, en manifiesta visión de Dios.'[21] This change of context is worked out thoroughly in the last five stanzas; but it is hardly a change of doctrine. The beatific vision as the ultimate goal of the soul's journey is not a notion alien to San Juan, but an integral part of his teaching.[22] Why should he not have changed his mind?

Jean Krynen has claimed that the new material in CB was added by two early-seventeenth-century writers, Tomás de Jesús and Agustín Antolínez, to combat certain erroneous elements in CA.[23] Antolínez (1554–1626) himself wrote a commentary on the *Cántico*, and eleven of the Sanlúcar annotations are said to reflect his teaching; while fifteen more come from Tomás de Jesús (1564–1627), who is said to have taught a different doctrine of mystical prayer from San Juan's. Krynen's thesis has been countered most effectively in a number of articles,

---

[21] CB 36.2.

[22] As in S 2.4.4, 9.3–4; CA 11.4; L 1.14.

[23] Krynen puts his case in 'Un Aspect nouveau des annotations marginales du "borrador" du "Cantique spirituel" de saint Jean de la Croix', *BH* 49 (1947), 400–21 and 53 (1951), 393–412. It is more fully developed in *Le "Cantique spirituel" . . . commenté et refondu au XVIIe siècle* (Salamanca, 1948). Bataillon, who had welcomed Chevallier's 'critical' edition of 1930 (see *BH* 33 (1931), 164–70), is more reserved about Krynen's claims (*BH* 51 (1949), 188–94).

using arguments both historical and doctrinal. For example, it is unlikely that Tomás de Jesús taught so different a doctrine; and the idea that the annotations were first developed by Antolínez and only then incorporated into CB is a tortuous one, because, as we have noted, there is a direct link only between the annotations and CB. That between the annotations and Antolínez is more tenuous, and is better explained by Antolínez's having used CB rather than vice versa. Moreover, it is hard to see why two different authors should have provided one set of annotations which are all developed in the same text (CB) in the same way.[24] By 1962, Krynen had developed a rather different theory, though still based on a doctrinal opposition between Tomás and San Juan.[25] A new mystical theory arose early in the seventeenth century, which he calls 'la mystique des lumières'. This accepted spiritual favours as a sign of God's grace and thus to be sought by the mystic, instead of negated, as with San Juan. Tomás de Jesús, charged with preparing San Juan's work for publication, is said to be the leader of this new era in Christian spirituality, and the 'profonds remaniements' to which he subjected San Juan's works show how he adapted them to the new way.

This hypothesis is a good example of the kind of arguments used to dispute the doctrine of CB; and rather than outline them all, the worth of this one will be tested. It is true that Tomás de Jesús was commissioned to prepare the works of San Juan for publication. But that had been in 1601, and the first edition did not appear until 1618, and then without the *Cántico*. Tomás withdrew from this task in 1604, and the part he played in preparing for the 1618 edition is far from clear.[26] Nor is the distinction Krynen makes between the teaching of San Juan and the 'mystique des lumières' convincing. The mystical tradition included both attitudes towards spiritual favours, with writers like Rolle stressing the light and joy of the spiritual life and taking a positive attitude towards them. As Wolters has pointed out in his introduction to the *Fire*: 'Clearly for some "the King's way of the Holy Cross" is so counterbalanced by "the joy that is set before them" that they attend but little

[24] The main replies to Krynen's argument are: Fr. Juan de Jesús María, 'La segunda redacción del "Cántico espiritual" y el comentario al mismo de Agustín Antolínez', *MC* 53 (1949), 13–37; and 'El "Cántico espiritual" de san Juan de la Cruz y "Amores de Dios y el Alma" de A. Antolínez', *EC* 3 (1949), 443–542 and 4 (1950), 3–70; and Fr. Simeón de la Sda. Familia, 'Un nuevo códice manuscrito de las obras de San Juan de la Cruz usado y anotado por el P. Tomás de Jesús', *EC* 4 (1950), 95–148; and 'Tomás de Jesús y San Juan de la Cruz', *EC* 5 (1951–4), 91–159.

[25] 'Du nouveau sur Thomas de Jésus', *BH* 64 bis (1962), 113–35.

[26] The mystery surrounding the first editions of the *Cántico* is discussed by P. Eulogio in 'Primeras ediciones del "Cántico espiritual" ', *EC* 18 (1967), 3–48; and *El "Cántico espiritual"–trayectoria histórica del texto* (Rome, 1967). It is a complicated issue, and will not be further discussed as it does not impinge directly on the question of CB's authenticity.

to the hardness of the way. For them it must be Rolle: it could not be Walter Hilton, *The Cloud of Unknowing*, or St. John of the Cross.'[27] It is incorrect to treat this 'mystique des lumières' as a new movement to be contrasted with the 'dark night' type of mysticism (and San Juan has plenty of moments when he dwells on the sweetness and joy also). Strange, too, that Krynen constructs most of his hypothesis from the 1618 edition of the works of San Juan—which did not include CA, let alone CB. He draws most of his evidence from the *Subida-Noche*. The examples he does give from CB relate not to some new teaching but to the change in context from this life to the next in the commentary on the last five stanzas of CB.[28] Only if that change were not the work of San Juan could such examples be cited to support the argument against CB.

What is needed, in view of the inconclusive nature of the manuscript evidence and the unsatisfactory argument against CB on doctrinal grounds, is a new method for testing its authenticity. Few writers on the subject have adopted a proper methodology; instead, there has been a tendency to snatch at isolated pieces of evidence which might support a given position. CB must be approached as a whole. Its additions and alterations can be isolated and tested for their authenticity against material indisputably by San Juan; but they must be seen within the totality of CB and not as individual case histories. Though this is a literary method, it can shed light on doctrine, because not only will the style of CB and other works be compared, but the content which the words are seeking to communicate.[29]

CB 11 provides a good test for this method. By examining the internal evidence of poem and commentary it can be clearly shown that CB 11 is the work of San Juan. The stanza is foreshadowed in CA 6.2:

Como las criaturas dieron al alma señas de su Amado mostrándole en sí rastro de su *hermosura* y excelencia, augmentósele el *amor* y, por consiguiente, crecióle el dolor de la ausencia . . . y como ue *no ay cosa que la pueda curar su dolencia sino la vista y la presencia de su Amado* . . . pídele en esta canción la entrega y possesión de su *presencia.*[30]

CB 11 is obviously a poetic version of this same thought. The commentary, too, contains many signs of the mind of San Juan, and there are several parallels in style and doctrine with his other works:

(i) In CB 11.3, three kinds of divine presence in the soul are distinguished. The first is essential presence, that is, the ontological dependence

---

[27] P. 29.

[28] Krynen, op. cit., fn 47, pp. 132–3.

[29] This next section is a fuller treatment of the method I first described in my article 'The authenticity of the second redaction of the *Cántico espiritual* in the light of its doctrinal additions', *BHS* 51 (1974), 244–54.

[30] My italics.

of every created thing on God: 'Con esta presencia les da vida y ser y, si esta presencia esencial les faltase, todas se aniquilirían y dejarían de ser.' Compare S 2.5.3: 'Y esta manera de unión siempre está hecha entre Dios y las criaturas todas, en la cual los está conservando el ser que tienen; de manera que si . . . faltase, luego se aniquilirían y dejarían de ser.' Not only is the same doctrine expounded; exactly the same verbs are used. The second kind of presence is through grace, given by God to those with whom he is pleased. It is not therefore, as the first, possessed in equal measure by all creatures, as S 2.5.4 also shows; and mortal sin deprives the soul of it, as in S 1.12.3. The third presence is 'por afección espiritual, porque en muchas almas devotas suele Dios hacer algunas presencias espirituales'. Here San Juan is thinking of a presence characteristic of the mystical way, which both he and Santa Teresa describe at such length. In other words, this passage in CB 11 crystalizes San Juan's teaching given elsewhere on God's presence in the soul.

(ii) CB 11.7 is typical of San Juan's teaching that suffering and death are gladly to be undergone for the sake of seeing the beauty of God, and expresses the mystical commonplace of dying in order to live in an acute form. The image of the 'espesura' in CA 35.11−13 contains a similar exposition of the soul's desire for suffering and death.

(iii) CB 11.10 contains a discussion of the idea that to see God is to die, developed from a Biblical text (Exodus 33:20) quoted earlier, in 11.5. The idea that man cannot look on God and live recurs throughout the Western mystical tradition. Some had thought that in highest rapture a man could actually see the essence of God, but by the sixteenth century, and certainly to San Juan's way of thinking, perfect vision was regarded as occuring only after death. San Juan quotes this text several times elsewhere.[31] CA 13−14.14−15 discusses two of the classic test cases: Elijah and the still small voice, and Paul's experience recounted in 2 Corinthians 12:4. 'Máteme tu vista' and its exposition thus stands within the tradition San Juan uses. But he goes further, distinguishing the old law of the Old Testament and the new law of Christ as marking different solutions to the question. CB 11.9: 'Pero hay aquí una duda, y es: ¿por qué los hijos de Israel antiguamente huían y temían de ver a Dios por no morir, como dijo Manué a su mujer (Iud 13, 22), y esta alma a la vista de Dios desea morir?' This same Biblical allusion, hardly a well-known one, occurs in S 2.24.2; while the first part of S 2.22 is also devoted to the unravelling of a 'duda', concerning those who sought visions under the old dispensation and those who in the new are to look to Christ alone. The parallel is not complete, as vision and visions of God are distinct categories in mystical teaching; but the theological principle is the same. Man's knowledge of God was incomplete, but is completed in Christ.

[31]   e.g. S 2.8.4, 24.2; 3.12.1.

(iv) An impressive stylistic parallel occurs in CB 11.10 and CA 35.5. The former reads: 'sería ella arrebatada a la misma hermosura, y absorta en la misma hermosura, y transformada en la misma hermosura, y ser ella hermosa como la misma hermosura, y abastada y enriquecida con la misma hermosura.' In CA 35.5 the word 'hermosura' is repeated some twenty times, in a passage which again demonstrates San Juan's fascination with the theme of divine beauty.

(v) CB 11.10: 'Pero el alma que ama a Dios, más vive en la otra vida que en ésta, porque más vive el alma donde ama que donde anima, y así tiene en poco esta vida temporal.' The idea that the true home of the soul is where she loves rather than lives is also found in CA 8.3: 'Es de saber que el alma más biue en lo que ama que en el cuerpo donde anima, porque en el cuerpo ella no tiene su vida, antes ella la da al cuerpo, y ella en lo que ama viue.' This is a commonplace theological principle of the time, which San Juan uses to justify the contemplative's attitude to life in the world.

(vi) Another well-worn theme is found in CB 11.11: the doctrine of the contraries. Here it is developed with regard to love, the one exception to the rule that contraries are cured by their contraries, an idea which occurs (without reference to the contraries) in CA 6.2 and 9.3, while the contraries are mentioned in many other places.[32]

(vii) CB 11.12: 'El amor nunca llega a estar perfecto hasta que emparejan tan en uno los amantes, que se transfiguran el uno en el otro.' This is reminiscent of the last three lines of stanza five of the *Noche oscura* poem:

> ¡Oh noche que juntaste
> Amado con amada,
> amada en el Amado transformada!

In his commentary on that poem, San Juan never reached the fifth stanza, but he would certainly have developed these words into a statement of mystical transformation. The CB examples uses 'transfigure' rather than 'transform', but the words are very similar and the meaning the same: the joining of the lovers in intimate union. The choice of word is undoubtedly dictated by the presence of 'figura' in the last line of the stanza being expounded. In CA 12.7 the union of the lovers is similarly pictured: 'Y tal manera de semejanza hace el amor en la transformación de los Amados, que se puede decir que cada uno es el otro y que entrambos son uno.'

In the face of such evidence, it is hard to see how anyone other than San Juan could have written either the stanza or the commentary in question. The method that has been used may now be extended to

---

[32] e.g. S 1.4.2, 6.1–3; 3.6.1, 19.4; N 2.5.4, 7.5, 9.2, 15.1, 21.2; CA 8.3, L 1.22–3; 3.18.

CB as a whole. It has the advantage of being firmly grounded in accessible material, and is not dependent upon hypotheses, like so much of the debate on manuscript transmission. Obviously, the whole extent of the CB changes cannot be covered, so the examples must be selective. Some are important, others apparently insignificant, because it is necessary to grasp that many of the changes from CA to CB are very small—rephrasing, clarification, addition of a few words—and that whoever was responsible for CB not only made major alterations but a very large number of minor ones, with little or no doctrinal bearing. They are as much a part of the problem of resolving CB's authenticity as the others, a point which has not been sufficiently realized. CB is not simply CA with a body of alien teaching introduced into it. It is a careful rewriting of CA, so that if the aim of the reviser of CA was to alter its doctrine, then it has to be explained why he also made many changes unrelated to such an endeavour. The following examples are intended to show how the material added to CA belongs to the recognizable style and teaching of San Juan.

(i) In CB 1.11 faith and love are called 'los mozos de ciego que te guiarán por donde no sabes, allá a lo escondido de Dios'. Compare S 1.8.3 and 2.3.4, which both use the example of the blind man's boy; and L 3.29: 'En este negocio es Dios el principal agente y el mozo de ciego que la ha de guiar por la mano a donde ella no sabría ir' (referring to the soul). Evidently this is one of San Juan's favourite pictures, though its precise value alters in its general use for describing the soul's progress when understanding is dimmed and faith the way to tread. The *Llama* parallel bears close resemblance to the CB teaching that ordinary knowledge cannot be the guide on this journey 'por donde no sabes' or 'a donde ella no sabría ir'. S 1.8.3 gives the Biblical source of the picture, Matthew 15:14. The blind man's boy was a stock literary figure, and a famous example of secular usage can be found in *Lazarillo de Tormes*.[33]

(ii) This same passage testifies to the inability of human understanding to reach God, an idea repeated even more forcefully in the CB addition 26.13:

Es de saber que la causa más formal de este no saber del alma cosa del mundo . . . es el quedar ella informada de la ciencia sobrenatural delante de la cual todo el saber natural y político del mundo antes es no saber que saber. De donde, puesta el alma en este altísimo saber, conoce por él que todo esotro saber que no sabe a aquello no es saber sino no saber.

Though the knowing/not knowing paradox is commonplace, it is repeated many times by San Juan: S 1.4.5, 'antes ha de ir no sabiendo que por saber'; 2.26.18, 'queriendo caminar a Dios por el no saber';

[33] *La vida de Lazarillo de Tormes*, ed. R. O. Jones (Manchester, 1963), pp. 9–16.

CA 38.13, 'entender no entendiendo'; and the *coplas* 'Entréme donde no supe'. CB and San Juan are again speaking with the same voice.

(iii) CB 1.14 describes the need for 'desnudez' from all things, and 'pobreza de espíritu' in the soul seeking God. San Juan is constantly pointing to the need for such poverty, as there can be no ultimate satisfaction in things created. Compare S 2.24.8, 'desundez de todas cosas, o pobreza espiritual'; 3.40.1, 'desnudez interior, que es la pobreza espiritual en negación de todas las cosas que puedes poseer'; and N 2.4.1, 'la purgación contemplativa o desnudez y pobreza espritual (que todo aquí casi es una misma cosa)'. Such expressions run like *leitmotivs* through the writings of San Juan.

(iv) CB 10.1–3 contains various analogies San Juan uses elsewhere. The sick soul, likened to a man who has lost his appetite for 'todos los manjares' is found, with verbal parallels, in N 2.19.1; the example of 'María Magdalena cuando con ardiente amor andaba buscándole por el huerto, pensando que era el hortelano' (John 20:15) is in N 2.13.7 as a case of 'embriaguez y ansia de amor'; and the picture of the city of the soul and the powers lurking outside the wall ready to attack it also occurs in CA 31.7.

(v) CB 13.1 adds a passage about the dark night, the most pervasive of all San Juan's symbols:

La causa de padecer el alma tanto a este tiempo por él es que, como se va juntando más a Dios, siente en sí más el vacío de Dios y gravísimas tinieblas en su alma con fuego espiritual que la seca y purga, para que purificada se pueda unir con Dios . . . Esle Dios intolerables tinieblas . . . porque la luz sobrenatural escurece la natural con su exceso.

There follow two Biblical texts, Psalms 96:2–3 and 17:12–13.[34] In N 2.5.3 the same two texts are used to illustrate exactly the same point, often in very similar words: 'tinieblas', 'escurece', 'purgada', 'cuanto el alma más a El se acerca'. Other features which give this passage its authentic ring are the suffering of the soul as it nears God (part of the dark night experience), the emptiness resulting from purgation of all affection for the creatures (S 1.5.2, N 2.6.4), and the traditional language of darkness and fire, juxtaposed, for example, in N 2.11.1, 7, and 12.1. Indeed, it would be hard to find a passage which sounds more like San Juan; but since it is a CB addition, it must be taken by opponents of CB's authenticity as a correction of his genuine doctrine and by Krynen, presumably, as an example of 'la mystique des lumières'! The addition is the more interesting because the *Cántico* is not dealing, like the *Subida* and *Noche*, with the symbol of the dark night, but with a

---

[34] The numbering of Psalms is according to the Vulgate, which is derived from the Greek Septuagint, as opposed to the Hebrew, which most English versions follow.

much more varied imagery in which no one symbol is the controlling one. It seems most unlikely that anyone who intended to combat San Juan's doctrine should have included in his correction so clear a statement of the terrors of the dark night.

(vi) In CB 16.2–3 material is added on the way the devil takes advantage of the prospering soul by arousing the subdued sensual appetites or causing it to sin. In such cases, the soul may call on angels to ward off the attack. This is also mentioned in N 2.23.4, where angels likewise appear as the soul's allies, as also in CA 7.6. In CB 16.6–7 the soul withdraws to find refuge from the devil: 'suele el alma con gran presteza recogerse en el hondo escondrijo de su interior'. Aminadab is quoted in illustration (Song 6:11), as in CA 39.3, and there the term 'escondrijo' also appears. But the closest parallel is N 2.23.4, which includes the CB experience of observing the devil attacking the soul: 'Y entonces todo aquel temor le cae por defuera'; compare CB 16.6: 'Y entonces padece aquellos temores tan por de fuera'.

(vii) CB 19.5 adds: 'Todo lo que se comunica al sentido, mayormente en esta vida, no puede ser puro espíritu, por no ser él capaz de ello.' The doctrine that in this life the flesh cannot bear purely spiritual communications because they are alien to it is often repeated by San Juan. Compare N 1.9.4: 'La parte sensitiva no tiene habilidad para lo que es puro espíritu . . . por no ser capaz el sentido y fuerza natural.'

(viii) CB 20–1.2 contains a significant addition about the betrothal and marriage, part of which runs thus: 'Teniendo ella [el alma] abierta la puerta de la voluntad para el por entero y verdadero *sí* de amor, que es el *sí* del desposorio, que está dado antes del matrimonio espiritual.' L 3.24–5 contains a similar passage, with the same repeated '*sí*' of consent: 'En el desposorio sólo hay un igualado "sí" . . . el "sí" acerca de todo esto en Dios . . . esto es haberle Dios dado en el "sí" de ella su verdadero "sí" y entero de su gracia.' What makes this coincidence the more striking, apart from doctrinal and stylistic parallels, is that the *Llama* and CB (if the work of San Juan) were given their final shape at about the same time.[35] CB must have been finished a little later, because CB 31.7 already mentions 'la declaración de las cuatro canciones que comienzan ¡*Oh llama de amor viva*!' Opponents of CB have to explain why its author should have gone to the trouble of including among his additions and corrections a reference to one of San Juan's own works which could not be included in CA because the work in question was not then completed.

(ix) CB 22.3, the expanded version of CA 27.3, adds 'meditación de las cosas espirituales' to the exercises of the purgative way. This small

[35] See Ruiz Salvador, *Introducción a San Juan de la Cruz* (Madrid, 1968), pp. 215–21, 249–52.

addition links with a distinctive feature of San Juan's teaching, which he was able to clarify from the confused way in which it reached him from the tradition. Meditation and contemplation are separate things. The time comes when meditation must cease, and give way to the truly mystical state of contemplation, which is a gift infused by God, not achieved by the soul. This terminology has a precise significance in San Juan's system, best seen in S 2.12–17, but more briefly, for the sake of comparison, in N 1.1.1: 'En esta noche oscura comienzan a entrar las almas cuando Dios las va sacando de estado de principiantes, que es de los que meditan en el camino espiritual.' In true contemplation the soul, emptied of all created images, waits in darkness for the Creator to visit her.

(x) CB 24.9 adds to the CA exposition of 'mil escudos de oro' a passage Krynen pointed to as a sign of Antolínez's influence, from his exegesis of Song 3:7:[36] 'Es el número cierto por incierto, como decimos mil soldados.' CB 24.9 has: 'Y dice que son mil, para denotar la multitud de las virtudes, gracias y dones de que Dios dota el alma en este estado; porque para significar también el innumerable número de las virtudes de la esposa, usó del mismo término.' There is a slight parallel, though Antolínez is dealing with 'sexaginta fortes' and only introduces 'mil' by the way, whereas San Juan's 'mil' is central. Moreover, San Juan is not concerned with Song 3:7, though the verse is mentioned to explain 'de oro', but with 4:4, the direct source of the image in his poem: 'Mille clypei pendent ex ea.' And there is a much closer parallel between this CB passage and CA 5.2 than between it and Antolínez. There San Juan himself writes: 'Por estas mil gracias que dice iba derramando se entiende la multitud de las criaturas innumerables; que por eso pone aquí el número mayor, que es mil, para dar a entender la multitud dellas.' In jumping at a weak example to support his own theory, Krynen has failed to see that the CB passage is much closer, with verbal parallels like 'innumerables' and 'multitud', to CA than to Antolínez.

(xi) One of San Juan's most characteristic theological points concerns equality in loving between the soul and God.[37] It is interesting, therefore, to find CB 27.1 and 28.1 referring to God's humility in raising the soul to be his equal: 'Y como no hay otra cosa en que más la puede engrandecer que igualándola consigo, por eso solamente se sirve de que le ame, porque la propriedad del amor es igualar al que ama con la cosa amada.' It is hard to imagine anyone other than San Juan writing these words; just as in CA 37/CB 38.3, where CB additions expand the 'igualdad de amor' theme from CA material, there is perfect harmony between the authors of both redactions.

---

[36] 'In lectulum Salomonis sexaginta fortes ambiunt ex fortissimis Israel.'
[37] This idea is examined more fully in Ch. 7, pp. 166–7 below.

(xii) The fact that the CB exposition of the last five stanzas refers to the beatific vision and not to this life was earlier found to be in accordance with San Juan's teaching and traditional theology. He was perfectly aware that experience of God in this life cannot compare with the glory of the blessed in the next. The argument of those who oppose CB's authenticity on doctrinal grounds rules out the possibility that San Juan himself revised CA because he wanted to systematize his teaching, apparently on the grounds that he could not have changed his mind. As long as his alterations are compatible with the doctrinal system, this seems an unwarranted supposition.

(xiii) CB 37.6 describes the ineffability of lofty experiences: 'Y el sabor de esta alabanza es tan delicado, que totalmente es inefable.' CB 38.4 makes the same point about the perfection of the spiritual marriage. This is another favourite theme of San Juan, as of most mystical writers: exalted experiences are beyond the reach of words. Compare CA 17.4: 'Y lo que Dios comunica al alma en esta estrecha junta totalmente es indecible y no se puede decir nada'; and CA 36.6 (peculiar to CA): 'Y el sabor y deleyte que también entonces recibe de nueuo, totalmente es inefable.' Because it is a commonplace theme, the close verbal parallels should be noted.

(xiv) CA 37/CB 38.2 offer differing interpretations of the image of the poem's 'día'. If the CB interpretation were alien to San Juan's pattern of thought, then here would be a strong argument against its authenticity. CA 37.2 inteprets 'día' as 'la limpieza y pureza que en el estado original la dio, o en el día de el baptismo, acabándola de limpiar de todas sus imperfecciones y tinieblas como entonces lo estaua.' It refers to the soul's re-entry into 'el estado de la justicia original', that is to its preternatural state in the restoration of man's lost paradise. CB on the other hand changes the interpretation to 'la gloria esencial para que él la predestinó desde el día de su eternidad.' Moreover, before this, CB has omitted its parallel to CA 31.9, which had referred to the state of the soul in union as 'una bienauenturada vida semejante a la de el estado de la inocencia'. It begins to look as if San Juan wanted to stress the idea of restored paradise and recovered innocence, while the author of CB removed these references, in favour of the theme of predestination to essential glory after death. But before such a conclusion can be drawn, it has to be established that this CB teaching is not part of San Juan's system. And this cannot be done. For what might have been a typically CA reference to the state of original innocence turns up in a CB addition, 26.14, at a different stage in the soul's progress; 'Está el alma en este puesto en cierta manera como Adán en la inocencia.' And the theme of 'gloria esencial', which seemed limited to CB, occurs in S 3.26.8, and 'predestinación' in CA 36.3: 'Y tiene muchos senos de juicios suyos ocultos de predestinación y presciencia en los hijos de los hombres.' There is therefore nothing foreign to San Juan's teaching in the CB changes here. Rather, this example shows once more how clearly the material of the last five stanzas has been restructured in accordance with their new meaning. The doctrines in fact are complementary. CA's 'estado original' and 'bautismo' refer generally to all souls, which stood in innocence before the Fall, as Adam, and do again when original sin is washed away in baptism. CB's changes refer to the particular destiny of each individual soul after death, as intended by God, frustrated by the Fall, but repaired through the atoning work of Christ.

(xv) The last few lines of CB 38.9 contain a miniature miscellany of typical expression of San Juan:

Aquel peso de gloria en que me predestinaste, ¡oh Esposo mío!, en el día de tu eternidad, cuando tuviste por bien de determinar de criarme, me darás luego allí en el mi día de mi desposorio y mis bodas y en el día mío de la alegría de mi corazón, cuando, desatándome de la carne y entrándome en las subidas cavernas de tu tálamo, transformándome en ti gloriosamente, bebamos el mosto de las suaves granadas.

Parallels to these expressions may be found as follows:

oh Esposo mío	CA 1.20
el día de tu eternidad	S 2.3.5
me darás luego allí	CA 37, lines 3–4
en el mi día . . . de la alegría de mi corazón	(Song 3:11) CA 21.7
desatándome de la carne	CA 1.2
las subidas cavernas	CA 36, lines 1–2[38]
tu tálamo	CA 15.2
transformándome en ti	CA 17.4
el mosto de las . . . granadas	(Song 8:2) CA 36, line 5

The number of such phrases in so short a space strongly suggests the hand of San Juan, not of another author correcting him.

A large number of points of contact between CB material and San Juan's undisputed works have now been examined. Direct verbal parallels do not occur in every case, though they are sufficient to provide weighty evidence for the authenticity of CB. But the essential conclusion to which they point is to a community of style and doctrine between CB and San Juan. It is that basic affinity which has been called into question, but which now emerges more strongly than ever. In each case the result has been the same. The CB additions exhibit characteristics of San Juan's prose style and nothing in them contradicts his doctrinal deposit. There are changes, certainly, but not the kind which require the hypothesis of another author. They reflect instead the different struc-

[38] Cf. L 3, line 3.

turing of CB undertaken by San Juan for reasons we shall later discover.
Thus the evidence these additions provide is, in my view, decisive in
demonstrating that CB is the work of San Juan and, together with the
failure of its opponents to construct a coherent, consistent, and
methodical case against it, sufficient to scotch the idea that anyone
other than San Juan was responsible for the second redaction of the
Cántico.

But the journey is not quite over yet. Two other lines of attack have
to be countered before CB's authenticity can be accepted. They stem
from the observation that there are inconsistencies within CB which a
revision might have been expected to remove; and that CA and CB treat
Biblical quotations differently.

Chevallier claimed that San Juan could not have written CB because
it contained a number of references to previous stanzas which had not
been corrected to accord with the new numbering system.[39] The
existence of such references cannot be denied. But San Juan abounds
in repetitions and digressions, and to assume that these uncorrected
references must be the work of another author is surely straining
credibility. In CA 13–14.17 San Juan introduces a long quotation from
Job 4:12–16 with the remark that first he will give it in Latin, then
Spanish, then expound it. This repeats his promise in the prologue,
which has not been fulfilled on a number of previous occasions in CA
(e.g. 7.3). If San Juan, therefore, is found repeating what his method is
to be yet from which he has already lapsed, consistency is not one of
his strong points. The fact that the expositions were written at different
times and in different places suggests he had not fixed on a plan for the
commentary until it became evident the whole poem was involved. This
may explain why no systematic outline of the treatise occurs until
CA 22, retained in CB 27. This would mark the point in the process of
writing the separate commentaries when San Juan first decided to weld
them all into one coherent structure. CA itself is not free from internal,
structural inconsistency, and similar lapses should not be used against CB.

But Chevallier is not even accurate. CB contains corrected as well as
uncorrected references. If his criterion is reversed, and authenticity
depends on there being no mistakes, then at least the corrected parts of
CB must be by San Juan! The uncorrected references are as follows:

(i) CB 18.3 retains CA 31.3's note on the change of speaker: 'En esta
canción la esposa es la que habla.' CA states this because for the previous
four stanzas the Esposo has been speaking. But this does not fit CB, in
which the Esposa has already been speaking for four stanzas (14–17)
when the note is made.

(ii) In the same passage, the Esposa wants to 'conservarse en la

[39] *BH* 24 (1922), 331–5.

seguridad . . . en la cual el Esposo la ha puesto en las dos canciones precedentes', which again suits the CA order, but not CB, where the Esposa has been creating such an atmosphere for her Beloved.

(iii) CB 14–15.17 calls 'Apártalos, Amado' the twelfth verse, whereas with the addition of CB 11 it should now be the thirteenth. The Segovia manuscript of CB has in fact corrected this point, unnoticed by Jaén— another, unexpected demonstration of the close link between CA Sanlúcar and CB Jaén.

(iv) CB 24.2 begins as CA 15.2: 'En las dos canciones pasadas ha cantado el alma esposa las gracias y grandezas de su Amado el Hijo de Dios.' This makes sense in the CA order, referring to the hymn to the Beloved's beauty in CA 13–14; but not in CB, where the two previous stanzas are spoken by him.

But other references have been corrected:

(v) CB 20–21.15, 18 (CA 29–30) contains references to another stanza, partly corrected, partly not. First, CB omits the CA description of the soul's entry 'en el ameno huerto desseado', as this does not occur until the following stanza in the CB enumeration. Then, inexplicably, in 20–21.18, CB adds 'siendo ella el huerto que arriba ha dicho'— in spite of the fact that it has just excised this very reference to the 'huerto', and in the next paragraph once again omits it. The evidence is thus indecisive, and the only reasonable explanation for such inconsistency is human fallibility.

(vi) In CB 20–21.3 are references to the preceding and following verses (19, 22–3) which make sense only in the CB order, and have thus been correctly added.

(vii) The references in CB 36.2 and 39.15 to the last few stanzas have been inserted in accordance with the new doctrinal scheme, referring to life beyond death.

(viii) CB 34.1 has a reference to 'la canción pasada' in which the soul has lamented her dark colouring. This fits only in the CB enumeration.

Apart from the equivocal example from CB 20–21, the general conclusion from these cross-references is that those in CA have not normally been corrected to apply to the CB order, but where CB has introduced fresh material, the references are always accurate. This is neither very surprising nor significant, and Chevallier was wrong to suggest it was conclusive evidence against CB. It merely points to the fact that whoever was responsible for copying CB from CA did not do his job thoroughly. If San Juan was not responsible for these lapses, then the corrector of his work whom the critics have proposed also failed to do his task properly.

The final area of debate concerns the use of Scripture in the two redactions. Baruzi, Chevallier, and Vilnet all point to aspects of CB's use of Biblical texts which appear different from San Juan's normal procedure.[40] The argument has centred on Biblical texts used in CB but not elsewhere in San Juan, and on the frequent omission of the Latin texts in CB when San Juan (ambiguously) states in the prologue: 'Llevaré este estilo, que primero las pondré la sentencia de su latín y luego las declararé al propósito del lo que se trajeren.'

P. Eulogio has studied the issue in minutest detail, and the conclusions he establishes answer in a thoroughly systematic fashion the suspicions others have expressed.[41] There are, as he demonstrates, certain norms in San Juan's use of Scripture. Paragraphs full of Biblical quotations and exegesis are followed by others with none, so that the distribution of Bibiblical material is uneven. Some texts are quoted much more than others, so that the incidence is irregular. CB shows the same characteristics as other works of San Juan. It is equally rich in use of Scriptural material, and contains, as they do, more texts used once only than texts used more than once. It does contain texts used nowhere else by San Juan, but this is true of all San Juan's authentic works. Distribution of texts is the same in CB as in the other works. Thirty-six Biblical books are not quoted in CB (but of these twenty-one never are at all by San Juan); four books quoted in CB (1 Chronicles, Nahum, Zephaniah, and Zechariah) are never quoted elsewhere. But the *Subida* yields eight such, so CB is typical and not exceptional in this.

Each Biblical quotation has five possible elements: an introductory formula, Latin text, phrase linking this to the Spanish, text in Spanish, and exegesis of the text. By detailed study of these five elements, P. Eulogio demonstrates convincingly that CB follows San Juan's norms in this respect too. Nor can the omission of the Latin texts in CB be used to support the theory that another writer produced it, without also bringing the *Subida* into suspicion. Latin versions and linking passages occur till S 2.28, when suddenly they are dropped, without explanation. CB normally retains the Latin texts carried over from CA but omits the Latin in new material. P. Eulogio suggests that for some unknown reason, San Juan changed his manner of quotation, providing the Latin versions in his earlier works (CA and the *Subida* as far as 2.28), and omitting it in his later ones (the rest of the *Subida*, CB, the *Noche* and *Llama*). The use of Latin in CB thus becomes a sign of its authenticity.[42] He concludes: 'Los elementos de los textos bíblicos atestiguan que el segundo *Cántico* reproduce fidelísimamente la línea de

[40] Baruzi, 'Le Problème des citations scriptuaires en langue latine dans l'œuvre de saint Jean de la Croix', *BH* 24 (1922), 18–40; Vilnet, *Bible et mystique chez saint Jean de la Croix* (Desclée de Brouwer, 1949); and Chevallier in his 1922 and 1926 articles.

[41] 'La Sda. Escritura y la cuestión de la segunda redacción del "Cántico espiritual" de San Juan de la Cruz', *EC* 5 (1951–4), 249–475.

[42] *San Juan de la Cruz y sus escritos*, pp. 356–9.

composición propia de San Juan de la Cruz, llegando a recoger con precisión matemática los rasgos, los errores, y las inexactitudes propias del Reformador del Carmelo.' His case is strengthened by Ledrus, replying to the peculiarities in CB's treatment of the Bible noted by Vilnet.[43] He shows how Vilnet's examples—verses and chapters not quoted elsewhere, texts used to sum up the meaning, the length of the Ezekiel text in CB 23, and of the sentence in the annotation to CB 1—can all be paralleled in San Juan and are not alien to his normal practice.

The conclusion is inevitable. None of the arguments put against CB's authenticity will stand. We have examined problems of manuscript tradition and the history of CB, style and doctrine in the two redactions, uncorrected references and use of Biblical texts. Not only do the arguments not stand, they turn out to provide evidence in favour of CB.

But why should San Juan have wished to revise his original *Cántico*? Before he begins to expound the verses, he adds to CB an 'argumento' describing 'el orden que llevan estas canciones'. This is 'desde que un alma comienza a servir a Dios hasta que llega al último estado de perfección, que es el matrimonio espiritual'. This is divided into three 'estados o vías de ejercicio espiritual', for 'principiantes', 'aprovechados', and 'perfectos'—the classical terminology of the three ways. As this is missing from CA, it looks as if CB is intended to provide a more systematic treatment of the mystical life. This suspicion is confirmed by the additions CB 22.3 makes to CA 27.3, which are nearly all connected with this more schematic approach: after meditation, the soul enters the 'vía contemplativa', and after the spiritual betrothal depicted in CB 13 it goes 'por la vía unitiva'. When we recall how the CA expositions began, quite haphazardly, it is not surprising that San Juan felt the need to bring more order into them.

This more systematic delineation of the stages in the spiritual life is the clue behind the reorganization of the stanzas. As the soul progresses, San Juan's clear teaching is that disturbances and demonic interferences recede. But the order of stanzas in CA makes this difficult to maintain, because the 'raposas' of CA 25 and the 'ninfas de Judea' of CA 31 represent just such troubles. This creates a tension between the CA poem and the commentary it has generated. CA 25 offers on the one hand 'turbaciones', on the other, 'suave deleite'. CA 31 urges the nymphs to grant the soul a peace she is long since supposed to have gained. Here the tension is explicit, and San Juan feels obliged to explain why the nymphs are distracting the soul which has already entered the 'ameno huerto desseado':[44]

---

[43] 'Les "Singularités" du second Cantique', *Gregorianum* 33 (1952), 438–50.
[44] CA 31.9.

Esta canción se a puesto aquí para dar a entender la quieta paz y segura que tiene
el alma que llega a este alto estado; no para que se piense que este desseo que
muestra aquí el alma de que se sosieguen estas mymphas sea porque en este estado
molesten, por que ya están sosegadas, como arriba queda dado a entender; que
este desseo más es de los que van aprouechando y de los aprovechados que de los
ya perfectos, en los quales poco o nada reynan las passiones y mouimientos.

The solution adopted by CB is to place this stanza earlier in the poem—
CA 31 suffers, with the following verse, the greatest displacement,
becoming CB 18. The above quotation can then be omitted, because
the problem it alludes to has been solved by the transposition of the
stanza to its new location. CA 31.9 speaks of the complete subjugation
of sense to spirit, which CB omits, as this is only reached at a later stage.
Similarly, the troublesome 'raposas' of CA 25 are moved back to CB 16,
where their distractions more properly belong. Just before this, CB 14—
15.28 develops an annotation from the Sanlúcar manuscript to the
effect that the sensitive part of the soul is not perfected until the
spiritual marriage, so that disturbances and demonic intrusions may
remain. The exposition of 'raposas' is then altered. Instead of trampling
the vines they are described as feigning sleep in order to surprise their
prey, which fits better with the way San Juan wants to describe the
sleeping senses which can be aroused to distract the soul.

These passages present the clearest examples of the tension between
the lyrical outpouring of the poem and the subsequent systematic
requirements of a treatise on the mystical life, which San Juan was never
able to resolve completely. CB was his answer, written to alleviate the
tension by giving the teaching derived from the poem a more coherent
structure and by altering the order of stanzas accordingly. The referring
of the last five stanzas to the beatific vision belongs to this same process.
CB covers the whole of the spiritual journey, 'desde que un alma
comienza a servir a Dios' (as the 'argumento' expresses it), to the
'manifiesta visión de Dios' (CB 36.2). Some of its alterations are far-
reaching; many others, very small. But they all belong to the sum total
of the CB changes, and it is the meaning of that total we have tried to
evaluate, not simply that of the more striking ones. There is, then, a
perfectly sound reason for San Juan's wanting to revise his first *Cántico*.
Like the *Subida-Noche* and the *Llama*, it had begun as a lyrical poem
and grew into a treatise deriving its teaching from the language of
poetry. Only the *Llama* really succeeds in holding the two aspects in
balance, because it is deliberately limited in its scope.[45] The *Subida-
Noche* soon abandons the pretence of expounding the poem, because

[45] In his prologue to the *Llama,* San Juan clearly states: 'estas canciones tratan
del amor ya más calificado y perficionado en ese mismo estado de transformación'.
There is therefore no attempt to relate the poem to the spiritual life in all its
stages.

all San Juan wants to say is contained in the first line, 'En una noche oscura', to which he persistently returns.[46] The *Cántico* wavers between poetic commentary and spiritual treatise because it is much longer than the other poems and because its imagery is so much more varied. The prose commentaries have to create order out of a lyrical outburst. Images, metaphors, and symbols have to be cashed. The instinct of the poet has to yield to the studied refelction of the theologian.

This transition has been finely analysed by P. Eulogio.[47] The poem, 'para llegar a su configuración actual de obra con intenciones doctrinales, ha pasado por largo e intricado proceso redacional.' This obvious point needs to be made because the opponents of CB's authenticity seem to have discounted the possibility that poem and commentary continued to develop in San Juan's mind after CA had been copied in the Sanlúcar manuscript. But the *Cántico* had grown and developed beyond the prison poem in ways the consequences of which San Juan had not fully appreciated when CA was finished. CB was written to rectify the situation. When the interests of poet and teacher meet, 'se entabla . . . una secreta y encondada contienda entre el tratadista metódico y el glosador de la poesía.'[48] The poem was not composed to fit a scheme; a scheme was worked around the poem, and when San Juan saw that his poem and his scheme were not always going in the same direction, he attempted to reduce the points of tension, by bringing his treatise into line with the mystical tradition of Western Christendom and making it cover the whole of the mystical journey. It is as simple and remarkable as that.

Meanwhile, the fundamental point of this chapter is in sight. It has been a long and roundabout way, but the only one which can establish the right conclusions. The best guide to San Juan as a poet is CA, because it reflects more nearly the original impulse to sing the divine love. But to appreciate his thought, there is every justification for turning to CB, because there is his final word on the *Cántico*, the word of a poet who is also a theologian.

---

[46] The commentary proper is restricted to N 2.4–25 (unfinished).

[47] 'La clave exegética del "Cántico espiritual" ', *EC* 9 (1958), 307–37 and 11 (1960), 312–51.

[48] Op. cit. (1958), p. 317.

4

THE LITERARY ORIGINS OF THE CÁNTICO

The poems of San Juan were rooted in his own experience. But the experiences out of which they grew needed to be clothed in words and concepts, and San Juan drew many of these from the wisdom of the past and of his own time. It is that process which this chapter seeks to understand, with particular reference to the inspiration San Juan drew from other literature. This will help to lay the foundation for appreciating how he forges the elements he has borrowed into so original a poetic creation as the Cántico. For a study of the literary sources of the poem achieves more than allowing the reader to feel his way into the atmosphere in which San Juan worked and to discover which authors to whom he is chiefly indebted. It can also permit us a rare glance into the poet's workshop, as we see the poet at his craft, shaping the material he has received into his own personal creation.

Though some work has been done to uncover the major area of San Juan's indebtedness to other poets, critics have not agreed about the relative importance of the various influences. The main issues raised have been the extent to which the Bible (and above all the Song of Songs) has been used by San Juan, the significance of Garcilaso and the Italianate poetry which came into Spain in the 1540s, and its later *a lo divino* versions, for understanding his sources, and the part played by popular poetry in his works.

The commentaries prove overwhelmingly that the Bible is San Juan's major source book. At every point he turns to it to illustrate and confirm the teaching he is expounding. Often the texts he introduces are directly related to the imagery he is explaining, or at least have some important word in common, particularly so in the *Cántico,* where the Song of Songs is far and away the most persistent influence. It is therefore obvious that the proper place to begin a study of its sources is the Biblical wedding-song. Yet there has been a strange reluctance to do this. Dámaso Alonso has done his best to uncover the most tenuous links between San Juan and Garcilaso, Sebastián de Córdoba, or popular poetry, but has avoided doing the same for the Song, though it yields much more fruit.[1] He merely states that the Song would have been a

[1]   *La poesía de San Juan de la Cruz* (Madrid, 1966), pp. 113–22.

ready-made source for the expression of mystical ideas in poetry, and gives a handful of images which have passed from it into San Juan, like the 'lámparas' in the *Llama,* and the 'cedros', 'almenas', and 'entre azucenas' of the *Noche.* This is not a satisfactory methodology, for in spurning the major source it runs the risk of attributing to other influences passages in the *Cántico* which are more justifiably understood as having their genesis in the Biblical Song.

P. Crisógono's account is also incomplete. He writes: 'muchas estrofas del *Cántico espiritual* no son más que bellísima traducción de versillos del epitalamio . . . por eso, no hay poesía que tanto se parezca a la hebrea como la de San Juan.'[2] This might be true of the images San Juan uses, but the most striking characteristics of Hebrew poetry, like the parallelisms running through the Psalms, are absent from his poems, and, paradoxically, it is the cultured Herrera who sometimes sounds Hebraic:

> Turbáron [se] los grandes, los robustos
> rindiéron [se] temblando, y desmayaron,
> y tú pusiste, Dios, como la rueda,
> como la arista queda
> al ímpetu del viento, a estos injustos,
> que mil huyendo de uno se pasmaron . . .
> Quebrantaste al dragón fiero . . .[3]

P. Crisógono gives very few specific examples of the way in which San Juan uses the Song. The only serious attempts to grapple with the extent of its influence on the *Cántico* have been the studies of Morales and Tillmans.[4]

What needs to be understood first is that the *Cántico*'s structure is quite closely modelled on that of the Song. In both works it is hard to follow any coherent, developing theme stanza by stanza; both are essentially a dialogue between *sponsus* and *sponsa*, but with a chorus which from time to time is questioned or interjects comments (Song 1:3; 3:6–11; 5:9, 17; 6:12; 7:1–5, 8:5, 8–9, 11; CA 2, 4, 5, 25, 29–31). In both, the parts spoken by each of the principal characters vary in length and are not always addressed directly to one another. Above all, both move around a focal point—the union of the lovers—rather than in linear progression from their meeting to the consummation of their love.

This is easily illustrated. There is, for example, a constant fluctuation between the presence and absence of the *sponsus.* In Song 2:4 the

---

[2] *San Juan de la Cruz,* ii. 31.
[3] 'Canción en alabanza de la divina majestad por la victoria del señor don Juan', lines 121–6, 131.
[4] Morales, *El "Cántico espiritual" de San Juan de la Cruz: su relación con el Cantar de los Cantares* (Madrid, 1971); Tillmans, *De aanwezigheid van het bijbels hooglied in het "Cantico espiritual" van San Juan de la Cruz* (Brussels, 1967).

sponsa says: 'Introduxit me in cellam vinariam; ordinavit in me charitatem', referring to him; at 2:8 he is shown approaching: 'Vox dilecti mei: ecce iste venit, saliens in montibus, transiliens colles'; and at 2:16 the *sponsa* claims 'Dilectus meus mihi, et ego illi'. Yet in 3:2 she is searching the city at night for him: 'Surgam, et circuibo civitatem; per vicos et plateas quaeram quem diligit anima mea.' The final chapter is particularly disjointed. The Song thus frequently changes tense and context within a very short space, and it is difficult to read it as a unity. Exactly the same process may be observed in the *Cántico*. Direct address of the Beloved is followed by asking the shepherds his whereabouts (CA 1, 2). A glance into the future (21) is followed by an account of something that had already occurred (22–3). A description of what seems to be consummation (17–18) is followed by verses which indicate that the consummation is still being delayed (29–31), after the description has been interrupted and only taken up again in CA 27. This constant fluctuation in time and place will be studied later in the analysis of the poem's mystery; for the time being, these examples show how closely the form and structure of the *Cántico* follows the Biblical poem.

But the pervasive influence of the Song is best seen in those large parts of the *Cántico* which grow directly out of it. The following table lists first the longer phrases San Juan has developed from the Song, then other elements they share.

CA		SONG OF SONGS
1. adonde te escondiste, Amado	1:6	indica mihi, quem diligit anima mea, ubi pascas
	5:17	quo abiit dilectus tuus
1. salí . . . clamando	3:1–2,5:6	quaesivi . . . vocavi
2. si por uentura vierdes aquel que yo más quiero, decilde que adolezco, peno y muero	5:8	si inveneritis dilectum meum, ut nuntietis ei quia amore langueo
3. buscando mis amores, yré por . . .	3:2	per . . . quaeram quem diligit anima mea
4. decid si por uosotros ha passado	3:3	num quem diligit anima mea vidistis
7. un no sé qué	6:11	nescivi
9. as llagado aqueste coraçón	4:9	vulnerasti cor meum
11. semblantes plateados	1:10	vermiculatas argento
12. apártalos, Amado, que voy de buelo	6:4	averte oculos tuos a me, quia ipsi me avolare fecerunt
15. nuestro lecho florido	1:15	lectulus noster floridus
15. de cueuas de leones	4:8	de cubilibus leonum
15. de paz edificado, de mil escudos de oro coronado	4:4	quae aedificata est cum propugnaculis; mille clypei pendent ex ea

16. las jóuenes discurren al camino	1:2–3	adolescentulæ . . . post te curremus
16. al adobado vino	8:2	ex vino condito
17. en la interior bodega de mi Amado beuí	2:4	introduxit me in cellam vinariam
	5:1	bibi vinum meum
17. el ganado perdí que antes seguía (also 19)	1:5	vineam meam non custodivi
18. allí me dio su pecho	7:12	ibi dabo tibi ubera mea
allí me enseñó	8:2	ibi me docebis
19. todo mi caudal en su seruicio	7:13	omnia poma . . . servavi tibi
21. en un cabello mío . . .	4:9	vulnerasti . . . in uno oculorum tuorum, et in uno crine colli tui
22. que en mi cuello . . . y en uno de mis ojos te llagaste		
24. no quieras despreciarme, que, si color moreno en mí hallaste . . . hermosura	1:5	nolite me considerare quod fusca sim
	1:4	nigra sum, sed formosa
25. cogednos las raposas, que está ya florecida nuestra viña	2:15	capite nobis vulpes parvulas . . . nam vinea nostra floruit
26. deténte, cierzo muerto; ven austro . . . aspira por mi huerto y corran sus olores	4:16	surge, aquilo; et veni, auster; perfla hortum meum, et fluant aromata illius
y pacerá el Amado entre las flores	2:16	dilectus meus . . . qui pascitur inter lilia
27. entrado se ha la esposa en el . . . huerto	5:2	veni in hortum meum . . . sponsa
27. el cuello reclinado sobre los dulces braços de el Amado	8:3	laeva eius sub capite meo, et dextera illius amplexabitur me
28. debaxo de el mançano . . . fuiste reparada donde tu madre fuera violada	8:5	sub arbore malo suscitavi te; ibi corrupta est mater tua, ibi violata est
allí . . . allí conmigo fuiste desposada	3:11	in die desponsationis illius
29. miedos de las noches	3:8	timores nocturnos
30. por . . . os conjuro	2:7	adiuro vos . . . per
que cesen vuestras iras, y no toquéis al muro, por que la esposa duerma más seguro	3:5, 8.4	ne suscitetis, neque evigilare faciatis dilectam, donec ipsa velit
31. o nymphas de Judea	1:4, 2:7 etc.	filiae Ierusalem
31. nuestros humbrales	7:13	in portis nostris
32. mira con tu haz	2:14	ostende mihi faciem tuam
35. vámonos . . . al monte u al collado	4:6, 7:11	vadam ad montem . . . et ad collem . . . egrediamur in agrum

36. a las subidas cauernas de   2:14 in foraminibus petrae, in
    la piedra . . . bien escondidas   caverna maceriae
36. y el mosto de granadas   8:2   et mustum malorum
    gustaremos   granatorum meorum dabo
                                          tibi
39. Aminadab . . . cauallería   6:11 quadrigas Aminadab

To this list may be added two examples of the *Cántico* and Song sharing the same grammatical constructions though a different vocabulary:

(i) the description of the Beloved in CA 13–14 in terms of several nouns with no connecting verb, parallels Song 5:10, 'Dilectus meus candidus et rubicundus'; San Juan had this in mind in 'Mi Amado, las montañas'.

(ii) the conjuration of animals and nature in CA 29–30 is modelled on Song 3:5 'Adiuro vos . . . per capreas cervosque camporum': 'Por las amenas liras y canto de serenas, os conjuro', In both these examples the number of things referred to by San Juan exceeds those mentioned in the Song.

There is also one pervasive theme common to both Song and *Cántico* not properly covered by the examples in the list—the theme of perfume and scent, present in CA 16, 26 and 31, and Song 1:2, 2:13, 4:11, 13–14. Moreover, there is a community of vocabulary between the two works, which reinforces the link already established:

CA		SONG OF SONGS	
1,12,29	cieruo	3:5 etc.	cervos
1,7,9,12,22	herido, llagan, vulnerado	4:9 etc.	vulnerasti (images of wounding)
3,13,29	montes, montañas	4:6	montem
3,21,31	flores	2:12	flores
11	fuente	4.12	fons
11,27	desseado	2:3	desideraveram
12,33	paloma, tortolica	2:10,12	columba, turturis
14,38	noche	3:1	noctes
14	aurora	6:9	aurora
15,29	leones	4:8	leonum
15	púrpura	3:10	purpurem
15	paz	8:10	pacem
16	emissiones	4:13	emissiones
24,35	hermosura	1:4	formosa
27,38	dulce	2:14	dulcis
29,35,39	aguas	8:7	aquae
30	muro	8:10	murus

33	socio	1:6	sodalium
33	riberas	5:12	rivulos
38	llama	8:6	flammarum

Apart from this overwhelming influence of the Song, there are places in the *Cántico* where other Biblical passages come to mind:

CA	BIBLE (VULGATE)
10. Y véante mis ojos, pues eres lumbre dellos, y sólo para ti quiero tenellos	Ps. 37:11 et lumen oculorum meorum, et ipsum non est mecum
13. los valles solitarios nemorosos	Num. 24:6 ut valles nemorosae
13. las ínsulas extrañas	Isa. 41:5 viderunt insulae ... extrema terrae
	Isa. 41:1 audite, insulae; et attendire, populi de longe
13. los ríos sonorosos	Ezek. 1:24 quasi sonum aquarum multarum
13. el silbo de los ayres	IIIK. 19:12 sibilus aurae tenuis
20 me hice perdidiza, y fui ganada	Mat. 10:39, 16:25–6 (losing one's life and gaining it)
33. la blanca palomica al arca con el ramo se a tornado	Gen. 8:11 (the dove's return to the ark with an olive branch)
CB 11 y máteme tu vista	Exod. 33:20 non enim videbit me homo, et vivet

Certain features about San Juan's use of this Biblical material help to show why it adds to, rather than detracts from, his poetic skill and originality.

First, Biblical sources are used with a varying intensity, sometimes appearing only as a faint echo of the Biblical poetry, as in CA 4, 7, 11, 32, and 38. CA 4 is a version of the question asked by the Bride in the Song (3:3), but verbal links are slight and San Juan has rearranged it and set it in a non-Biblical context (the source of CA 4–5 is more likely to be found in the *Confessions* of St. Augustine). CA 7 contains the characteristic language of wounding and the famous 'no sé qué'; CA 11, the one word 'fuente'. These may well come from secular poetry, though given the extent of the Song's influence in the *Cántico* it is reasonable to assume that where a word or phrase could stem from the Bible or a secular source, it is the former which has inspired San Juan. CA 32 has only 'mira con tu haz'; and CA 38 again has symbols not necessarily Biblical in inspiration but in San Juan's case likely to be so ('noche', 'llama', and the adjective 'dulce', so characteristic of the tradition of Garcilaso). On the other hand, other stanzas contain a much greater concentration of Biblical material. CA 15 is wholly constructed out of disparate elements from the Song, and 26–8 have only a few phrases which do not arise directly out of it. CA 36, with its entry into the caves and tasting of pomegranate juice, shows a similar pattern. The influence of the Song is rarely very far away, therefore, though sometimes it is concentrated, at other times slight. From CA 4–9 particularly it plays a secondary part, yet, strangely, these stanzas (6, 8–9 especially) are lacking in what we recognize as most characteristic of San Juan, and most original about his poetry.

Second, San Juan weaves the Biblical material which has inspired him into the whole texture of the poem, and frequently places phrases from the Song in the company of those from another poetic tradition. CA 2, for example, invokes the shepherds, a general picture probably belonging to sixteenth-century pastoral poetry. But the last three lines develop an idea present in the Song. In CA 25 this works in reverse. The Song has inspired the first two lines (the vixen in the vineyard), but the rest of the stanza is a picture compounded of San Juan's own imagining (the bunch of flowers, solitude on the mountain). CA 12 is a more complex piece of interweaving. The first line and a half, spoken by the Bride, grow out of the Song and so in part does the Bridegroom's reply; but in fact it is an involved series of interrelated images drawn from several places. Behind it lies Song 2:9, the picture of the stag-Beloved peeping through the window. But San Juan has made him a wounded stag, both because he is touched by the arrows of love and, as Christ, has been wounded for our transgressions.[5] He depicts him on the hillside (Song 2:17) but also in the fresh air, a detail perhaps suggested by the Bride's 'vuelo' (from Song 6:4), which is presumably the reason for the stag's appearance. Though the kernel of the stanza is in the Song, it has grown almost beyond recognition. CA 31 shows the same process of interweaving at work: the perfume, nymphs and 'humbrales' come from the Song, but San Juan associates them with amber, flowers and roses, and introduces a reference to 'arrabales', whereas the Song describes a circuit of the city by night in search of the Beloved. The transition from 'filiae Ierusalem' to 'nymphas de Judea' is also interesting in that San Juan avoids the obvious translation 'hijas' and instead uses a word with roots deep in pagan poetry. CA 33 demonstrates how he weaves together different Biblical passages. 'Haz' and the dove can be found in the Song, but the dove image is developed first according to the Genesis story of the flood, and then in a secular manner.

[5]   The wounded-stag motif, possibly with the same religious significance, occurs in the Portuguese *cantigas de amigo*: see, e.g. 'Tal vai o meu amigo', by Pero Meogo (*Oxford Book of Portuguese Verse*, pp. 19–20).

A third characteristic of San Juan's use of the Song is seen in CA 3, 13–14 and 29–30. Here we find a heaping up of symbols, enough to baffle the most sensitive reader. Some are Biblical, others have no definite source and belong to the poetic background of the age. 'Montes', 'riberas' and 'flores' all occur in the Song; 'fieras', 'fuertes' and 'fronteras' can be found in the Bible but are not necessarily taken from it. In 13–14 most of the images have some Biblical connection, except the paradoxical 'música callada' and 'soledad sonora', which belong more to a poetry delighting in such ambiguities, like the *Cancionero*, or Petrarchan poetry. CA 29–30 contains a mixed collection of animate and inanimate objects, Biblical and non-Biblical. The 'canto de serenas' is the most obvious of the latter and is found next to the 'amenas liras' of secular lyrical poetry and enclosed by the Song's 'miedos de las noches' and 'os conjuro'. Such a juxtaposition of images from distant sources seems to cause San Juan no embarrassment at all. In the commentary, he treats them all on the same level. So his use of the Song and the Bible is happily married to non-Biblical material in the *Cántico*.

Fourth, and most important of all, he uses the elements taken from the Song with complete freedom, which ties in with one of the principles behind his exegetical method. In S 2.19.1–7 he gives examples of Biblical prophecies never literally fulfilled, which must therefore be interpreted in other ways, 'porque . . . el principal intento de Dios en aquellas cosas es decir y dar el espíritu que está allí encerrado, el cual es dificultoso de entender, y éste es muy más abundante que la letra y muy extraordinario y fuera de los límites de ella'. Such an approach allows considerable flexibility in interpretation. San Juan does not take Biblical expressions and introduce them into his poem like alien plants, isolated from their environment; he adapts them so that they are part of the poetic world he is creating. Sometimes, he takes a phrase and does little more than translate it or arrange it so that it will scan or rhyme. 'Lectulus noster floridus' becomes 'nuestro lecho florido', which serves perfectly well as an heptasyllabic line. 'Capite nobis vulpes parvulas . . . nam vinea nostra floruit' translates well into two lines of the *lira* more or less as it is 'Cogednos las raposas, / que ya está florecida nuestra viña.'

But more often, San Juan allows himself complete liberty. Not only does he integrate material from the Song with passages from secular traditions, he also makes considerable alterations to the Latin texts themselves, changing speaker, context, tense and meaning at will. In CA 18 the Bride reports in the third person and a past tense what Song 7:12 and 8:2 refer to the future and in direct speech: 'ibi dabo tibi ubera mea' and 'ibi me docebis' become 'allí me dio su pecho' and 'allí me enseñó', as the soul looks back to her betrothal. The image of Song 1:5 is altered in CA 19 from the Bride no longer tending her vineyard to the neglect of her sheep. Although the pastoral is strongly characteristic of the Bible (Psalm 23; John 10.1–16), there is no need to dwell on its significance in sixteenth-century literature. And although there are viticultural references elsewhere in the *Cántico* (CA 16, 25), here, for some reason best known to himself, San Juan has chosen to alter the imagery. Further examples are not hard to find. The Bridegroom's words in Song 4:9 are given to the Bride in CA 21–2. In Song 4:16, both north and south winds are summoned; CA 25 calls on the 'cierzo muerto' (the addition of 'muerto' emphasizes the undesirability of the wind) to cease and the south wind only to blow—more understandable perhaps in Spain than in Palestine. Song 5:2 shows the Beloved having entered his garden, as the Bride desires a verse earlier. In CA 27 this very important moment is described by the Beloved, in reported speech, and without specifying as the Song does, that it is *his* garden. CA 28's reference to the betrothal is transposed from a chorus comment (Song 3:11) about the king's betrothal to a description of that of the lovers as a past event, given by the Bridegroom to the Bride. Something almost incidental in the Song is thereby elevated into a position of great importance in the *Cántico*, because the betrothal is one of the main stages in the spiritual journey San Juan was later to describe. Hence any reference to it in a sacred text, however veiled, would be seized on as an authority to corroborate the experience. Finally, Song 5:9 makes the bridegroom exclaim that the Bride has wounded him to the heart. Understandably, San Juan ascribes this intense emotion to the Bride (CA 9); it is she who is wounded by love for him, rather than he for her, as she strays among the flowers.

These, then, are some of the places where San Juan retains the core of a passage from the Song, but turns it to his own purpose. In other places, his freedom in altering has a more directly poetic function: changes in vocabulary, omissions and amplifications, to aid scansion and rhyme. The Song has two main expressions for the Beloved, the short 'dilectus meus' and the longer 'quem diligit anima mea'. San Juan has equivalents for both, but uses whichever suits his purpose, not the one found in the source passage. CA 1's 'Amado' replaces the longer version of its source (Song 1:6); on the other hand, the 'aquel que yo más quiero' in CA 2 is more suitable for him than the simple 'dilectus meus' of Song 5:8. CA 15 presents an interesting example of this freedom. 'Edificado' has clear roots in Song 4:4's 'aedificata', but there it is not peace which is involved. San Juan has chosen to introduce 'paz' to replace the more bellicose 'propugnaculis' of the Song, and to use the more poetic 'coronar' for the Song's 'pendent'. His addition of 'de oro' to the Song's already hyperbolic picture provides a further extravagance—all to describe the lovers' bed! He wants to stress its peace and beauty, whereas the Song in his source is not describing the

bed at all, but the neck and necklace of the Bride. CA 24 also demonstrates how San Juan can amplify a brief phrase from the Song. 'Quod
fusca sim' becomes 'si color moreno en mí hallaste', a curiously prosaic
expression, lacking the terseness of 'fusca', and appearing to indicate
some blemish. It is hardly suprising to find San Juan referring it to the
stain of sin in his exegesis; and his amplification helps to underline the
idea, which might have been overlooked.

In CA 28, San Juan intends to sharpen the allegorical contrast which
was present in the traditional interpretation of Song 8:5: Eve, the
mother of mankind, who ate from the tree and Christ, born of Mary,
redeeming mankind on the tree of Calvary. The Latin text describes
the violation of the mother and the arousal of the daughter, the Bride,
at the same place—one of the most erotic passages in the poem. In
characteristic Hebrew fashion, 'ibi corrupta est mater tua' is balanced
by 'ibi violata est genitrix tua', repeating the same idea, with no mention
of repairing any damage done. Instead of this twofold insistence on
violation, San Juan emphasizes a contrast: 'y fuiste reparada' where
the mother had been violated. In appearance, it is only a small change;
but it alters the sense of the original and enables San Juan to squeeze
a great deal of meaning from it. His freedom is further exemplified by
the way he draws into one section of his poem elements from unrelated
parts of the wedding-song. In CA 26, the blowing of the breeze comes
from Song 4:16 but the Beloved feeding among the flowers from 2:16;
in 36, the cave image comes from 2:14, and the tasting of pomegranate
juice from 8:2. In both cases, the unrelated material of the Song is
joined by the simple conjunction 'y', as though it belonged together.
The most striking example of this process is CA 15, a whole stanza
constructed out of disparate images from different parts of the Song
and all pressed into service to describe the bed: 'lecho florido' (1:15),
'cueuas de leones' (4:8), 'edificado' and 'mil escudos' (4:4), and 'púrpura'
(3:10).

From this evidence it is clear that San Juan took considerable
liberties with the Biblical text in the creation of his poem. He used the
Song not as a whole, but as a quarry from which he could draw his
poetic material. He was not interested in preserving the sequence of
images he found in the Song, but in the evocative quality of each, and
where he thought it right he reshuffled them and altered them. Certainly
his is a borrowed language, but he has made it his own, because he
controls the images and redirects their tremendous power into the
channels he has prepared for them.

Morales states that in his works San Juan has 1,583 explicit and 115
implicit quotations from the Bible. This should act as a warning not to
overestimate the importance of non-Biblical sources in San Juan, for
they come only in single figures. Literary critics have, however,

concentrated on studying the secular poetic influences on him, and their findings must now be considered, in order to establish the precise nature and extent of his links with secular sixteenth-century poetry.

San Juan does mention Boscán—once. Before he starts the commentary proper on the *Llama de amor viva* he writes: 'La compostura de estas liras son como aquelles que en Boscán están vueltas a lo divino, que dicen: *La soledad siguiendo, | llorando mi fortuna, | me voy por los caminos que se ofrecen*, etc., en las cuales hay seis pies, y el cuarto suena con el primero, y el quinto con el segundo, y el sexto con el tercero.' The authenticity of this statement has been called into dispute, as it seems to have been suppressed at some point during the seventeenth century; but it is now accepted as authentic, as it appears in practically every manuscript of both redactions of the *Llama* commentary, and certainly in all the weightier ones. It proves that San Juan was familiar with the divinized version of Boscán and Garcilaso made by Sebastián de Córdoba and first published in 1575.[6]

Why should San Juan go to such trouble to locate the source of the *Llama* in this way? Córdoba's version of Garcilaso's *Canción segunda* is found exactly as San Juan quotes it (Gale, p. 123). But it is hardly the source for his poem. He cites it because it is his metrical model, because its metre is unusual for a *lira*, with six lines and an abCabC rhyme scheme—though this is only the first part of the thirteen-line *canción*, which continues cdeEDfF.[7] San Juan therefore bases the metre of his *Llama* on part of a verse in the divinized version of Garcilaso's *Canción segunda*. There is no question of the *Llama* being influenced by this work in any other way, for it betrays no links with it in style, vocabulary, or imagery. There is no reason to be surprised at the reference to Boscán when the poem under question is by Garcilaso: the works of the two poets, having been published together, were frequently referred to in the sixteenth century as 'un Boscán'.

San Juan presumably included this note because he was aware that his poem used a metre rarely found in the *lira*, and he wanted to provide some sort of justification for it from another poet, an 'authority', perhaps, just as he corroborated his own mystical experience by authorities like Scripture and the Fathers. That he should have felt the need to justify a metrical innovation suggests that the devout readers for

---

[6] *Las obras de Boscán y Garcilasso trasladadas en materias Christianas y religiosas* (Granada, 1575 and Zaragoza, 1577). I have used the latter edition, which is in the Bodleian Library; its foliation becomes increasingly chaotic towards the end. Córdoba's versions of Garcilaso have recently been edited by Gale, *Garcilaso a lo divino* (Madrid, 1971), and where appropriate, references will be given from this, though it does not cover the much larger number of poems by Boscán divinized by Córdoba.

[7] Unusual, but apparently not unique. See Orozco, *Poesía y mística* (Madrid, 1959), pp. 130–1.

whom poem and commentary were intended knew more about poetic forms than one might have suspected, and also that he was acquainted with some at least of the technical aspects of the poetry of his age. Interestingly, too, he quotes from Córdoba rather than Garcilaso, who would have suited his purpose equally, as Córdoba had not altered the original metre. There are a number of possible reasons for this: he may not have known Garcilaso well enough in the original and possessed no copy of his works; he may have disapproved of Garcilaso's secular love poetry and found Córdoba's versions more edifying; or he may have referred to the *a lo divino* poem because it would have been familiar at least in a household like that of the devout Ana de Peñalosa, to whom the *Llama* was dedicated. All these reasons may be true: there is no way of telling. None the less the fact that San Juan preferred the divinized version is of itself significant.

The influence of divinized poetry on San Juan is not restricted to the *Llama*. A number of his lesser poems are written in a more obviously divinized style than the *Noche*, *Llama* or *Cántico*. The theological *romances* on the Trinity, the *coplas* 'Vivo sin vivir en mí', 'Entréme donde no supe' and 'Tras de un amoroso lance', the 'Pastorcico' poem and the *glosas a lo divino* 'Sin arrimo y con arrimo' and 'Por toda la hermosura' all show more clearly than the major poems that San Juan contributed to the tradition of divinized poetry. It is therefore reasonable to conclude, from these and from the *Llama* reference, that San Juan was familiar with the work of the divinizers.

Since Dámaso Alonso's *La poesía de San Juan de la Cruz* (1942), it has generally been accepted that San Juan was influenced by Garcilaso not so much through a direct knowledge of his poetry as through Córdoba's divinized versions. The idea was not new, as it had already been mentioned by P. Gerardo, Baruzi and P. Crisógono.[8] But they had not discussed the subject in any depth and were content with generalities. Dámaso Alonso, however, subjected the relationship between San Juan and Córdoba to a more critical appraisal, and it seemed as though San Juan's poetry could be understood in a new light, one which made it comprehensible as a product of its time. Gale, for example, states: 'El mayor interés histórico de ésta [la obra de Córdoba] consiste en haber sido fuente de inspiración para . . . San Juan de la Cruz, facilitándonos así un punto de comunicación textual entre el verso erótico y profano de Garcilaso y la poesía mística de San Juan'.[9]

---

[8]   See P. Gerardo de San Juan de la Cruz's three-volume edition of the *Obras* (Toledo, 1912–14), II, 387, note 1; Baruzi, *Saint Jean de la Croix et le problème de l'expérience mystique* (Paris, 1924), pp. 115–16; and P. Crisógono, op. cit., II, 23–6.

[9]   Gale, op. cit., p. 7.

Dámaso Alonso found the clue to the presence of this influence on San Juan in certain words used in the *Cántico* which were typical of the lexicon of Garcilaso but alien to the predominantly Biblical imagery of San Juan: the 'nymphas' of CA 31 and 'Philomena' of CA 38. He might have added a third, the 'canto de serenas' of CA 30. How could so deeply Christian a poet feel able to use such pagan words without offending himself and his readers? The answer lay in the work of men like Córdoba, who had spiritualized the erotic connotations of Boscán and Garcilaso and rendered them palatable to the most discriminating of tastes. It was as though the missing link between Garcilaso's sensual love poetry and San Juan's sensual mystical poetry had at last been discovered, a link which some critics questioned, but which most have assumed to exist ever since.[10]

The whole question of *a lo divino* literature is still, however, under discussion. Glaser has given examples of hitherto unknown works of this genre, while Crosbie argues that, at least until the middle of the sixteenth century, divinization was more or less accidental and spontaneous, and there was no systematic attempt to improve the secular poets.[11] Córdoba was an exception, but was not imitated. Many divinizers merely used the opening line or two of a poem, probably to show off their compositions to a well-known tune, since most of the *contrafacta* were intended to be sung. He questions the moral aim of Córdoba and points to words in the 'epístola prohemial a los lectores', where Córdoba writes: 'Comencé casi burlando algunos sonetos y canciones'; though one wonders how seriously this is to be taken. It may simply be a conventional disclaimer, like the famous one made by Fray Luis de León of his poetry. A sterner tone is soon to the fore, in a letter addressed to the reader by D. Fernando de Herrera, canon of Úbeda: 'Viendo quan comun y manual andava en el mundo el libro de las obras de Boscán y Garcilasso . . . que, aunque son subtiles y artificiosas, son dañosas y pestilenciales para el ánima, y debaxo la suavidad y dulçura del estilo tan alto en su modo está la serpiente engañosa' (f.7r; Gale, pp. 86-7). Obviously his views were very different from those of his poet namesake in Seville!

But it is easy to make assumptions; harder to prove them to be true. One of the parallels between Córdoba and San Juan cited by Dámaso Alonso—probably the closest of them all—was Córdoba's version of lines 449-51 of Garcilaso's *Égloga segunda* and San Juan's 'Pastorcico' poem.

[10] For example, Allison Peers, 'The alleged debts of San Juan de la Cruz to Boscán and Garcilaso de la Vega', *HR* 21 (1953), 1-19, 93-106; and P. Emeterio de Jesús María, *Las raíces de la poesía sanjuanista y Dámaso Alonso* (Burgos, 1950).

[11] Glaser, '"El cobre convertido en oro": Christian "rifacimentos" of Garcilaso's poetry in the sixteenth and seventeenth centuries', *HR* 37 (1969), 61-76; and Crosbie, 'Amoral "a lo divino" poetry in the Golden Age', *MLR* 66 (1971), 599-607.

Blecua, however, has shown that San Juan's real source lay not in Córdoba but in some anonymous *redondillas* which he remodelled; and Dámaso Alonso has accepted this.[12] Blecua's discovery should be taken as admonitory: the originally suggested parallel seemed close enough to prove Dámaso Alonso's claim, yet this turns out to have been erroneous. Great care needs to be taken before accepting any such parallels as admissible evidence. The findings which follow are based on a thorough investigation of Córdoba's work, which has yielded only a few possible links between it and the *Cántico*:

(i) f.5^V: 'y aviendo ya passado como dizen en flores gran parte de mi vida'; also f.188^r: 'y aquel de Garcilaso entre sus flores'. For flowers as symbolic of vain pursuits, CA 3: 'Ni cogeré las flores'. For use of the repeated future in CA 3, compare f.29^{r-v}: 'También yré derribando/al mundo y la carne fuerte,/venceré de los que vencían,/y entenderé lo que valen.'

(ii) f.9^V: 'como el ciervo sediente'; compare CA 1: 'como el cieruo huiste' and 12: 'el cieruo vulnerado'.

(iii) f.11^V: 'Yo como la tortolilla/que huye alegre vivir,/y con su ansioso gemir,/se lamenta y se amanzilla,/para su dolor sentir.' Compare CA 33–4, the 'tortolica' and the solitude she seeks.

(iv) f.18^V: 'Tan herida el alma tengo'; compare CA 1:'auiéndome herido'.

(v) f. 19^V: 'Calla, me dize perdido/no dexes la compañía'; compare CA 20: 'pues ya si en el exido/de oy más no fuere vista ni hallada,/diréis que me he perdido'. See also f.53^r: 'Eme perdido queriendo/mas no puedo yrme ganando/estoy sin fuerças llorando'.

(vi) f.21^r: 'tornas al humilde altivo/con tu canto de Serena'; compare CA 30's reference to the 'canto de serenas'.

(vii) f.123^r, f.142^r: 'los montes, y los valles y los ríos/alábele la noche con el día'; compare CA 13: 'Mi Amado, las montañas . . . los valles . . . los ríos' and CA 29: 'montes, valles, riberas'.

(viii) f.134^V: 'y así la celestial caballería/gozaban del Señor'; compare CA 39: 'y la cauallería'.

(ix) f.172^r: 'que perdida del bien la esperança/al monte y al collado más supervo/llamaréys todas juntas a porfía.' Compare CA 35: 'al monte u al collado'.

(x) f.193^{r-v}: 'Iuntos a alguna fuente nos yremos/por donde el agua murmurando vaya/y combidarnos a que nos sentemos/su cristalina lustre.' Compare CA 11: '¡O christalina fuente!'

[12] Blecua, 'Los antecedentes del poema del "Pastorcico" de San Juan de la Cruz', *RFE* 33 (1949), 378–80. The *redondillas* are not dated, but are said to belong to the second half of the sixteenth century. See also Dámaso Alonso, op. cit., pp. 193–6 (fn 81).

(xi) f.202^r: 'y por aquel ameno y sancto huerto'; compare CA 27: 'en el ameno huerto desseado'.

To these may be added three which might have influenced other poems of San Juan:

(xii) f.76^v: 'el fuego de amor bivo,/el que en el cielo tiene su morada'; compare the start of the *Llama*: '¡Oh llama de amor viva!'

(xiii) f.123^r: 'como en lamar después de la tiniebla/pone alboroço el asomar de día,/y entonces fue plazer la noche escura'; compare the start of the *Noche*: 'En una noche oscura'.

(xiv) f.244^v (Gale, p. 186, lines 536–7, 545–7): 'Ésta me hizo al fin que me saliesse/por el silencio de la noche escura/ . . . allí entre dos almenas hize assiento/y acuérdome que ya con ella estuve/la [*sic*] noches del verano al fresco viento.' Compare *Noche* 1: 'En una noche oscura/ . . . salí sin ser notada'; 6: 'Allí quedó dormido/y yo le regalaba,/ y el ventalle de cedros aire daba'; and 7: 'El aire del almena'.

This is a rather meagre harvest in view of the expectations aroused. Dámaso Alonso himself only found a handful of cases where there was any likely influence of Córdoba on San Juan (and one of these, as we have seen, has had to be discounted). Of the 'tema de la fuente' (x), he says: 'En la ascendencia pastoril del *Cántico*, es tan viejo como la literatura bucólica en el mundo' (p. 52). Though it is qualified by the same adjective as San Juan uses, 'cristalina', this commonplace description is given to the 'lustre' rather than to the 'fuente', as in San Juan. The 'canto de Serena' (v) and the 'Filomena' and 'ninfas' which occasionally appear in Córdoba and were viewed as strangers in the *Cántico* must also be judged entirely conventional. They may originally stem from pagan poetry, but had long since been accepted into the poetry of Christian Western Europe, and would have caused no scandal to the pious. The other examples yield the same scanty fruit. In nearly all of them the links are commonplace and show no significant parallels. The 'flores' of (i) is a good example, while the repetition of the future verbs is no more than a common rhetorical device. The two poets share only 'yré', otherwise the verbs and their objects are different. The 'cieruo' (ii) merely reflects the age-old use of the hart in Psalm 42 (Vulgate 41). The mountains, valleys and rivers (vii) again are too common in poetry to provide any definite links with San Juan; while Córdoba himself has been influenced by Song 4:6 (ix) and he and San Juan share the same source. The 'caballería' (viii) could stem from the 'quadrigas' of Aminabad in Song 6:11, but more probably from the vision of the celestial army seen by Elisha and the young man in II Kings (Vulgate IV) 6:17–18.

Only (v) seems worth noting. Though there are no verbal parallels with CA 20, the theme is the same: the loss of former companions because of love, and their comments. It is not a distinctive enough parallel to demonstrate certain dependence; all that can be said is that it is the once place where Córdoba might justifiably be considered the source for a passage in the *Cántico*. Even so, San Juan uses the idea in a different context and develops it in his own way, and the unusual word 'exido' is not present in Córdoba. Nor are the examples relating to the *Llama* and *Noche* more promising, with the possible exception of (xiv), for which Garcilaso's original must also be considered.

But another point needs stressing, equally significant in showing how little San Juan has in common with Córdoba. Anyone who ploughs his weary way through the seemingly endless pages of the latter's work will quickly realize that it leaves a very different impression from San Juan's. Córdoba's versions are predominatly introspective, overburdened with sin and guilt and anxiety to repent; they are melancholy, gloomy, analysing human vice in its many forms, dark in colour, miserable in tone. The finest passages, oases in a barren desert, come where Garcilaso and even Boscán have been left well alone and allowed to speak with their original voices. San Juan's poetry, on the other hand, and particularly the *Cántico*, is light and colour, beauty and love: a world shot through with joy and delight, in which flowers, birds, animals, rivers, mountains, forests, breezes, and flames all join to celebrate an affirmation of live lived in union with its source. In other words, there is a tremendous gulf between the two. Córdoba is a moralist, and not a very impressive one; San Juan is a mystic, given to flights of rapture and exuberance of language. It must therefore be concluded that in spite of the importance ascribed to Córdoba as an influence on San Juan's poetic formation, an examination of his divinized Boscán and Garcilaso fails to produce anything more than a series of shared commonplace words and themes, and perhaps one case of an indirect parallel. The view which has become so widespread, that San Juan was deeply indebted to Córdoba, needs serious modification.

If this is so, does San Juan owe anything directly to Garcilaso? No evidence exists that he ever read him, though many critics have presumed he did, probably before 1568, when San Juan finished his training at Salamanca. But it is no more than a presumption. There is, of course, the question of the *lira*. Garcilaso had introduced it into Spain in his celebrated *Canción quinta*, 'Si de mi baxa lira', from which the form took its name. It is the metre San Juan uses for his three major poems. But many years had passed since the *lira* first appeared in Spain, and it had been widely imitated. Luis de León springs readily to mind, but his poetry was not published until 1631, though it had circulated privately among his friends and admirers at Salamanca. A recent attempt to prove that Fray Luis was used by San Juan as a source may look attractive on the surface, but closer examination shows it unconvincing.[13]

According to Orozco, the *lira* was already being used in convents and monasteries for the singing of spiritual songs by the time San Juan began to write, and he makes a study of what he terms 'poesía tradicional carmelitana'.[14] In 1576 the works of Fr. Jacopone da Todi were published at Lisbon in a Spanish translation, and Orozco calls the fourteenth 'Canto' 'una poesía mística escrita en liras y además impresa', and the whole work the kind of book a monk might well have carried around with him. There is also the record of the verse San Juan was sung by the Beas nuns, though in P. Silverio's text it cannot be called a *lira*, as it has nine syllables in the second line and eight in the third.[15] It is hard to be sure about the ancestry of the *lira* as it reached San Juan, but it is at least possible that he had encountered it in more spiritual poets than Garcilaso.

Earlier critics referred to Garcilaso's influence in a number of passages from San Juan's poetry. Baruzi mentioned examples like the adjective 'nemoroso' (CA 13 and the shepherd of that name in the first two eclogues) and the invocation of CA 29–30 and lines 239–43 of the first eclogue. P. Crisógono only found parallels with the *Llama*, in the shared vocabulary of 'encuentro', 'tela', and 'mano delicada, blanda'. Some of these have been discounted because they are too commonplace or essentially Biblical in inspiration. Dámaso Alonso prefers to speak of the 'ambiente garcilasesco' of the *Cántico* and *Llama*: of the latter, he states that the first two verses 'en su giros, en su vocabulario, en su imaginería,

---

[13] F. García Lorca, *De Fray Luis a San Juan: La escondida senda* (Madrid, 1972). There is no doubt that some contact existed between the two men, but we can only be sure of this towards the end of their lives, when the works under question were already written. San Juan was at Salamanca while Fray Luis taught there; both were imprisoned, though for different reasons and at different times; both shared a deep love for the Bible and particularly the Song of Songs, which Fray Luis translated and expounded; Fray Luis edited the works of Santa Teresa, and San Juan knew of this (CB 13.7); both were poets and theologians, though Fray Luis had a much wider range of interests; and Fray Luis, towards the end of his life, became involved with the problems of the Carmelite Reform. But García Lorca has almost entirely ignored the major problem of dating. Can San Juan, as a Carmelite student, really be expected to have been in the intimate circle of those to whom Fray Luis read his poems, supposing that he had written any of the influential ones by 1568, when San Juan left Salamanca? And how feasible is it that San Juan should have read Fray Luis's manuscript Spanish *Cantar* (and perhaps his manuscript *liras*) or his Latin *In Canticum Canticorum* (not published till 1589) and assimilated them, before he was arrested late in 1576? The only evidence we have (see p. 3) suggests that San Juan read very little apart from the Bible. Moreover, to what extent can the similarities García Lorca has noted be explained by the fact that both authors are using a common source—the Songs of Songs? These questions need tackling before any firm conclusions can be drawn. I am surprised in view of their common interests, how little like each other they are.

[14] Op. cit., ch. 2, especially pp. 132–3.

[15] BMC 14, 169.

respiran esencias de Garcilaso'.[16] They do perhaps come closer to Garcilaso than anything else San Juan wrote, yet, because of their religious setting, they are quite distinctive.

As for the atmosphere of the *Cántico*, Garcilaso must in any case come a very poor second to the Song. There are pastoral elements in CA 2, soliloquy and appeal to the Beloved in 6—11, and various images, especially in CA 13, 33 and 38, which might all suggest a link with him. Dámaso Alonso uncovered only one example where he felt that Garcilaso was directly influencing San Juan's *Cántico*: the lines in CA 38 which run 'El aspirar de el ayre,/el canto de la dulce Philomena', which he related to lines 1146—7 of the second eclogue. San Juan uses a number of images from lines 1146—53, which run:

> Nuestro ganado pace, el viento espira,
> Filomena sospira en dulce canto
> y en amoroso llanto s'amanzilla;
> gime la tortolilla sobre'l olmo,
> preséntanos a colmo el prado flores
> y esmalta en mil colores su verdura;
> la fuente clara y pura, murmurado,
> nos está combidando a dulce trato.[17]

Alonso suggested that the juxtaposition of the blowing wind and the sweet song of the nightingale in CA 38 showed that these lines lay behind San Juan. There is a fairly clear parallel, closer than those discussed from Córdoba, and closer here to Garcilaso's original, as Córdoba omits the reference to the nightingale. Moreover, the picture of the meadow covered in flowers in CA 4: 'o prado de verduras/ de flores esmaltado', shares four important words with Garcilaso, 'prado', 'flores', 'esmaltar', and 'verdura'. Allison Peers discounted this as a conventional description, and certainly each poet could have arrived at it independently; but a stronger case can be made for Garcilaso's influencing of San Juan's poetic diction in this case than in most others. Other possible links are fortuitious. The turtle-dove is depicted differently in the *Cántico* and probably has a Biblical origin; the fountain acts as a mirror there, whereas Garcilaso's invites pleasure; and even the blowing of the wind can be traced back to Song 4:16. If San Juan did use these lines, then his procedure was the exact reverse of his use of the Song. There he selects elements from the eight chapters and brings them together in his own chosen way. Here he would be taking a consecutive passage from Garcilaso and scattering its images across his poem. It may fairly be concluded that there is some influence of Garcilaso's second eclogue on CA 4 and 38, but that any other apparent points of contact should be ascribed to a common poetic tradition reaching back far beyond Garcilaso.

[16] Op. cit., p. 32.
[17] The edition used is that by Rivers (Madrid, 1974).

There are other signs of this tradition in the *Cántico*. In CA 8, the old commonplace beloved of the mystics is expressed by San Juan as 'no viuiendo donde viues', and develops into a conceit involving the arrows of Cupid:

> y haciendo por que mueras
> las flechas que reciues
> de lo que del Amado en ti concibes.

But San Juan complicates the traditional image. The arrows which bring death are caused by the Beloved's absence, in which she 'lives but does not live', and by the fleeting glimpses she has had of him on his passage through creation. They have caused her to 'conceive' some indefinable part of him ('lo que del Amado') in herself, and it is this conception, in which both physical and spiritual meanings coincide, that is causing her death. The whole stanza is a rhetorical question asked of 'vida', who is responsible for the dying of the soul by continuing to live. Its syntax is difficult, because the last two lines seem to be the object of 'haciendo', and the 'por que mueras', which follows it, the result of that object. The traditional picture of wounds of love and Cupid's darts is still recognizable, but given a most unusual treatment.

CA 11 and 19 are likewise based on two ancient elements, used by poets from Theocritus onwards: the Lover gazing into the water (here, a fountain); and lovesick shepherds neglecting their flocks.[18] Again, San Juan develops the underlying ideas in his own manner, and proves quite original. CA 11 is an elaboration of the picture of the shepherd (or Polyphemus) who gazes into the water and sees his own reflection, showing that he isn't so bad-looking after all. With San Juan it is the Bride who gazes into the 'christalina fuente', with all the symbolism of those words in Christian literature, desiring to see there reflected the eyes of the Beloved. She does not catch sight of her own beauty, but longs for a glimpse of the Beloved's eyes, which CA 12 gives us to understand is granted to her. Her former companions may chide her (CA 20), but she has chosen her path. San Juan does not depict the effect this has on the flocks and countryside (compare *Polifemo* 21), except indirectly, in CA 19's 'ya no guardo ganado'. There is little doubt that here San Juan is echoing this prestigious tradition, and that secular poetic themes do therefore exert some influence on the *Cántico*.

There are also one or two traces of popular poetry in it. Much popular poetry was anonymous, so it is themes rather than specific authors that are said to have influenced San Juan. Dámaso Alonso believes that CA 24's 'No quieras despreciarme,/que si color moreno en mí hallaste' may come from the *Cancionero*, in which this was a prominent theme; but

---

[18] Compare Garcilaso, *Égloga primera*, lines 169–82, 189–96; *Égloga segunda*, lines 910–985. He also treats the theme originally, especially in linking it with

the *Cántico* version has strong links with Song 1:5, just as the 'no sé qué' has with 6:11, though it too is present in popular and courtly poetry. Perhaps the Song of Songs itself influenced the popular poetry of an earlier age; certainly in Spain, where Jews and Christians counted it among their sacred books, and Muslims also shared a heritage of erotico-mystical literature from the Ancient Near East, its literary influence ought not to be underestimated.[19]

The dove of CA 33—4 has also been claimed as an example of popular influence, though the bird appears in the Song (2:12) and also in Boscán and Garcilaso. Cossío suggested that the sixteenth-century poets were influenced by the ballad 'Fontefrida':

> Fonte-frida, Fonte-frida,
> Fonte-frida y con amor,
> do todas las avecicas
> van tomar consolación,
> si no es la Tortolica
> que está viuda y con dolor.

But 'Fontefrida' is not the first example of this theme in literature, so there is no *a priori* reason for supposing it must be the source for San Juan's turtle-dove, or anyone else's. As Bataillon has observed, San Juan 'se mueve a sus anchas en el simbolismo que le suministra la tradición.'[20]

In the commentary, it is clear that San Juan is drawing on ancient lore: 'Es de saber que de la tortolica se escriue que, quando no halla al consorte, si ne asienta en ramo uerde, ni beue el agua clara ni fría, ni se pone debajo de la sombra, *ni se junta con otras aues*'.[21] This derives from Christian exegesis of the Song of Songs, and probably from pre-Christian writers on natural history. The tradition was of enormous authority and can be found as far back as Origen's commentaries on the Song, *c.* A.D. 240. On Song 1:9 he writes: 'They say it is the nature of the turtle-dove that the male bird never mates with any female but one,

---

Albanio's madness in the second eclogue. But San Juan's treatment is too different to suppose that he is here directly influenced by Garcilaso. In Góngora's *Fábula de Polifemo y Galatea*, 21, 49, and 53, the theme reappears in a different setting and it reaches into English literature in, for example, Marvell's 'Damon *the Mower*', V—VIII, and Milton's *Paradise Lost*, Book IV, lines 453—65.

[19] See *The Jewish Poets of Spain*, ed. Goldstein (Harmondsworth, 1971); especially poems by Danash ha-Levi Ben Labrat, Samuel ha-Nagid, Solomon ibn Gabirol, and Judah ha-Levi.

[20] 'La tortolica de *Fonte-frida* y del *Cántico espiritual*', *NFRE* 7 (1953), 305. See also Cossío, 'Rasgos renacentistas y populares en el "Cántico espiritual" ', *Escorial* 25 (1942), 205—28. The ballad is quoted from Menéndez Pidal's text in *Flor nueva de romances viejos*.

[21] CA 33.5: the italicized words come from a marginal annotation in the Sanlúcar MS. and pass, slightly changed, into CB.

and the female similarly will not suffer more than a single mate; so that, if one of the pair be killed and the other left, the survivor's desire for intercourse is extinguished with its mate.' Later, on 2:11, he continues: 'This bird spends its life in the more hidden and remote localities, away from crowds; it loves either mountain wastes, or the secret parts of the forests, is always found far from the multitude, and is a stranger to crowds.'[22] It is within such a tradition, rather than from one ballad which also reflects the tradition, that we should look to understand from where San Juan drew his material. He must have heard such illustrations used as *exempla* in sermons and homilies: the spoken word must have been an important influence on him, particularly in the context of a worshipping Christian community. But oral transmission, of course, by its very nature, cannot be detected in San Juan. Unless it is written down, it vanishes for ever.

Popular poetry, then, has left little trace in the *Cántico*. Its influence is strongest in the forms he chooses for his lesser poems—the *glosas* and *romances*—which also owe more to *a lo divino* literature than the major works. In the *Cántico* prologue San Juan himself outlines his sources: mystical experience, the holy doctors, things written for beginners, scholastic theology, personal contacts, Scripture, and ecclesiastical tradition. Compared with this background, the influence of secular poetry, even of the divinizers, is very thinly spread. This is perhaps truer of the *Cántico* than of any other of his poems; certainly it shows the closest relationship to the Song. But that should cause no surprise. Córdoba was not the originator of spiritual interpretations of secular love poetry. In the Song, San Juan found a poem understood *a lo divino* in Jewish and Christian thought for centuries. For a man of his obvious poetic sensibility, the Song, with its powerful evocative appeal, must have been far more attractive than the pedestrian efforts of a Sebastián de Córdoba, and in any case, it was authoritative, because it was part of the canon of sacred literature. The supremacy of the Song as a source for the *Cántico* is undeniable. But, whether using specific texts or general themes, whether inspired by sacred or secular sources, always it is San Juan who is the poet, speaking to us through his ancestors, yet nonetheless singing a new song.

---

[22] Origen, *The Song of Songs: Commentary and Homilies*, trans. Lawson (London, 1957), pp. 146, 241.

5

TOWARDS AN EVALUATION OF THE *CÁNTICO*

For some three hundred years after San Juan's death, his poetry was almost completely ignored. He is not mentioned in the early histories of literature, like Pouterwek's *History of Spanish and Portuguese Literature* (1823) and Sismondi's *De la littérature du midi de l'Europe* (1829). Ticknor treats him as a didactic prose-writer, though remarks that his poetry is 'marked by great felicity and richness of phraseology'.[1] It is with Menéndez Pelayo that modern appreciation of San Juan's poetry really begins. Comparing it with that of Luis of León, he wrote:

> Pero aún hay una poesía más angélica, celestial y divina, que ya no parece de este mundo, ni es posible medirla con criterios literarios, y eso que es más ardiente de pasión que ninguna poesía profana, y tan elegante y exquisita en la forma, y tan plástica y figurativa como los más valiosos frutos del Renacimiento. Son las *Canciones espirituales* de San Juan de la Cruz . . . Confieso que me infunden religioso terror al tocarlas. Por allí ha pasado el espíritu de Dios, hermoseándolo y sanctificándolo todo.[2]

Following in the wake of this confession, many modern critics have come to the same conclusion, at least about the *Noche, Cántico,* and *Llama* poems, and have called them some of the greatest poems of Spanish literature. Dámaso Alonso's evaluation is not untypical: 'San Juan de la Cruz es un maravilloso artista literario y el más alto poeta de España.'[3] Most recently, Brenan has called him 'one of the supreme lyric poets of any age or country'.[4]

Understandably, perhaps, there has been a persistent tendency to describe or eulogize San Juan's poetry, rather than subject it to serious critical examination, and this inability to probe his poetic creativity has affected even the best *sanjuanista* scholars.[5] P. Crisógono could not resist the temptation to generalize: the poetry has no 'voces rebuscadas: todas son llanas y comunes, pero nobles . . . palabras dulces y sonoras,

---

[1] *History of Spanish Literature*, 3 vols (London, 1863), iii. 208.
[2] As quoted by Alonso, op. cit., pp. 17–18.
[3] Ibid., p. 178.
[4] *St. John of the Cross* (Cambridge, 1973), p. 3.
[5] This process reached a climax in 1942, San Juan's quatercentary, when many articles were published in his honour but none actually analysed his poetic craftsmanship. See the articles in *RE* i (1941–2) for good examples (details in bibliography).

de voces suavísimas y delicadas', and 'No existe poesía de menos artificio que la de San Juan de la Cruz'.[6] But can 'adamabas', 'Aminadab' and 'un no sé qué que quedan' really fit such a description? And, as we shall see, few poets display greater mastery over a wide variety of poetic techniques than San Juan.

Some of Dámaso Alonso's findings have shed light on the way the poetry works. One of his major discoveries was the irregular distribution of adjectives and verbs in the *Cántico*. No adjectives occur until CA 11, and then a great concentration of them from 13–15. This hastens the pace of the opening stanzas, depicting the anxious search for the Beloved; but when he is glimpsed, the Bride can dwell on his beauty and the adjective comes into its own, delaying further action and inviting the reader to concentrate on the scenes which unfold to reveal 'Mi Amado'. Thus, San Juan passes rapidly through the natural scenes of CA 3–5 but lingers to enjoy their beauty in 13–15, because the search is over. This movement between concentrations of verbs and adjectives is typical of the *Cántico* and can also be found in the *Noche*'s last three stanzas. It may be added that verbal activity predominates in CA 17–26, 31–2, 35, 37 and 39, with a corresponding scarcity of adjectives. Alonso describes this feature as 'la ondulación entre un trayecto *a*, caracterizado por la escasez de verbos o de adjetivos, y otro *β*, en donde esos mismos elementos se amontan.'[7] His suggestion that this is linked with progress in the mystical life—no adjectives in the purgative way, more in the illuminative and unitive—does not, however, match the later parts of the poem, where there is often a dearth of adjectives, although the fruition of love is being described. But the Bride's search is more generally reflected in this undulation, in that when she lingers over the Beloved adjectives are prominent, and when the history of the encounter is being related, verbs are to the fore, as one might expect. His own imaginative picture of San Juan's poetry is telling: 'una hoguera, con intervalos pausados o un saltar frenético de las llamas, como una hoguera bajo el viento.'

Apart from this valuable contribution, Alonso also mentions a number of more obvious features, like the famous 'no sé qué que quedan' cacophony and the 'en soledad' anaphora (CA 7, 34). He finds little of interest in metre and rhyme; he points out some examples of alliteration and paradox, and the more developed conceits, like that in CA 8; and he refers to the mixture of popular and courtly vocabulary: 'exido' and 'majadas' on the one hand, 'vulnerado', 'nemoroso', and 'emissiones de bálsamo' on the other, together with a good sprinkling of Biblical words.

---

[6] Op. cit. ii. 186–7, 221.
[7] *Poesía española* (Madrid, 1950), p. 305; as also the next quotation.

Jorge Guillén, for whom San Juan 'es el gran poeta más breve de la lengua española, acaso de la literatura universal', has also made some interesting observations of a general kind, especially about imagery, allegory, and symbolism—the concrete imagery San Juan prefers, the small amount of allegory which is clearly present in the poems (such as the 'christalina fuente' in CA 11, and the references in CA 28), and the way in which some of the symbols, such as night and flame, are intimately related to the experiences being described. He calls the *Noche* the purest of the three great poems and explains: 'Y "puro" apunta aquí a una calidad desprovista de toda sospecha de retórica'—an observation which, it will become clear, cannot be substantiated for the *Cántico*.[8]

In this study of San Juan's poetry, Brenan, following clues given by Lowes in his *The Road to Xanadu*, relates the process psychoanalysts have discovered in dream symbolism and term 'condensation', to San Juan's treatment of his raw material. Thus the images and symbols he uses do not often have a simple, single source but are compounded of many different elements from different sources which San Juan has encountered and which have already begun to fuse together in his imagination—certainly a more illuminating approach to the question of sources and his use of them than most critics have been able to provide:

What he extracted from a poetic text was not its power of evocation as poetry, but an image or episode which had a special significance for him because it accorded with those images he had collected to express his central mystical theme of the road to union. No poet borrowed more from other poets, yet none was more original because before be began to write all the work of transmutation into his own categories had been accomplished.[9]

But we shall discover that in other respects Brenan's account of San Juan's poetic technique is open to serious question.

In order to understand and evaluate the achievement of San Juan, the *Cántico* must be studied in depth and from different angles. It will not be enough simply to describe his techniques, for description and evaluation are not the same task, and a stylistic analysis is incomplete unless accompanied by an attempt to penetrate the techniques to see why the poem is so highly praised. In the following study of these elements, it will be suggested that San Juan deliberately used particular techniques to create the effects he required; in other words, that his poetry was not the spontaneous overspill of profound experiences, but an artistic creation in its own right, in which any such experiences are moulded into poetry of the highest craftsmanship.[10]

[8] *Lenguaje y poesía* (Madrid, 1969), pp. 75–6, 78.
[9] Op. cit., p. 125.
[10] Formal rhetorical terms will normally be given in Latin and Greek, following the classification of Sonnino, *A Handbook to Sixteenth-Century Rhetoric* (London, 1968).

I

The *Cántico* leaves an overwhelming impression of mystery behind it. Why does the poem so puzzle its readers?

First, it shows considerable disruption in structure, theme, and imagery. No scene is set at the start; instead, the poem plunges into a dramatic complaint, which may have been going on for some time. There is no recognizable *exordium* or *conclusio*, no logical movement from one place or event to the next; instead, a bewildering array of images which causes the reader to lose his way almost at once. Rarely is it clear who is addressing whom, and about what.[11]

The baffling nature of the poem becomes clearer through a closer analysis of this last point. The first four words imply the existence of an absent Beloved who, at some moment in the past, has hidden from the Bride: she has set out to find him, but has failed. Such is her opening complaint. In the second stanza she turns to address the shepherds and moves into the present tense (though somewhat uncertainly because of the unusual 'fuerdes' and 'vierdes') to inquire where he might be. In CA 3, she seems to be informing herself of her intentions (*praeparatio*) though she could still be addressing the shepherds. Next (4) she turns to the woods, thickets, and meadow to ask if they have witnessed the Beloved passing by; and after their affirmative reply, she returns to her complaint (6–7) and says that her quest has discovered the 'mil gracias' he has strewn along his way, which only deepen her wound. The complaint, now more of a soliloquy, continues in 8, and 9–10 again castigate the Beloved. Until this point it is not too difficult to follow the thread of a story: a lament to the absent Beloved, which only increases the suffering of the Bride.·

But now the poem becomes more disjointed. There has been mystery already, because the identity of the protagonists has not been revealed, nor the reason for the Beloved's vanishing, nor for Nature's assuming the power of speech (*conformatio*). In 11, the Bride, gazes into the 'christalina fuente', longing to see there reflected the eyes of her Beloved 'de repente'. This phrase should act as a signal, for 'suddenly' she cries out: 'Apártalos, Amado, que voy de buelo.' Without any warning, her wish has become reality: she sees the eyes before her, though this is not stated explicitly. San Juan merely suggests this through the enclitic pronoun '-los', which can only refer back to 'los ojos desseados', the sight of which she cannot now bear. Rarely can so insignificant a part of speech have been endowed with such tremendous content, for it alone marks the end of the Bride's quest and the first appearance of the Beloved in the poem: a most startling example of *defectio* (*ellipsis*). The

---

[11] Some of the characteristics are reminiscent of certain ballad techniques which create similar effects of drama, tension, and mystery, exemplifed so well in the famous 'Romance del infante Arnaldos'.

source (Song 6:4) has nothing of this dramatic impact—it is San Juan's own invention.

And at this abrupt point of transition, we lose control of the poem. The complaint is over; something happens; she cannot bear it, she flies, and is summoned back by the Beloved, who now speaks for the first time, as the wounded stag who appears on the hill-side in the breeze stirred up by her flight, to take refreshment. For the first time in the poem, the Bride and the Beloved are described in images, the dove and the wounded stag; and the poem now dissolves into a torrent of images, as the Bride attempts to convey the beauty of the Beloved. It is as though his appearance, with the word 'paloma' rather than 'Esposa' on his lips, acts as a release mechanism for the store of images held in check throughout the Bride's complaint. The reader begins to delight in the lyrical scenes the images convey (13–14), for their own sake. In much the same way, when the Bride describes their bed (15), the onrush of images—lions' dens, royal purple, peace, the thousand golden shields surmounting it—defies any attempt to form a coherent picture of it.

Then suddenly, another picture flashes on to the screen, young girls running in the Beloved's tracks, towards a 'spark' and 'spiced wine'. No sooner are they introduced than they vanish, with no explanation of their identity or meaning, and the reader is pulled backwards in time as the Bride describes to some unspecified audience an event in a wine-cellar which led to her betrothal (17–18). It is curious that this was not stated earlier, because from the initial complaint it seemed unlikely that their relationship was so intimate. Only now can the poignancy of the Bride's situation be fully appreciated—and the poem has run nearly half its course! In 18–19 she again addresses an unspecified audience, yet by 21 is directly addressing the Beloved, in the first person plural, and referring to some joint activity—gathering flowers and entwining them in a strand of her hair. This is the cue for another glimpse into the past (22–3), before a return to the present (24) in an appeal to the Beloved not to despise her for her dark colouring. This strikes a strange note, in view of the intimacy already achieved in 17–18 and 22–3.

Another turning-point is reached in 25. The Bride asks for the vixen (their one and only appearance) to be chased away, but by whom we are not told. Here San Juan remains faithful to his source (Song 2:15): 'Capite nobis'. The verbs in this stanza come in a bewildering variety of tenses and moods, with different subjects, none of which is concrete save 'nuestra viña'. In 26 the Bride appeals to the north wind to cease and the south wind to blow through the garden, which she enters in the next stanza. The Beloved now makes his longest intervention in the poem, describing her entry into the garden as accomplished and depicting her at rest in his arms. Then he switches back in time, as the Bride had done, to relate a mysterious event beneath an apple-tree, in

which the attentive reader can hardly fail to see an allegorical reference
to the fall of Eve in the garden of Eden and the redemption on the tree
of Calvary by Mary's son. It refers at 18, to the betrothal, which only
increases our bewilderment as this now appears to have taken place in
two distinct locations: in the wine-cellar, and under the apple-tree. But
the Beloved quickly returns to the present and his attention focuses on
a host of animals, places, and emotions, which are ordered not to
disturb the Bride's repose.

For two stanzas the Bride speaks again. First she commands the
'nymphas de Judea' to depart, beings who appear for the first and last
time here. They are troublesome, for an unknown reason, yet were not
invoked by the Beloved when he ordered disturbing elements to leave.
Either his invocation did not work, or the Bride is repeating it in another
form. In CA 32, for the first time since 24, she addresses the Beloved,
but still in the imperative. It is unclear what she wants him to do: look
at the mountains 'y no quieras decillo'. The 'lo' does not seem to refer
to anything specific. 'Mas mira las compañas/de la que ua por ínsulas
estrañas' is also puzzling. If this is the Bride, what is she doing in far-off
places when she was last seen at rest in the Beloved's arms?

San Juan offers no explanation. The Beloved makes his last speech, a
report of the dove's return to the ark and the turtle-dove's to her mate,
referring, presumably, to the Bride but apparently repeating what 27
has already described as accomplished: the Bride's entry into union
with the Beloved. In 35 she speaks for the last time and concludes the
poem. Again, the tenses are confused: first person plural, present subjunctive (35), future (36), and conditionals with an imperfect and a
preterite (37). The Bride is outlining to the Beloved plans for future bliss
in secret places. 38, with no main verb, defines the 'aquello' of 37 in a
series of pictures; and the poem ends with a tableau depicting some
past event, seemingly unconnected with anything.

From this summary, it should be abundantly clear why it is so hard
to follow any thread through the poem. Changes of speaker, audience,
tense, location; large numbers of unrelated images; paradox, logical
nonsense, constant uncertainty on the reader's part as to the exact
meaning—the whole poem is constructed in this extraordinary manner.
In parts it is almost impressionistic in feel; in other parts, it seems to
be using a sixteenth-century equivalent of modern cinematographic
technique: flashbacks introduced without warning, events implied rather
than stated, characters introduced in passing, focused upon briefly,
then discarded. No sequence of events can be followed except through
small groups of stanzas, because the thematic progress of the poem is
constantly being interrupted by glances into the future or past, and by
fragments of conversations and comments. There is no ordered progression in time, place, or argument, except the very basic one that at the

beginning the Bride is searching for her Beloved and at the end she is united with him. The over-all impression is one of a large number of beautiful fragments pieced together but never fitting properly. In this the *Cántico* faithfully reflects it model, but manages to be more complex and elusive in a much shorter span. It is therefore most unusual, perhaps unique, in the poetry of the Golden Age, for such a technique is wholly out of keeping with the predominant classical and Renaissance ideas about poetry.

But the sense of mystery is more pervasive than this. It arises not only from the structure of the poem, but directly out of the text. Consider the effect produced by the large numbers of vague paraphrases in it (*circumlocutio, periphrasis*):

2	aquel que yo más quiero
6	decirme lo que quiero
7	un no sé qué
8	de lo que del Amado
23	adorar lo que en ti vían
32	y no quieras decillo
	de la que ua por ínsulas estrañas
37	aquello que mi alma pretendía
	aquello que me diste el otro día

to which may be added other curiously vague lines:

17	ya cosa no sabía
18	y yo le di de hecho
	a mí, sin dexar cosa
39	y nadie lo miraua

These contrast sharply with the richness of imagery elsewhere.[12] This predilection for vague expressions with 'lo que' and 'cosa' is partly explained by the circumlocutions for the Beloved used in the Song, but is more thoroughgoing than the simple 'quem diligit anima mea'. Its effect is to draw attention away from anything concrete, like a person or an event, and render them intangible, and therefore mysterious. What the Bride wants to hear, what she has conceived, what she has seen in the Beloved's eyes, what he must not say, and what her soul has been claiming and received 'el otro día', all remain unstated, and the reader seems to be invited to colour the indefinable from his own imagination.

This is the more impressive because of the richness of colouring elsewhere. It is as if San Juan were saying that however vividly he can describe the love he is celebrating, there is ultimately in the poem something which cannot be captured by such means, a part of the total

---

[12] Garcilaso also uses vague paraphrases, e.g. 'Canción segunda', line 52; and 'Canción tercera', line 26.

picture which can only be left blank, or at best provided with a few brush-strokes. Several of these vague expressions occur at the end of verses, so that the effect is one of building up the tension towards some point, which then dissolves into the indefinable. This is surely the poetic counterpart, the 'balbucir', of San Juan's insistence, with other mystics, on the ineffability of the mystical encounter. Outbursts of exuberant language (like CA 13–15) are counterbalanced by a language which can no more than stammer, because it is inadequate to capture the experience it seeks to communicate.

The sense of mystery is further heightened by the shifting location of the poem. Just as vague paraphrase is used to intensify the mysterious atmosphere, so is the adverb 'allí', repeated three times in CA 18:

> Allí me dio su pecho
> allí me enseñó sciencia muy sabrosa . . .
> allí le prometí de ser su esposa.

It refers to the wine-cellar of the previous stanza, while in 28 it can only be to the apple-tree:

> allí comigo fuiste desposada,
> allí te di la mano . . .
> donde tu madre fuera vïolada.

In 36–7 we find:

> y allí nos entraremos . . .
> allí me mostrarías . . .
> allí tú, uida mía . . .

—the lofty caverns of stone. Each place must have a more than literal meaning: you don't get betrothed in a wine-cellar and under an apple-tree, nor is a dark cave a good place for showing anyone anything. For this reason, and through its insistent repetition, 'allí' acquires a power of its own, a combination of all these places and more, as the locus for some extraordinary event which must continually be approached in different ways because it is so momentous. In fact, 'allí' itself comes to be a symbol, the answer to the first word of the poem, '¿adónde?', but an answer ambiguous in the extreme.

Nor can any one place be called the scene of the *Cántico*'s action. This contrasts sharply with the normal practice of sixteenth-century Spanish poetry, and to see how far San Juan creates his own poetic world we may compare his procedure with that of Garcilaso's description of the scene in which his third eclogue is set—the traditional *locus amoenus* (*topographia*). After the customary dedication, Garcilaso begins:

> Cerca del Tajo, en soledad amena,
> de verdes sauzes ay una espessura
> toda de yedra revestida y llena,
> que por el tronco va hasta el altura

> y assí la texe arriba y encadena
> que'l sol no halla passo a la verdura;
> el agua baña el prado con sonido,
> alegrando la yerva y el oýdo.[13]

This perfect cameo, evoked in considerable detail, introduces the story by depicting a nymph rising out of the water, combing her golden tresses, and looking on the meadow with its flowers and shadows. Once the scene is set, the story unfolds.

But San Juan has nothing like this. From CA 2–5 the setting is drawn on a large-scale canvas: hills, mountains, river banks, fortresses, frontiers, woods, thickets, and meadows—a broad vision of the natural creation, with all these elements taking an active part in the drama. The picture of the Beloved in 13–14 is similarly illustrated with mountains, lonely wooded valleys, rivers, breezes, night, without being in any sense the description of a particular scene. The end of the poem has this same broad context: mountains, hills, water, lofty caverns, calm night. These places contrast sharply with a group of much smaller ones which assume great significance in the poem: the fountain (11), the bed (15), the wine-cellar (17), the apple-tree (28), the garden with its wall, vines, and roses (25–31). The poem therefore moves between two extremes, macrocosm and microcosm, one moment contemplating the whole realm of nature, and the next, concentrating on one tiny place. This fluctuating setting only increases the sense of mystery in the poem.

This is increased further by the obscure meaning of some passages—*ambiguitas* (*amphibologia*). Strict ambiguity occurs only once, CA 17's 'En la interior bodega/de mi Amado beuí', where the latter phrase could either qualify 'bodega' (I drank *in my Beloved's* wine-cellar) or modify 'beuí' (in the wine-cellar I drank *from my Beloved*). San Juan opts for the second interpretation in the commentary; otherwise, there is no way of telling which meaning is intended, as both make good sense. But there are also paradoxical lines in the poem, like 8's '¡o vida!, no viuiendo donde viues', 20's 'me hice perdidiza, y fui ganada', and 38's 'con llama que consume y no da pena'. These are fairly straightforward examples of *contrapositum* (*syneciosis*), in which two opposites are placed together. In 24 the lines 'ya bien puedes mirarme/después que me miraste' are so odd as to qualify as near-paradox, while there is a general obscurity of meaning in parts of the poem, like 12, 15–16, 21–4, 28–32, 37–9. Literal interpretation of such verses is meaningless. In 21 the garlands of flowers are supposed to be entwined in one strand of hair, which is impossible. In 22 the Bride claims she has wounded and imprisoned the Beloved, whereas the rest of the poem gives a different impression. In 29–30 it is hard to imagine how mountains, valleys, banks, ardours, and watchful fears can be angry, let alone touch a wall.

---

[13] lines 57–64.

Through such examples, the conviction grows that whatever meaning is to be found in such passages, it lies beyond normal comprehension and cannot be grasped without some clues offered to solve the mystery.

Another reason why the poem mystifies is its mixture of courtly, cultured language with the popular and rustic, and of the language of West and East. Words like 'adamar', 'adobado', 'bálsamo diuino', 'nymphas de Judea', 'haz' and 'Aminadab' indicate a poetic world different from the familiar one of the Golden Age. But there are other signs that the *Cántico* does belong to its age: its pastoral elements, landscape, shepherds, doves, and flowers, its language of wounding and dying, the flame which burns painlessly. Images familiar to Golden Age readers are set next to unfamiliar ones. There are nymphs, but from Judaea; there is a bed, but with lions' dens, purple, and golden shields; there are roses, thickets, springs; but also pomegranates and amber. San Juan appears to make no distinction between images taken from the poetic tradition of the West and those taken from the oriental, Biblical tradition. They all serve his purpose. The provenance of the image does not govern its choice; rather, he bombards the reader's imagination with one image after another, even if they belong to different poetic worlds, in a language so rich that it becomes impossible to savour any one picture because the next one is already pressing in upon it. Again, 13–15, 29–30, 35–6, and 38–9 are the most striking examples. The reader cannot reflect on them all. Instead, like the brilliant colours of the kingfisher, they leave the impression that something incredibly beautiful has flown by, though too swiftly for each of the colours to be distinguished and enjoyed at leisure.

Nowhere is the *Cántico*'s elusiveness greater than in the last three stanzas. CA 37 begins 'alli', in the caverns of the previous verse, and consists of two actions, a showing and a giving, neither of which is defined, and the objects of which are described only in the vaguest of paraphrases, 'aquello que mi alma pretendía', and 'aquello que me diste el otro día' (perhaps 'la mano', given in 28). It is the barest verse in the poem, consisting mainly of pronouns, adverbs and verbs. The contrast with 38 could hardly be greater, for this is an attempt to give detail and colour to that skeleton of a stanza. It presents a series of related images: the breeze blowing, the nightingale singing, the groves in the calm night, the burning but painless flame. Now, it is all nouns and adjectives, and there is no main verb, no action, no participation of the Bride and her Beloved; simply a series of beautiful scenes unfolding to define 'aquello'. Yet we are no closer to understanding what this 'something' really is.

The last stanza begins with a parenthetical comment 'Que nadie lo miraua'. The 'lo' seems to refer to the scene just described, but ought to be understood in terms of the desire for solitude and privacy expressed by the lovers in 25, 31, 34, and 36. The imperfect tense is used throughout the stanza, and this insistence on the past tense is strange. Attention is still being focused on 'aquello que me diste el otro día'. It is at that past moment that Aminadab did not appear, and the cavalry descended to the waters. From the point of view of temporal succession, therefore, 36 marks the end of the poem, with its promise of a future ascent to the lofty caverns; after this, San Juan retreats again into the past, which is apparently to be repeated in that promised future. The *Cántico* thus ends inconclusively, looking backwards to the event hinted at in 37 and forwards to its repetition. Then a startlingly new element is introduced (*improvisum*): 'Aminadab tanpoco parecía'; introduced as casually as if he were expected, an old friend. But his identity is not revealed, except as someone undesirable. His presence no doubt is explained by his appearance in the Song, but that does not help us to understand why San Juan has delayed it till the last possible moment. In the Song, he appears in the company of his horsemen, and San Juan has obviously remembered this, because he proceeds to conclude his poem with a military image. Surely this is the least expected of pictures at this point in the *Cántico*, for since CA 32 all disturbances have been absent, and the atmosphere is one of peace and serenity. To end this poem, San Juan has chosen to introduce a new character, fresh images and a quite unexpected action. This leaves the reader with the feeling of being stranded, and in vain he searches for any clue to bring him back to earth. Here the elusiveness of the poem reaches it culminating point, utterly mysterious, almost other-wordly in atmosphere, the most tantalizing part of a poem which hides so many secrets.

In view of all this, one wonders how accurate Brenan is in claiming of the *Cántico* that 'there is nothing vaporous or imprecise in its lanugage or imagery.' He also writes:

There is another feature that one cannot fail to notice—the distinctness and precision of the language. As each verbal note is struck, another follows without blurring or overlap. The words are clear, clean, almost transparent, yet sufficiently full for their purpose: each phrase is perfectly articulated and there is no continuous mood or overtone flowing through the stanzas and blurring their particular effects as in Garcilaso's poetry.[14]

A mood of mystery pervades the *Cántico*, and while there is a richness of language in many stanzas, there is also a stammering, uncertain language, imprecise, indistinct, which is deliberately employed to help in creating this mood.

II

Yet all the time there is another process at work in the poem, pulling it away from fragmentation and towards its own kind of unity. San Juan

[14] Op. cit., pp. 123, 116.

controls the fragments and relates them to one another, and helps us to recognize that the poem does belong together and is meant to. So it becomes possible to speak of the unity of the *Cántico*, to which several factors contribute.

There is its use, throughout, of the language of the Song, part of the reason for its unfamiliarity to the modern reader. Even those factors which accelerate the poem's tendency towards fragmentation act, paradoxically, as a unifying factor, because they affect the whole poem, not just one part of it. And it has one central theme, the love of the Bride and the Beloved, to which every fragment is related. But there is more than this to its unity. A large number of images are used more than once in the poem, with a cumulative effect, which deepens the mysterious meaning of each:

1, 12, 29	cieruo
2, 12	otero
3, 13, 25, 29, 35	monte, montaña, montiña
3, 29, 33	ribera
3, 4, 21, 26, 31	flores
5, 24, 35, CB 11	hermosura
11, 22, 23	ojos
5, 38	soto
12, 33	paloma
12, 13, 29, 38	ayre
13, 29	valle
13, 32	ínsulas estrañas
15, 29	leones
15, 29, 38	noche
16, 26, 27	huerto
22, 27	cuello
23, 24	gracia
25, 31	rosas, rosales
29, 35, 39	aguas

Different parts of the poem are drawing on the same treasury of images, so that in spite of its apparent disjointedness, it can be experienced as one world.

But the poem's unity is best seen in the careful series of links between stanzas, sometimes widely separated, sometimes close together. In CA 1 the Beloved is already likened to a stag, which prepares the way for his description of himself as 'el cieruo vulnerado' in 12. We have seen how the initial 'adónde' is answered by the repeated 'allí', and how the same event, the betrothal, is referred to in 18, 28 and 37. There are other links between separated stanzas:

25   en tanto que de rosas
31   en tanto que en las flores y rosales

25   y no parezca nadie en la montiña
39   que nadie lo miraua

32   escóndete, Carillo
36   cauernas . . . que están bien escondidas . . .

In the last two cases, the second example shows how the wish of the first has been or will be fulfilled.

There are many verbal links between the verses which reinforce the unity of the poem. The 'Amado' of 1 is echoed by 'aquel yo más quiero' in 2, the 'auiéndome herido' by 'adolezco, peno y muero'. 3 and 4 are linked by the natural landscapes they portray, with 'flores' in both; while the question at the end of 4, 'decid si por vosotros ha passado', is answered in 5: 'passó por estos sotos con presura'. The 'sanarme' of 6 harks back to the theme of wounding, prominent again in 7: 'y todos más me llagan'. The 'mil gracias deramando' is taken up in 7:

> Y todos quantos vagan
> de ti me van mil gracias refiriendo . . .

8–10 belong together because they all express the Bride's complaint to the Beloved, directly or indirectly, and contain three sets of antitheses: living and dying (8), healing and wounding (9), vision and lack of vision (10).

But even in the more fragmented parts of the poem, this unifying process is at work. 11 links with 10 and 12 through their common theme of seeing the Beloved's eyes:

> 10. Y véante mis ojos
> 11. si . . . formases de repente
>   los ojos desseados
> 12. Apártalos, Amado . . .

12 is addressed to the Beloved, while 13–14 describe him, and pick up one of its images:

> 12. al ayre de tu buelo
> 13. el siluo de los ayres amorosos . . .

13–15 share a syntactical peculiarity, the omission of the copulative verb 'to be':

> 13. Mi Amado, las montañas . . .
> 14. la noche sosegada
> 15. Nuestro lecho florido,
>   de cueuas de leones enlaçado . . .

and so on. 15 and 16 seem to be quite separate, yet they too share a syntactical feature, the four prepositional phrases in each verse:

> 15. de cueuas de leones
>   en púrpura tendido
>   de paz edificado
>   de mil escudos de oro coronado
> 16. A zaga de tu huella
>   ... al camino
>   al toque de centella
>   al adobado vino ...

This last image introduces the 'interior bodega' of the next stanza.

Between 17–20 is a complex series of inter-relationships. 17 has a concentration of words with a stressed final syllable: beuí, perdí, allí, dí, mí, mio, enseñó. Although in themselves they are not unusual, such a concentration is striking, especially as they are not used for rhyming, but occur within the verse lines, forming their own contrasting rhythm. The sharp sounds underline the precise, defined events to which they refer, and look like a deliberate technique to isolate these significant moments in the Bride's life. 19 appears to shift the scene dramatically, but its 'ya no guardo ganado' harks back to 17's 'y el ganado perdí'. Meanwhile, a series of temporal clauses binds it to the next stanza:

> 19. ya no guardo ganado
>   ni ya tengo otro officio
>   que ya sólo en amar ...
> 20. pues ya si en el exido
>   de oy más no fuere vista ...

while the last three lines of 20 all relate to earlier material:

> 20. diréis que me he perdido;
>   que, andando enamorada,
>   me hice perdidiza, y fui ganada.
> 17. el ganado perdí
> 19. ya no guardo ganado
>   ya sólo en amar es mi exercicio ...

Themes of gain, loss and love continue through these otherwise disjointed stanzas, and there is a deliberate play on the ambiguity of 'ganado', as a noun meaning 'flock' and the past participle of the verb 'ganar', 'gained' (*antanaclasis*).

A further complex pattern of relationships can be discerned in spite of the tenuous links in content between 21–4, through a long series of 'en' clauses, which is still being echoed in 25–7:

> 21. en las frescas mañanas
>   en tu amor
>   en un cabello mío
> 22. en solo aquel cabello
>   en mi cuello
>   en él preso quedaste
>   y en uno de mis ojos

23. su gracia en mí
    lo que en ti vían
24. si color moreno en mí hallaste
    en mí dexaste
25. en tanto que de rosas
    en la montiña
26. deténte . . . ven . . . entre
27. entrado . . . en el ameno huerto . . .

It is as though the 'en' sound is being continually repeated in preparation for the all-important entry into the garden in 27. This remarkable accumulation of phrases (*acervatio, polysyndeton*) might seem excessive when so isolated, a recipe for bad poetry; but it is achieved so unobtrusively that to my knowledge it has never been noted before.

These stanzas are also bound together by a careful balancing of first and second person singular pronouns, intensifying the intimacy of the dialogue, especially in 23, and by an extraordinary series of internal rhymes: a detailed analysis of these two points will be made in due course.[15] 22 and 24 are united by their common use of 'aste' as a rhyme, while 22–4 use various forms of the stem of 'mirar' (*adnominatio, polyptoton*): 'mirástele', 'mirabas', 'mirarme', 'miraste'.

The 'huerto' of 26 anticipates that of 27, and the adjectives which describe it, 'ameno' and 'desseado', have links with other parts of the poem, the 'amenas liras' of 30, the 'ojos desseados' of 11 and the 'socio desseado' of 33. The rest of the poem shows less of this interconnection between stanzas, because it falls into well-defined groups which are not, however, separate entities. From 28 to 34 a series of pictures is presented, including the flashback technique in 28 (compare 5, 17–18, 22). 29–31 enumerate the elements which might disturb the Bride's repose, while 32–4 are characterized by a stress on hiddenness, secrecy, and solitude, issuing in love. 35 leads into 36 through the conjunctive 'y luego', and 36 into 37 through the 'allí' anaphora. 38–9 both depend, as was demonstrated, on the last line of 37 and should not be understood in isolation from it.

In all these ways, San Juan can be discerned building bridges between the separated elements of the *Cántico*. They are never very obvious, but enough to mean that anyone who studies the poem carefully will realize that it is not a series of unrelated fragments. The atmosphere of mystery, the strange world conjured up through the imagery and fragmented scenes, is constant throughout; the same stammering language is found at the end (37) as at the beginning (7), and the singing language likewise (38; 13–15). Flowers and perfume, mountains, islands, water, breezes, stags, doves, eyes are found across the whole poem; and through it all, the same disconcerting tension between the familiar and the unfamiliar. In the CB arrangement of stanzas, some of the links described above are

[15] See below, pp. 108–112.

broken, as when the 'huerto' of CA 26–7 is split between CB 17 and 22, and the syntactical links between CA 13–15 are broken into CB 14–15 and 24. This only serves to emphasize the priority of CA when approaching the *Cántico* as a poem.

III

The reader of the *Cántico* must enter the strange world which San Juan has created. On the one hand, the meaning is puzzling and points beyond the words. On the other, he finds familiar images but set in this unfamiliar world, and therefore images forged anew. By setting them in a quite unexpected environment San Juan is able to redeem the tired images of his age, which its sun, moon and stars, ice and fire, wastelands and flowers, darkness and light, and allow them to speak again with power, because they have been liberated from their conventional places and can be appreciated again.

But there is something more than decorative imagery to the poems of San Juan. Critics have also referred to his use of an allegorical or symbolic language, and the effect this has on the poetic diction and the meaning of his poems. It is time to look more closely at this important, though difficult area of literary study.

There is no defined boundary between allegory and symbolism, but the area in which the division between them becomes most apparent is that of the relationship between the language as it appears in the work of literature and the meaning that language is intended to convey. In allegory there should be a one-to-one relationship between the image and the meaning it contains, and in order to follow the meaning of a work it is necessary to decode each image in turn, since it stands for something else which the author wanted to communicate. With symbolic language, no such procedure is possible, because the symbol acquires a life of its own and contains within itself various meanings and levels of understanding. There has been a tendency, noted by Fletcher, to call allegory bad and symbolism good, but allegory is rarely present in its extreme form, and the studies of Honig and Fletcher have, in their different ways, stressed the creative power of allegory and its value as a literary vehicle for conveying ideas.[16]

Now the *Cántico* cannot in the strictest sense be called an allegory because the poem itself cannot be interpreted in such a way that each image refers to another reality in some kind of logical sequence of thought, and San Juan's own commentary shows that he was well aware of this. It contains allegorical elements, notably CA 28, and it is also true to say that the commentary uses an allegorical technique in many places, but never in such a way that the *Cántico* could be classified as

---

[16] Honig, *Dark Conceit* (New York, 1966); Fletcher, *Allegory* (Ithaca and London, 1970).

an allegory.[17] Many of the images in the poem do not have a single interpretation, and they move closer to a symbolic form of language.

For example, it is impossible to state exactly what 'flores' in the poem stand for. If it were an allegory they would refer to the swift passage of time, or the decay of earthly beauty, and the lesson could be deduced: gather them, because soon they will be gone; or, do not put your trust in the fleeting beauty of created matter. But there is no obvious identification of the *Cántico*'s flowers with any such conventional meaning. They mean the sum total of their uses in the poem, and more, for the mind cannot grasp their whole significance and the reader's imagination adds all the associations the image has for him, particular flowers he has seen and enjoyed, their colour, scent, and shape. The flowers of the *Cántico* (CA 3–4, 21, 26, 31) are not flowers of wasted youth or fading beauty, but simply 'flores'. The onus of perceiving their significance rests on the reader, for San Juan does not prescribe an interpretation for the image, as an allegorist might; he allows the reader to picture it and its meaning transcends any one interpretation and suggests more than it states, which is the way of the symbol.

San Juan's most famous symbol is the dark night. Baruzi writes: 'Par un prodige de l'imagination mystique, la nuit est à la fois *la plus intime traduction de l'expérience et l'expérience elle-même.* Elle est . . . incommensurable avec toutes ses significations et mérite d'être appelée, au sens technique du mot, un symbole.'[18] Night, as a fundamental human experience, is a word which speaks to everyone. It appears three times in the *Cántico*: CA 14's 'noche sosegada', 29's 'miedos de las noches veladores', and 38's 'noche serena'. Even here, it passes beyond any simple definition and assumes a life of its own. It is not the 'night of sin' or the 'night of grief', but a category of human experience which covers a large variety of meaning and overtones and acquires an inexhaustible depth, in the *Subida-Noche* above all. It is impossible to state what exactly this 'noche oscura' is: sin, ignorance, spiritual darkness, fear, secrecy, suffering, faith, God—it is all these seemingly incompatible meanings and more. It is less pervasive in the *Cántico* but approaches symbolism in the 'noche sosegada' and 'serena', in which the adjectives suggest that part of the symbol 'night' which is calm and peaceful. As such, the reader is freed from the tyranny of forcing it to stand for one particular calm and peaceful thing, and it opens out before him, waiting for him to enter into its profundity.

The *Cántico* contains other symbols too, the most telling being the breeze, the water, and the mountains. The first appears in CA 13's 'siluo de los ayres amorosos', the 'cierzo' and 'austro' of 26, the 'ayres' of 29 and the 'aspirar del ayre' of 38. It is almost bound to convey the notion of intangibility, and San Juan must have been aware of its

---

[17] See Ch. 6, pp. 126–132.   [18] Op. cit., pp. 322–3.

theological connotations, through the wind/spirit ambiguity of the Greek *pneuma* and the Hebrew *ruah*. But because sometimes it is unwanted ('cierzo' and 29's 'ayres'), sometimes connected with love (the other examples), no precise significance can be given to it. It gathers these meanings together and is raised to something approaching symbolism. If it were confined to one equation, like 'wind = nothingness', the image could not play on the reader's imagination and might fail to move him. The difference is well illustrated by the caverns in the *Cántico* and *Llama*. CA's 'subidas cauernas *de la piedra*' simply adds a detail to the image, which still remains mysterious. The latter's 'profundas cavernas *del sentido*' explains it—the caverns stand for the senses—and the mystery is gone. Such explanations are normally reserved by San Juan for his commentaries, and that is surely one of the reasons why his poetry does not suffer with the passage of time as has, for example, Herrera's, with its endless variations on literary conventions like the icy fire paradox.

The same points can be made for the mountains and water in the *Cántico*, but there is no need to dwell on it. Instead, they can serve to introduce the related problem of the depiction and function of the natural world in the poem, which also has symbolic features. Nature has always been a favourite subject of poetry and the natural world has yielded a storehouse of images. It can be the backdrop of some action, or participate in it (the pathetic fallacy, for example). It then fulfils a particular and to some extent predictable function within the poem. Garcilaso's sensitivity to nature is revealed throughout his work. He allows it to play its part in the scenes of human love he creates, so that it becomes more than mere ornament. In the third eclogue he draws a startling contrast between its beauty and the death of the nymph:

> cuya vida mostrava que avia sido
> antes de tiempo y casi en flor cortada;
> cerca del agua, en un lugar florido,
> estava entre las yervas degollada
> qual queda el blanco cisne quando pierde
> la dulce vida entre la yerva verde.[19]

The image of the bud 'casi en flor cortada' prepares the way for the horrific 'degollada', one word which bears the full tragedy of death in an otherwise idyllic scene. The scene itself harks back to the *locus amoenus* of line 57, 'Cerca del Tajo, en soledad amena'; while the simile chosen to picture this death, the song of the dying swan, is melodious

---

[19] lines 227–332. The reading 'degollada' and its meaning has been the subject of controversy since the sixteenth century. 'Whose life revealed that she had been/ before her time and almost in flower cut down;/ Near to the water, in a flowery place,/ she lay among the grasses beheaded/ as the white swan when she loses/ her sweet life among the green grass.'

and devoid of all brutality. Nature is beautiful, death an ugly intruder; and the poet's anguish is communicated powerfully through the violent contrast between the delicacy of the scene and the horror of the event which has taken place there.

Another way of relating nature to love was to describe the fruitfulness of nature when love was requited, and its barrenness when it was not. Garcilaso again provides good examples. Nemoroso's lament at the end of the first eclogue depicts 'la escura, desierta y dura tierra' (line 281), and lines 239–407 intensify his desolation after Elisa's death by evoking this cruel landscape. The amoebic song which concludes the third eclogue contrasts Tirreno's vision of the beauty and fertility of nature with Alcino's landscape of sterility, storm, and darkness, because Flérida returns Tirreno's love, but Filis does not return Alcino's. Each lover looks out upon the natural creation, and in it sees a confirmation of the idyllic nature of love fulfilled or of the cruelty of love which is spurned.

It is clear from the images and symbols already mentioned that nature is a pervasive force in the *Cántico*, the main source of images and directly evoked in several places (CA 4–5, 13–14, 21, 25–7, 33–6, 38). But the world which is created in the *Cántico* is startlingly different from the kind of use of nature we have briefly examined in Garcilaso as typical of sixteenth-century treatment of the natural world at its best. Nor does any other Golden Age poet create a world anything like it, not even Fray Luis, who drew so much inspiration from the Song of Songs. Nature here is not a passive spectator, but neither is she a mirror of men's moods. Nature does not provide the colouring for human emotions, but seems rather to be a participant in the unfolding drama, a protagonist independent of the others. In this sense she is 'outside' the poem's action: not as a passive onlooker, but as a force to be reckoned with in the course of the search the poem is describing.

To begin with, nature is endowed with the power of speech (*conformatio*). Woods, thickets, and flowery meadows are questioned to see if the Beloved has passed through them, and they give an affirmative reply (4–5). Those with some theological perception begin to suspect that San Juan is expressing in poetry the doctrine that the presence and being of God may be read in the natural order. The creatures, as his creation, must testify to his existence. But it still strikes a strange note in the poetry of this age. The apostrophe of the fountain in 11 is more conventional: the fountain remains silent, and the reply comes from the Beloved, who corroborates the testimony of the natural creation.

The images of 13–14 again take the reader far beyond the accustomed use of nature in providing descriptive pictures of human beauty (eyes like suns, breasts or hands like snow or lilies). The Beloved is identified through nine images, six from the natural order. His beauty

is such that the Bride cannot restrict herself to simile, frequent in the
Song (e.g. 4:1–5), or to conventional metaphor, but instead pours out
her love as if to say that it cannot be confined within such limits. In
this respect, San Juan uses language more radically than Góngora.
Góngora was to stop referring to eyes like suns, and call them simply
suns, suppressing the first term of comparison in the simile. But after a
while, when one becomes accustomed to this technique, aimed at
revitalizing the language of poetry when many poetic conventions had
become exhausted, the effect is lost and suns become as ordinary as
eyes. San Juan conserves the sense of wonder. He sets down the central
figure, the Beloved, and next to him, without any verb to connect them,
mountains, valleys, rivers, islands and breezes. One Beloved, and such a
wealth of beauty in him that it requires the whole realm of nature even
to approach expressing it.

Nature is a protagonist in the drama in 25–6 and 29–30. The vixen
spoiling the vines have to be chased away, a cold wind has to be stopped
and a warm one summoned to blow through the garden. Certain elements
appear inimical to the Bride's quest (vixen, north wind), others, friendly
(south wind, garden, scents). In 29–30 a host of creatures and natural
phenomena threaten the Bride's slumber and are ordered to desist. By
contrast, nature is used in the last few stanzas to describe the place of
ineffable delight, with its hill, pure flowing water, hidden caverns, and
thicket. Nature, therefore, has a divided function in the poem, sometimes an aid and sometimes a hindrance to the desired union.

Nor is there a normal hierarchy of beings. Alongside the Bride and
Beloved are all sorts of creatures, animate and inanimate, some of
which appear only fleetingly, others, more persistently. None is as
important as the two main protagonists, but all are treated as though
they participate in the same level of being, the same cosmos, where
men and women, animals, forests, mountains, and a great array of other
objects express feeling and directly engage in action bearing on the
poem's progress. It is a vision of the world quite foreign to the one in
which the reader lives, and it does not behave in a unified fashion but is
itself in tension. It cannot be easily imagined because it contains such
disparate elements—not only mountains, rivers, and flowers, but also
lions, vixen, sirens, Judaean nymphs, and cavalry. San Juan is clearly
not using nature as a backcloth to the story he has to tell, nor as a
reflection of the human emotions which unfold in its telling. He uses
images from the natural creation because they all belong to the one
creation which testifies to its Creator, and because each is endowed with
a mysterious significance even he may not have grasped entirely in the
making of the poem. In a word, it is not nature as the poets of his age
(or perhaps any other) portrayed it: it is a created world, part of his
total symbolic creation, contributing to the depth and mystery of the

poem. Such a remaking of the world, pointing to a meaning beyond that of the everyday world, itself becomes symbolic as we stand on the threshold between the real and the ideal and wonder how the values and the being of the latter can illuminate and relate to the former. Fletcher writes: 'Christianity sees the creation of the world as an establishment of a universal symbolic vocabulary.'[20] San Juan would have agreed, though in other words. As he read the Bible, and sought to penetrate beneath the surface literal meaning to the allegorical and mystical core, he began to enter the ideal world, the mystery of which was mediated through the hidden meaning of the sacred text. And his symbolic world, with its different hierarchy of being, and its elements which might appear to be images but in fact were bearers of the truth about the creation, arose, we can be sure, out of such a procedure. If there is allegory in the *Cántico*, then it has led to a recreation of the natural order, and made possible 'a cosmic view of the intrinsic relationships of all objects and beings'.[21] The poem itself becomes a symbol for another, better world.

IV

But if San Juan is master of a broad canvas like this, he is also meticulous about the details. In order to create his masterpiece, he uses a great number of poetic techniques. Referring to the difficulty in translating San Juan's poems adequately into English, Brenan speaks of the 'luminous purity and simplicity of his language . . . precise and economical and completely lacking in rhetorical constructions and in amplifying nouns and adjectives.'[22] The implication of such statements (and other critics have written to the same effect) is that he arrived spontaneously and accidentally at the intensity of language he uses, employing no deliberate techniques to achieve it. That may be the impression with which his poetry leaves us; but though he did not share Herrera's concern for a language worthy of the age and fit to rival the language of antiquity, there are signs enough that he was familiar with the art of rhetoric; so many, in fact, that the chances of his having hit upon them all fortuitously and with such evident skill seem remote.

In its forensic origins, rhetoric had a suasory purpose to convince the listener of the truth being uttered. In terms of poetry, one might say that it helps the reader to experience what the poet intends him to. At its simplest, it renders more memorable a particular sequence of words, underlining and reinforcing them in ways not normally present in ordinary speech or writing. It intensifies language, controls it more carefully. There are many techniques that can be used, as the sixteenth

[20] Op. cit., p. 131.   [21] Honig, op. cit., p. 180.
[22] Op. cit., p. xii.

century perhaps knew better than our own, and each has its own method for so doing. Hyperbaton, for example, by disrupting the expected sequence of words, forces the reader to pause and reflect in order to assimilate the meaning. The power of language is renewed, because the reader has to reconstruct sense from the disordered pattern, and he is surprised into concentrating more keenly on the words, especially those important ones which are made to stand in strong positions in a line of poetry, when normal syntactical practice might cause them to be overlooked. In a similar way, alliteration reinforces words. Random groupings will rarely contain many identical vowel or consonant sounds, whereas the poet, by exercising control over the selection and placing of his words, can bring them into closer relationship and greater prominence.

In the *Cántico*, variety is introduced by two groups of opposing tendencies, each created through use of certain techniques: the polarity between the dynamic and the static, and between long, flowing lines and short, separated elements.

Stanzas 1–5 are dynamic: the action moves rapidly from the Beloved's disappearance in the past to the Bride's initiatives in searching for him. The verbal element is very much to the fore: escondiste, dexaste, huiste, auiéndome herido, salí clamando, eras ydo; fuerdes, vierdes, quiero, adolezco, peno, muero; buscando, yré, cogeré, temeré, passaré; decid, ha passado; deramando, passó, yéndolos mirando, vestidos dexó. Particularly striking is the large number of present participles, some related to past events, and these continue into 7: van refiriendo, déxame muriendo, balbuciendo. After this, they disappear (except 20's 'andando'). This concentration serves to underline the continuing quality of the actions described, implying that past actions were of some duration and present ones have been going on for some time. They also contrast vividly with the suddenness and decisiveness of the Beloved's disappearance and the Bride's search: escondiste, huiste, dexaste, salí, yré, cogeré, temeré, passaré. San Juan's choice of verbal forms reflects the main theme of these verses: a sudden flight and consequent search, and an ongoing wounding and grieving.

But 6–11 represent a distinct change. Having reached the point where the creatures have given their testimony of the Beloved's passing by, San Juan concentrates his attention on the inward state of the Bride. This has been delayed till now, instead of articulated right from the start, so that the force of ¡Ay! comes with an even greater explosion of feeling. The poem moves into a static period, that is to say, the action is not forwarded at all, because this is a time of intense introspection for the Bride. From the emotional point of view it is the most highly-charged moment in the poem and many rhetorical devices are used to heighten the acute suffering of the Bride. The theme of these stanzas, the wound the Beloved has left in her and he alone can heal, is approached in many different ways to emphasize it (*commoratio, epexergasia*). There are rhetorical questions (*interrogatio, erotema; quaestium, pysma*) in 6, 8–9, requiring no answer but underlining the Beloved's departure, and increasing emotion with images of wounding and dying and the less conventional, more violent 'y no tomas el robo que robaste' (*adnominatio*). In 6, 8, and 11 are examples of *exclamatio* (*ecphonesis*) combined in the last two cases with *aversio* (*apostrophe*) addressed to 'vida' and 'christalina fuente'. 7, through the repeated 'y', makes effective use of *acervatio* (*polysyndeton*), joining all the lines of the stanza into one prolonged outburst of grief. The rhetorical question in 9 is *provocatio* (*proclesis*), arousing an adversary with what in this case amounts to a vehement accusation. 10 contains *querimonia* (*memphis*), as the Bride makes her complaint and appeals for help; while 11 has *obsecratio* (*deisis*), the expression of her earnest prayer. To this already charged language may be added the fact that several verbs are in the imperative, and no time is spent pausing to describe anything. So it becomes clearer how San Juan actually creates the relentless and powerful appeal to the absent Beloved and the desperation of the Bride as she turns for succour to herself, to him, and to the fountain. Her condition does not alter through these stanzas—nothing happens to change it. Some of these techniques are found in other parts of the poem—the exclamation in 31, *percontatio* (*exetasis*) in 2, where the Bride reveals her own suffering through inquiring of the shepherds where the Beloved has hidden.

12 is strongly dynamic. The flow of the poem is abruptly interrupted by a series of rapid events expressed in a highly elliptical manner, causing the Bride to pass in the compass of a single stanza from depths of grief to great elation. In place of anguished exclamations, she pauses to contemplate the inexpressible beauty of the Beloved. Noun and adjective predominate; indeed for three stanzas (13–15) there is no main verb, the two verbs present ('recrea', 'enamora') being both adjectival in function, qualifying the 'cena'. 15 is part of this lyrical outpouring, as it has the same grammatical structure: the lovers' bed is defined in a series of images and no verb. The over-all effect of these three stanzas is diminished in CB by the removal of one of them (15) to another place (24), one of the few places in which the superiority of the CA poem can be detected. Here, for the first time in the poem, large numbers of epithets and adjectival phrases colour the descriptions. After the accumulation of sibilants in 13, the effect of 'la noche' at the beginning of 14 is calming and evocative. Although the 's' sound is still predominant, most of the nouns are in the singular, creating a different kind of picture from the expansive whispering landscapes of 13. These three stanzas move gradually from macrocosm to microcosm, the natural creation at one extreme, the lovers' bed at the other. They are a telling

example of Peacham's definition of *conglobatio* (*systrophe*), as quoted by Sonnino:[23] 'many definitions of one thing yet not such definitions as do declare the substance of a thing by the kind and the difference, which the art of reasoning doth prescribe, but by others of another kind all heaped together.'

After this lyrical pause, the poem describes a series of events: young girls running, events leading to the betrothal recalled from the past (*recordatio, anamnesis*). The outstanding feature of 17–18 is a series of verbs in the first and third persons singular of the preterite which highlight decisive events relating to the betrothal: beuí, perdí, enseñó, di, prometí. 19–20 are more static, another pause for reflection after this journey into the past. From this point, the action of the poem is more intimate and largely dynamic, though the contrast with the static is not as marked as before. This is only to be expected, for once the crisis point in 12 has been reached, the subsequent lyrical outbrust concluded, the necessary details about the past revealed, the scene is almost entirely set in the present and future and moves towards its mysterious conclusion. The one real exception is 38, with its series of pictures defining 'aquello que me diste el otro día'. The technique here is similar to that in 13–15: nouns and adjectives, with no main verb.

The second polarity lies between passages which run in long, flowing lines, and those broken up into short groups. San Juan uses two main devices to ensure a smooth flow of words: repeated conjunctions (*acervatio*) and enjambement. The whole of 7 is linked as a single unit through the three 'y's:

> Y todos quantos vagan . . .
> y todos más me llagan,
> y déjame muriendo . . .

It is a simple, but effective technique. Those who tell of the Beloved cause the wound to deepen, and what they stammer leaves the Bride dying. A similar prolongation of the complaint is achieved in 10 with two 'y's and two 'pues'. In 32, the flow is maintained by the contrast between 'y mira' and 'mas mira', welding together otherwise separate elements into one action, not a series of disjointed ones; and further examples can be seen in 22, 27, 30, 34, 36, and 39.

The use of enjambement is more striking. Among other things, it helps to break up the very steady rhythms of individual lines, as San Juan rarely departs from a regular 2–6–10 stress in hendecasyllables and 2–6 in heptasyllables. This ought to make the poem monotonous, as a repetitive rhythm in music might prove excessive. But the poem was not written in line-by-line units, rather phrase by phrase; and San Juan often extends his phrases over the lines. There is a close parallel with music,

[23] Op. cit., p. 58.

in that bar lines rarely mark the end of musical phrases, but are conventional markings of musical punctuation which the phrases straddle
quite happily. For example, in 9 the phrase divisions fall '¿Por qué/ pues
as llagado aqueste coraçón/ no le sanaste?'; and in 23, 'y en eso/ merecían
los míos/ adorar lo que en ti vían'. Sometimes, two lines flow naturally
into one another.

> 2. si por uentura vierdes
>   aquel que yo más quiero

> 32. mas mira las compañas
>   de la que ua por ínsulas estrañas . . .

This is particularly noticeable in 11, when the conditional clause
occupies the remaining four lines after the apostrophe of the fountain,
in one long sigh:

> ¡si en essos tus semblantes plateados
> formases de repente
> los ojos desseados
> que tengo en mis entrañas dibuxados!

In 13–14 each line represents a separate entity except 14's

> la noche sosegada
> en par de los levantes de la aurora . . .

Night is more closely defined than any of the other images in this
section, as if to underline its special significance for San Juan. CA 14–
15.23 (and the CA parallel) relate this description to the distinction
between the three parts of night, after dusk, midnight, and before dawn.
The appearance of two lines so closely joined in a part of the poem
where each line is more or less self-contained adds a flowing quality to
a passage which might otherwise be monotonous with its repeated
single-line images; and it acts like a musical crescendo, expanding and
dying away again into 'música callada'.

30's opening conjuration, 'por las amenas liras/ y canto de serenas',
forms a long phrase which runs over the line division for the first time
since the end of 28.[24] This helps to establish the contrast with 29: all
the creatures which threaten the Bride's repose are separated by
commas, whereas the powers helping her are united by 'y' and cross the
boundary of the line. Only once is the enjambement such that it inter-
rupts normal sequence by separating an epithet from its noun:

---

[24] Unless no comma was intended between 'ardores,/ Y miedos de las noches
veladores.' BAC has none, but is not faithful to the manuscripts. Sanlúcar, difficult
to decipher at this point, seems to lack the comma, but Jaén certainly so separates
'ardores' from 'miedos'. In any case, San Juan's commentaries in both redactions
prove he did not intend 'ardores' to be connected with 'miedos'.

> 36.   Y luego a las subidas
>   cauernas de la piedra . . .

The impetus of the first line is carried over strongly into the next, and the end of the line is meaningless as a division in sense.

Such examples show how San Juan achieves a musical flow of words and frees the poem from any rhythmical monotony. Groups of two, three, and four lines form complete units, and phrases are not bound by the line divisions. But in other places the opposite can be seen, short, staccato phrases, with verses arranged in series of single lines or broken up into very small units. Two rhetorical techniques are used to achieve this. The first is *dissolutio* (*asyndeton*), an absence of connecting particles, predominant in those verses which are primarily enumerative, 3, 13–15, 16, 29–30, 38. The second is *articulus* (*brachylogia*), in which images are heaped up and single words separated by commas. The best example is 29:

> A las aues ligeras,
> leones, cieruos, gamos saltadores,
> montes, valles, riberas,
> aguas, ayres, ardores . . .

Others are found in 3, 13–15, and 26. Though San Juan concentrates less on techniques which break up the flow, stanzas like 29 create a very different impression from those characterized by long, smooth phrases. He is able to wield language in such a way that he can highlight the static and dynamic parts of his poem and create the effects of harmonious progression or measured pause, according to its needs. These polarities introduce great variety into the texture of the poem, which is never allowed to settle down for too long into one kind of style.

But he uses many other technical devices in the *Cántico*, and they may conveniently be divided into those which deal with sounds, repetition, balance, and disruption.

Concentrations of one vowel or consonant are frequent. In 1 'i' is to the fore: escondiste, gemido, huiste, herido, salí, ti, ydo; as in 37: allí, mostrarías, pretendía, darías, uida mía, diste, día. The 'i' preponderance is achieved partly through all the rhymes containing a stressed 'i' and partly throughout repeating the sound in other parts of each stanza. Not only does it add sharpness and brightness of tone, it helps to underline the insistence of the action—the Bride's search in 1, the indefinable gift of 'aquello' in 37. It is a similar technique to the repetition of a certain musical note in the course of one melodic phrase, and only works if it is not overdone. In 2, rarely for San Juan, 'e' is dominant: fuerdes, otero, vierdes, quiero, adolezco, peno, muero. Just as an important instruction may need to be repeated, so by the insistence on the 'e' sound attention is drawn to the gravity of the situation here described.

The use of the three similar verbs at the end is *interpretatio* (*synonymia*) if their meaning is to be more or less identical, or *traductio* if, as in the commentary (CB 2.6), they are carefully to be distinguished.

In 17–18 'i' is again the dominant sound, especially in the final stressed syllables; while in 20 there is a fascinating tension between the 'i' sound, underlining the element of loss, and the 'a', underlining the element of finding:

perdido   hallada
hice perdidiza   andando enamorada, ganada

31 and 33 both show a preponderance of the smoother, warmer 'a': rosales, ámbar, morá, arrabales, queráis, tocar, humbrales; and the measured and lovely

La blanca palomica
al arca con el ramo se a tornado . . .

It should be noted that there is nothing in the actual 'i' or 'a' sound, save perhaps a certain sharpness of the one and mellowness of the other, which actually creates a particular impression. The function of their concentration, as with other rhetorical devices, is not by themselves to create an atmosphere which would not otherwise exist, but to make more memorable one which is already implicit but needs to be stressed.

The same is true of *alliteratio* (*parimion*). There is nothing inherent about a 'q', except the explosive quality it shares with other consonants (though less so in Spanish than English), which is bound to produce a hiatus, as in the celebrated 'no sé qué que quedan balbuciendo'. Here, the meaning of 'balbucir' is itself represented in the text, through the 'stammer' of the repeated 'que'. But there is another 'que' concentration in 2, which leaves a different impression: 'aquel que yo más quiero'. This reinforces the power of the Bride's love and is not like the interruption of the stammer in 7.

This is even truer in the sibilants. If it were the case that 's', for example, conjured up the sound of bees, as in Garcilaso's 'un susurro de abejas que sonaba', why is it that English chooses 'm' and 'n' to create the same effect (the murmuring of innumerable bees)? The concentration of sounds is there to stress what is already suggested to the imagination by the picture the poet is drawing. 4–5 and 13 contain large numbers of sibilants: bosques, espesuras, plantadas, verduras, flores esmaltado, si uosotros, passado; gracias, passó, sotos, presura, yéndolos, sola su, vestidos los, hermosura; las montañas, los valles solitarios nemorosos, las ínsulas estrañas, los ríos sonorosos, siluo, los ayres amorosos. In 5 there is a secondary alliteration with 'p': passó por, presura. The theme of 4–5 is the abundant testimony left by the Beloved of himself in his passage through creation. It is conjured up primarily by the imagery, only secondarily through alliteration, which helps the mind to capture the images more vividly. Similarly in 13 the Bride praises the Beloved in extravagant terms because of the great love she has for him, and it is these images that first inspire the reader's response, while the alliteration serves to direct his attention more closely to the relationship of the images and the scenes they evoke.

There are two other important cases of alliteration. The consonant 'f' is repeated in 3 in the objects of the last three verbs, making them more forceful: flores, fieras, fuertes, fronteras. The parallel form of the verbs likewise reinforces the intentions expressed: yré, ni cogeré, ni temeré, y passaré. In 11 there is a group of 'v' sounds: voy, buelo, buéluete, cieruo vulnerado, buelo. The sound itself is not suggestive of flight or of stags returning, but the concentration of 'v's in this place brings into close relationship a number of different words, stemming from 'ir', 'volar', 'volver', 'vulnerar' and 'ciervo'.

Internal rhyme is another sound technique employed to great effect by San Juan. Like regular rhyme, it creates relationships between sounds at certain intervals, but it occurs where normally there would be none. It thus establishes a link with the other words in a stanza which rhyme in expected places, at the ends of lines, and echoes them or points to those to come. In the last line of 1 we read 'salí tras *ti* clamando'. The idea of going forth is linked by the repeated sound to the object of the journey, the Beloved. The last line of 15 contains another echo: 'de mil escudos de *oro coro*nado'; and there are also assonant groups, like 4's 'plantadas por la m*ano* del Am*ado*', 25's 'está ya florec*ida* nuestra v*iña*', and 28's 'deb*axo* de el manç*ano*'. In rhetoric, the repetition of the same sounds at the beginning and middle or middle and end of a unit is *regressio* (*epanodos*).

But there are more striking examples. In 17–18 the repeated stressed 'í' sounds set up a complex series of internal rhymes in the first halves of lines which contrast sharply with the rhymes stressed on penultimate syllables at the ends of lines:

> 17. de mi Amado be*uí* . . . sal*ía* . . .
>   y el ganado perd*í* . . . segu*ía*.
> 18. All*í* me d*io* su pecho,
>   all*í* me enseñó sciencia muy sabrosa,
>   y *yo* le *di* de hecho
>   a m*í*, sin dexar cosa;
>   all*í* le promet*í* de ser su esposa.

The cumulative effect is unusual, in its establishing of two distinct rhythmical patterns which complement one another. In 4 we find:

> plantadas por la mano del Am*ado*;
> o pr*ado* de verduras
> de flores esmalt*ado*

which together with the 'mano-Amado' assonance and the rather similar 'plantadas' form a series of closely related sounds replying to one another across three lines of poetry and creating a sense of unity, harmony and balance. The enjambement of the beginning of 30 also contains an internal rhyme which joins the two lines into one harmonious phrase:

> Por las ame*nas* liras
> y canto de ser*enas* . . .

But most remarkable of all is the effect in 21—2. If all rhymes are placed at the ends of lines, the passage would look like this:

> 21. en tu amor florecidas
>   y en un cabello
>   mío entretexidas.
> 22. En solo aquel
>   cabello
>   que en mi cuello
>   bolar consideraste,
>   miráste-
>   le en mi cuello
>   y en él
>   presso quedaste,
>   y en uno de mis ojos te llagaste.

This intricate pattern of sound relationships is itself interwoven in the way the word 'entretexidas' suggests, so that the lines themselves display the meaning of the word. The main rhymes are each foreshadowed by being introduced in the middle of the preceding line ('cabello', 'cuello', '-aste'). The effect of rewriting the stanzas in this way is immediately apparent. The natural structure of the *lira* is destroyed and replaced by something which though still technically a *lira* functions on a much more complex plane. The 'aste' sound introduces a further series of rhymes in the middle of 22, while the '-ello' group is in full swing, and the beginning and end of lines 2—3 form a mirror image:

> en mi cuello . . . consideraste
> miraste . . . en mi cuello . . .

It hardly seems likely that such technical accomplishment should be accidental. San Juan may not have worked it out in detail beforehand, but he must have sensed how extraordinarily appropriate this interrelation of sounds was to convey to picture of intertwining flowers he had drawn.

The repetition of the same words and sounds gives this passage, and others in the poem, an almost liturgical ring. Such repetitions, as is well known, can induce states of trance through the potency of words insistently chanted. San Juan would have encountered something of this in the daily monastic offices, with their liturgical language and daily recitations, and he must have been particularly sensitive to the power of words to mystify and move. We might also remember that the one thing he was not short of in prison was time. It is in the techniques of repetition that he uses that the liturgical feel of his poetic diction is most apparent, like the 'estando ya mi casa sosegada' at the end of the first two lines of the *Noche* and the 'aunque es de noche' and its variants as the refrain in 'Que bien sé yo la fonte'.

In the *Cántico* the repeated 'allí' of 18 and 37 becomes a kind of invocation, while the long lists of images in 13–15 and 29–30 sound like elements in a mysterious prayer chanted to a world beyond our own. The pleonastic accusative of 'el robo que robaste' has a Hebraic ring about it (cf. Psalm 96:1; Malachi 3:3); but the supreme example is the *repetitio* (*anaphora*) of 34:

> *En soledad* biuía,
> y *en soledad* ha puesto ya su nido,
> y *en soledad* la guía
> *a solas* su querido,
> también *en soledad* de amor herido.

San Juan has enough poetic sensibility to know that such a device must be used cautiously and would be spoiled by adherence to too rigid a pattern. This is characteristic of his other poems, notably in the slightly varied refrains of the 'Fonte' and 'Pastorcico' poems, which avoid any mechanical usage. Here, after the first three lines, he replaces the expected 'en soledad' by the synonymous 'a solas' (*traductio*), so that the insistence on solitude is reinforced by a second manner of expressing it. In the last line, 'en soledad' recurs but is moved towards the middle of the line, so that the reader has to wait for what he suspects is to come. This is deliberate, because 'en soledad también' would make equally good sense, though not poetry; and by moving it, San Juan is also able to allow the preposition to echo the conjunction: 'tambi*én en*'. It is in such slight alterations that San Juan reveals his poetic skill most plainly. He knows that a simple repetition would be too mechanical, and he hides his technique by varying it sufficiently so that it does not obtrude upon the reader.

There are large numbers of repetitions within the *Cántico*. Some of the images he uses, as we have seen, occur in several places. But if one were to have to point to the outstanding feature of San Juan's poetic technique in this poem, it would surely have to be the huge number of phrases introduced by conjunctions or prepositions which run in parallel above all in the middle section of the work:

> 10.   pues que ninguno basta . . .
>   pues eres lumbre . . .

15. de cueuas de leones . . .
    en púrpura tendido,
    de paz edificado,
    de mil escudos de oro coronado.
16. A zaga de tu huella
    . . . al camino
    al toque de centella,
    al adobado vino . . .
19. Ya no guardo ganado
    ni ya tengo otro officio,
    que ya sólo en amar . . .
20. Pues si ya en el exido . . .
21. De flores y esmeraldas,
    en las frescas mañanas . . .
    en tu amor . . .
    y en un cabello mío . . .
22. En solo aquel cabello
    que en mi cuello . . .
    . . . en mi cuello,
    y en él presso quedaste.
    y en uno de mis ojos . . .
23. su gracia en mí . . .
    por esso . . .
    y en eso . . .
    lo que en ti vían.
24. . . . en mí hallaste,
    ya bien puedes mirarme
    después que me miraste,
    . . . en mí dexaste.
25. en tanto que de rosas
    . . . en la montiña.
26. . . . por mi huerto
    . . . entre las flores.
27. Entrado se ha la esposa
    en el ameno huerto desseado,
    y a su sabor reposa . . .
    sobre los dulces braços . . .
29. A las aues . . .
30. Por las amenas liras . . .
31. en tanto que en las flores . . .
    morá en los arrabales . . .
33. al arca con el ramo . . .
    al socio desseado
    en las riberas . . .
34. En soledad . . .
    y en soledad . . .
    y en soledad . . .
    a solas . . .
    también en soledad de amor herido.
35. . . . en tu hermosura
    . . . en la espesura.
36. Y luego a las subidas
    cauernas de la piedra . . .

> 38. en la noche serena
>   con llama . . .

One of the chief characteristics of the *Cántico*, therefore, is this use of long chains of phrases, usually adverbial, which add to the liturgical ring of the poem, like those found in some psalms and canticles (such as the *Benedicite* and *Gloria in excelsis*). The astonishing thing is that in spite of them there is no monotony; indeed, except in the most obvious example (34), they have not even been noticed before, though they form the main component of several stanzas.

Another feature worthy of attention is the contribution made to the intimacy of the dialogue by careful balancing between first- and second-person-singular pronouns and verbs:

1. *te* escond*iste*, *me* dex*aste*, auiéndo*me* herido, sal*í* tras *ti*
6. sanar*me*, entregar*te*, quier*as* embiar*me*, decir*me*
7. de *ti me* van, más *me* llagan, déxa*me* muriendo
9. *as* llagado, san*aste*, *me* le *has* robado, dex*aste*, tom*as*, rob*aste*
10. véan*te mis* objos, para *ti* quier*o*
21. en *tu* amor, en un cabello *mío*
22. en *mi* cuello conside*raste*, mirás*te*le en *mi* cuello, qued*aste*, en uno de *mis* ojos *te* llag*aste*
23. Quando *tú me* mirab*as*, su gracia en *mí tus* ojos, *me* adamab*as*, los *míos* adorar lo que en *ti* vían
24. No quier*as* despreciar*me*, en *mí* hall*aste*, pued*es* mirar*me*, *me* mir*aste*, en *mí* dex*aste*
28. co*migo* fu*iste* desposada, *te* di, fu*iste* reparada, *tu* madre
37. *me* mostrar*ías*, *mi* alma, *me* dar*ías*, allí *tú*, uida *mía*, aquello que *me diste*

This concentration, naturally, occurs in dialogues between the Bride and the Beloved, even where, as at the beginning, the Beloved is absent. When, verbally and visually, first and second person elements are found in close proximity ('de ti me van', 'véante mis ojos', 'allí tú, uida mía'), San Juan is demonstrating the theme of the poem, the union of the one with the other.

Other techniques of balance used by San Juan involve parallel and antithetical forms. The only perfect parallel is 35's 'al monte u al collado', though 37 contains close ones:

> Allí me mostrarías / aquello que mi alma pretendía
> y luego me darías / aquello que me diste el otro día.

28 contains the deliberate antithesis 'y fuiste reparada/ donde tu madre fuera violada', mirroring the theme of the verse: the violation has been repaired where it occurred, under the apple-tree, '*allí . . . donde*'. It is particularly significant in view of the underlying theology of Fall and

Redemption, developed from St. Paul's doctrine of recapitulation and interpreted by St. Irenaeus.[25] By contrasting the two actions in this way, San Juan is able to say through the medium of poetry what theologians may take much longer to explain less forcefully.

One antithesis merits special attention, the paradoxical 'música callada' and 'soledad sonora' of 14. This is more than the conventional paradox: normally, music is not silent nor solitude sonorous, but rather the other way round. San Juan combines paradox with transposition of adjectives, adjectives which themselves are hardly commonplace, since 'callada' and 'sonora' have their own evocative power and contrast with more conventional transpositions like Góngora's 'púrpura nevada' and 'nieve roja' in the *Polifemo* (14). San Juan did not need to introduce paradox or transposition to strengthen an otherwise commonplace piece of poetry: it is strong already. Once more, he seems to be suggesting mystery: what music is this, which is silent? what solitude, which is vibrant with sound? There are traces here of neo-Platonic notions about the music of the spheres, to which he may be alluding. But it is the mystery of the Beloved's identity which is his chief concern—one who transcends the ordinary categories of experience and can only be described in terms which defy them. It is not that San Juan is playing games with language or avoiding expected forms to free us to appreciate what might otherwise have been too predictable: he is making language itself the servant of the encounter with the Beloved. Without any awareness of San Juan's explanation of the poem in his commentaries, such phrases cannot fail to impress the reader as remarkable, anticipating in some ways a use of language Góngora was to develop to an incredible degree, and in others, pointing to something beyond the reach of words.

San Juan's sensitivity to the power of language is also well demonstrated where he distorts the syntax of his sentences. He makes considerable use of this technique of disruption to ensure that important words are placed in significant positions and that the reader's attention is drawn to them, forcing him to stop and think. The 'prado-esmaltado' internal rhyme in 4 could not have been achieved except by altering the normal sequence of words, by retarding the second past participle:

> o prado
>> de verduras
>> de flores
> esmaltado . . .

Syntactical distortion is more noticeable in the following stanza:

> con sola su figura
> vestidos los dexó de hermosura.

---

[25] See Romans 5, and *Contra haereses* v. 19 (LCC 1).

The significant 'vestidos' and 'hermosura' occupy the most stragetic positions in the lines, beginning and ending, and this also leads to a slight echo effect in '-dos los'. The placing of 'sola' is emphatic, and underlines the creative power of the Beloved. 19 contains a good example of hyperbaton:

> Mi alma se ha empleado
> y todo mi caudal en su seruicio . . .

The twofold subject is split in half and straddles the verb, expressing the total self-giving of the Bride. Her soul is given over to serve the Beloved, and that is strong language. But evidently it is not enough, for she adds 'y todo mi caudal', as if she felt that her self-giving had not been adequately expressed by the first phrase.

In the second line of 23, the word order is object, subject, verb: 'su gracia en mí tus ojos imprimían'. The line is unusual in containing in close proximity pronouns of all three persons. It makes no sense until it is realized that 'su' anticipates the subject, 'ojos'; '*their* grace on me your eyes imprinted'. This is clear from the Sanlúcar manuscript, where 'tu' is used in place of 'su', to simplify the syntax, but has been corrected to 'su' and remains so in the commentaries. Normal syntax is in fact turned round: 'tus ojos imprimían su gracia en mí', though more immediately comprehensible, has been cut in two and reversed, perhaps for the sake of the rhyme, perhaps to indicate the primacy of 'gracia', which contains obvious theological overtones.

The beginning of 27 marks a turning-point in the poem, as the Bride enters the garden. The fundamental idea is entrance, and the first word expresses it at once, causing a dramatic displacement in the normal order of words: 'Entrado se ha la esposa'. The syntax of 29–30 is also noteworthy. For six and a half lines nouns are piled up in a long list (Quintilian's *synathrismos*), before any subject or verb appears. Then, subject, verb and object are all compressed into two short words, 'os conjuro', an extreme contrast with the extensive list which has preceded them. The verb has to be understood for each element in the list (*zeugma*). The effect is exactly that required by the sense of the passage: a chaotic accumulation of things, followed by a very short, sharp, precise command, calling them to order. Finally, by delaying the verb in 33, the central idea of finding is held back until the end of the stanza:

> y ya la tortolica
> al socio desseado
> en las riberas verdes a hallado.

All the incidental information is known—who, whom, and where—but until the last word is reached, the meaning cannot be gauged.

V

The task of evaluating the *Cántico* can never be covered exhaustively or definitively. But during this exploration of its inner works, certain pointers have emerged which support the assertion that it is a very great work of art. It is, for example, abundantly clear, despite many critics, that San Juan is a master of poetic techniques who handles a large number of rhetorical devices to great effect. He is a skilled manipulator of language, taking full advantage of its flexibility and ambiguity to express himself more tellingly. He does not wear his artistry on his sleeve, but hides it deep within the poem, so that only a long and pains-taking search discovers it. Through these rhetorical figures, so finely employed, he intensifies the power of language to convey the experience to which the *Cántico* bears such eloquent witness. He is therefore to be judged great as a practitioner of the art of poetry. This is perhaps the most surprising finding of this study. While it remains true that his poetry is unique in the Golden Age, at least he shares with his contem-poraries an awareness of what rhetoric, in the broad sense, can achieve, and thus needs to be understood in the light of his earlier training in sacred eloquence.[26] The picture of an isolated man who happened to write marvellous poetry is not an adequate explanation of the facts. The quantity of rhetorical figures used, and the quality of usage, demand a different account of San Juan the poet. He is not a poet by accident, but by craft.

But there is more to his achievement than this. For one thing, he never allows the *Cántico* to settle into any one pattern for long. It is for ever moving between different polarities, and cannot be defined in such a way that its genre is immediately grasped. For each characteristic an opposite can be found: a language which sings, and one which stammers; a rhythm of smooth, flowing lines, and one of detached, staccato phrases; times when the vast panorama of creation is evoked, times when attention is fixed on one small place, the polarity of macrocosm and microcosm. There are moments when the reader of sixteenth-century poetry finds himself on familiar grounds, but there are also moments, often in close proximity, when the poem is strange, unfamiliar, out of place as a child of its time or indeed of any. There are moments when it seems to scatter into disjointed fragments, but also signs that it is one unified creation.

So it happens that the poem lives and thrives on these tensions, challenging and stimulating the reader at every turn. This capacity to suprise and cause wonder must be counted as one of the reasons why the *Cántico* can still be read today with pleasure and with awe. San Juan does not allow his readers to control his poem, by taking them along

---

[26] See Ch. 1, pp. 17–18.

paths they know to the next expected moment. The poem is beyond the immediate grasp of any mind; it is obscure poetry, antedating the conscious obscurity of Góngora yet in many ways going further, for it is the subject matter itself which is its cause, as San Juan states in his prologue: 'las cuales semejanzas no leídas con la sencillez del espíritu de amor e inteligencia que ellas llevan, antes parecen dislates que dichos puestos en razón'.[27] One of the joys of poetry is precisely this ability to add something, the 'no sé qué', to the words men use so carelessly and insensitively, and cause them to be imprinted upon the mind and uplift the emotions.

Through the *Cántico* runs a pervading sense of mystery. It is present in its meaning and its extraordinary structure. Through the mystery come hints of the inexpressible, for the poem itself confesses that some experiences are beyond the power even of poetry to capture. It can only hint at them, through the vaguest of paraphrases, or by a desperate attempt to pile up image upon image and thereby approach the un-approachable. It is a comment on the failure of language itself when it reaches out into such areas. Only on one or two occasions (the 'Amado' of 4—5 who clothes creation with beauty by a glance, the allegory of 28) is this explicit from the poem's content. More usually, it is suggested by the poem's inability to capture the experience and reduce it to words. This confession strikes a poignant note, because of all forms of the written word it is poetry which most successfully probes into truths beyond the reach of descriptive or analytical prose. So, even without a knowledge of the commentaries, it is clear enough from the poem itself that even when it has exhausted the limits of language it has not exhausted the experience which that language has been pressed into service to convey. One is reminded of T. S. Eliot's lines in *Four Quartets*:[28]

> ... Words strain,
> Crack and sometimes break, under the burden,
> Under the tension slip, slide, perish,
> Decay with imprecision, will not stay in place,
> Will not stay still.

Few poets, whether of the sixteenth century or any, have sung of the joys of consummated love at such length as San Juan. Their themes are mostly its pursuit and its loss (as in CA 1—11). Perhaps that is why San Juan encounters the problem of the limits of language. Pursuit and loss can be conveyed in words; ongoing fruition is a different matter.

San Juan's use of a symbolic language also lifts the poem out of our reach—and his—because the symbol has a life of its own, and prescribes

[27] 'If these similitudes are not read in the simplicity of spirit of love and understanding which they contain, they will seem more like nonsense than expressions reasonably ordered.'
[28] 'Burnt Norton', lines 149—53.

no meaning for the reader. It is our point of access into the *Cántico*'s world, because it relates to our experience as well as being part of that world. By the use of symbols, the two worlds—his and ours—begin to coincide, and the reader is invited to participate in them both. The contrast with the verses of Sebastián de Córdoba could hardly be greater. It marks the gulf between the mediocre and the great. Córdoba begins his version of Garcilaso's first eclogue thus:

> El dulce lamentar de dos pastores,
> Christo y el peccador triste y lloroso . . .

The mystery is gone. In the second, the characters represent the sensual part of man, reason, the soul, and grace: allegory at its least creative. To drive the lesson home, Córdoba defines exactly what he means, and squeezes the poetry out of it. San Juan senses that poetry did not need such exhaustive interpretation; other mediums were more suited to that. Man the sinner or lover could respond better if he had to make his own interpretation. In that sense, there is a continual dialogue in the *Cántico* between poet and reader. San Juan does not draw a detailed map and hope that the reader will follow the route stage by stage. He draws in some of the fundamental lines, some elements from his own imagination, and allows the reader to colour in the rest for himself. This partnership of poet and reader, in which each has something to contribute for the poem to be complete, is a rare and precious achievement of San Juan.

Great poetry should surely provoke this response. It should take a man out of himself and his world and lift him into its own, but with his mind and emotions intact, so that the dialogue between the poet's imagination and the reader's can begin. The poet's contribution to humanity is the way he makes this possible by creating poetry out of the raw materials of language and experience. The greatness of San Juan is that in showing us images of haunting beauty he makes this possible to such a high and rich degree.

6

THE POEM AND THE COMMENTARIES

If mystical inspiration in San Juan was associated with the writing of poetry, it also led him in another direction, far removed from the imaginative, symbolic world of the *Cántico* poem, to the analysis and systematization of his experience. Experience needs interpetation, and for this task he had to use language in a different way. He had to leave behind imaginative, creative, symbolic thinking and use a language which explained, clarified, and made some kind of order out of his material. The beginnings of this process have already been discussed, in the way in which the commentaries themselves first arose.[1] The purpose of this chapter is to provide some account and evaluation of the relationship between the poem and San Juan's explanation of its meaning, in view of the commonly maintained opinion that poem and commentary inhabit quite separate worlds; and because this represents, as far as we can tell, his final intentions as an interpreter of his own poem, the CB version will be the basis of the discussion.

But not even in this redaction can the commentary be called wholly systematic. As one becomes more and more familiar with the text, it becomes apparent that there are three main strands at work in it, pulling the commentary closer to or away from the original poem. There is the *lyrical thrust*, where poem and commentary stand closest together; the *interpretative function*, sometimes explaining the images, sometimes interpreting them as part of the spiritual life; and the *systematic approach*, in which the commentary moves furthest away from the poem and could have been written in isolation from it. Sometimes the strands are so interwoven that they can hardly be separated; but on many occasions one is predominant and for a while controls the course of the work.

I

The commentaries are usually described as methodical treatises, dull to read, which entirely lack the lyrical intensity of the poem. Brenan describes San Juan's prose style as 'plain and direct and ... lacking in the rhetorical tropes and latinisms which abound in most of the devotional

[1] Ch. 2, pp. 26–32.

books of that age.'[2] But the lyrical outpouring is not exhausted by the poem and carries over into the CB commentary.

On several occasions, for instance, lines from the poem are echoed at some distance for their original appearance. CB 1.10 points to the 'caverna de la piedra' in which Moses hid, reminiscent of the 'subidas cauernas de la piedra' of CA 36. CB 6.2 contains a passage studied earlier which is almost word for word the theme of CB 11.[3] CA 38.9 has both the 'subidas cavernas' and the 'mosto de las suaves granadas', while 24.6 retains the long summary of images in CA 13–14 (the mountains, wooded valleys, and so on) which had concluded that passage in the CA commentary (CA 15.6) but in CB is divorced from that context and comes upon the reader at a much later point. Finally, CB 31.10 has a CB addition with the words 'andando de él enamorada', harking back to CA 20/CB 29 and their 'andando enamorada'. This referring back to lines of poetry is not restricted to the *Cántico*: in the prologue to the *Subida*, 'más claro que la luz del día' reminds one of the *Noche*'s 'más cierto que la luz del mediodía'; and the stammer of CA 7, 'un no sé qué que', is partly present in N 2.7.6. From time to time, therefore, San Juan allows lines inspired by his poetry to creep into the commentaries even though they are not being expounded at these points.

The lyrical thrust is also noticeable in the large number of similes and *exempla* he employs, particularly when he works them out at greater length than is strictly necessary, and takes an obvious pleasure in choosing the right words for his picture:

A manera de ciervo que–cuado está herido con yerba–no descansa ni sosiega buscando por acá y por allá remedios, ahora engolfándose en unas aguas, ahora en otras, y siempre le va creciendo más en todas las ocasiones y remedios que toma el toque de la yerba, hasta que se apodera bien del corazón, y viene a morir.[4]

CB 20–21.14 is interesting because it introduces a picture which is in no sense derived from the poem, to illustrate the commentary: 'A manera del sol cuando de lleno embiste en la mar esclarece hasta los profundos senos y cavernas y parecen las perlas y venas riquísimas de oros y otros minerales preciosos'. CB 20–21.16 describes the effect of music: 'Así como la música de las liras llena el ánima de suavidad y recreación, y le embebe y suspende de manera que le tiene enajenado de sinsabores y penas'; and adds that the sirens' song 'es tan sabroso y deleitoso al que le oye, de tal manera le arroba y enamora que le hace olvidar como transportado de todas las cosas'–a rare glimpse into San Juan's feelings about an art which moved Fray Luis de León so greatly.

The example of the 'tortolica' who has not found her mate (CB 34.5)

[2] Op. cit., p. 141.   [3] Ch. 3, p. 45.
[4] CB 9.1; Peers, ii. 221. References are to Allison Peers's translation of the works of San Juan, 3 vols. (London, 1953).

has already been mentioned, and its reference to green branches, clear, cold water and shade endow it with a lyrical quality which extends beyond the descriptive imagery of the poem.[5] Finally, in CB 39.8, San Juan writes about the nightingale, which 'se oye en la primavera, pasados ya los fríos, lluvias y variedades del invierno, y hace melodía al oído, y al espíritu recreación'. The word order at the end of the period betrays the same care in placing words already seen in the poetry. If San Juan had written 'y recreación al espíritu' he would have constructed a satisfying parallelism, but something tells him he can do better, and he achieves a beautifully balanced climax to his sentence:

> melodía
> al oído,
> y al espíritu
> recreación.

Other similes and *exempla* used are: the solitary stag (CB 1.15), the phoenix (1.17), desire for food, health, foothold (9.6), water thrown on the forge (11.1), the stone travelling to its centre, wax receiving an impression (12.1), the breeze refreshing the weary, cooling love's fire (13.12), vixen feigning sleep (16.5), lions in their dens (24.4), spiced wine (25.7), sun shining through glass, coal and fire, star and sunlight (26.4), human affection (27.1), the bee extracting honey (27.8), the low-flying bird who catches the eagle (31.8), Christ the inexhaustible mine (37.4), pomegranate pips (37.7), fire turning coals to ash (39.14). The traditional origin of most, if not all, of these is obvious; though Brenan's remark that 'his comparisons and similes are of a homely kind and drawn from daily life' does not do them justice.[6] What is interesting is that San Juan should still feel it necessary to introduce fresh pictures and comparisons, as well as expanding ones suggested by the poem, in order to illustrate his meaning further. His prose is not simply cashing the images the poem provides: it is extending them and adding to them from beyond the poem.

But the lyrical momentum reaches deeper into the commentary. There is one passage which stands out above all others as the supreme example of lyrical prose: San Juan's exposition of the first three lines of CB 14 (CA 13.6–8), first noted by Baruzi as an exception to the rule that allegory predominates in the commentary:[7]

> Mi Amado, las montañas.

6. Las montañas tienen alturas, son abundantes, anchas, hermosas, graciosas, floridas y olorosas. Estas montañas es mi Amado para mí.

---

[5]   P. 79–80.
[6]   Op. cit., p. 141.
[7]   Op. cit., p. 358. For translation of the quotation, see Peers, ii. 249.

Los valles solitarios nemorosos.

7. Los valles solitarios son quietos, amenos, frescos, umbrosos, de dulces aguas llenos, y en la variedad de sus arboledas y suave canto de aves hacen gran recreación y deleite al sentido, dan refrigerio y descanso en su soledad y silencio. Estos valles es mi Amado para mí.

Las ínsulas extrañas.

8. Las ínsulas extrañas están ceñidas con la mar y allende de los mares, muy apartadas y ajenas de la communicación de los hombres; y así, en ellas se crían y nacen cosas muy diferentes de las de por acá, de muy *extrañas* maneras y virtudes nunca vistas de los hombres, que hacen grande novedad y admiración a quien las ve.

It would require too much space to make as detailed a stylistic analysis and evaluation of the prose commentaries as of the poem. But in lyrical prose passages like this it is not hard to show a close relationship between the poetry and the prose. A number of lines can be isolated, for example, which could well have stood in a *lira*:

> son abundantes, anchas
> floridas y olorosas
> los valles solitarios
> de dulces aguas llenos
> y suave canto de aves
> y deleite al sentido
> descanso en su soledad y silencio
> y allende de los mares
> muy apartadas y ajenas
> de la comunicación de los hombres
> cosas muy diferentes
> virtudes nunca vistas de los hombres
> novedad y admiración a quien las ve.

The striking number of such rhythmically balanced phrases is well beyond the bounds of accidental usage and suggests that the *lira* rhythm itself has influenced the prose. The rhetorical figure employed, *compar* (*parison*), balances different parts of the sentence by using the same number of syllables in each.

This passage stands out because San Juan does not attempt to cash the images. He prefers to amplify them, rather than extract their precise significance, and makes the same kind of figurative assertion as in the poem: 'Estas montañas es mi Amado para mí.' This contrasts markedly with his normal procedure, as in CB 24.6, where these same images receive an exact meaning:[8]

Porque acaecerá que vea el alma en sí las flores de *las montañas* que arriba dijimos, que son la abundancia y grandeza y hermosura de Dios; y en éstas entretejidos los lirios de los *valles nemorosos,* que son descanso, refrigerio y amparo; y luego allí entrepuestas las rosas olorosas de las *ínsulas extrañas*, que decimos ser las extrañas noticias de Dios.

[8]   Peers, ii. 302.

Although the lyrical element is still strong, and 'flores', 'lirios', and 'rosas' are added to the original images, each one is now provided with its own theological function within the commentary.

But CB 14–15.6–8 is not the only example of the lyrical momentum prolonged into the commentary. 2.8 contains a series of balanced clauses (*metabole*):

que, pues *adolezco*	y Él solo es mi salud,	que me dé mi salud;
y que, pues *peno*	y Él solo es mi gozo,	que me dé mi gozo;
y que, pues *muero*	y Él solo es mi vida,	que me dé mi vida.

Only one word per clause changes in each line. The verbs in the first clause are those of the poem. Apart from the parallel structure, there is also an antithesis between the state the verbs express, and the health, joy, and life the Bride seeks. The influence of the *lira* may likewise be discovered in other passages. CB 31.10 adds a passage which contains rhymes, and may be set out as follows:[9]

> En lo cual se podría
> considerar el gozo, alegría
> y deleite que el alma
> tendrá con este tal prisionero,
> pues tanto tiempo había
> que lo era ella de él,
> andando de él enamorada.

Likewise the turtle-dove *exemplum* of CB 34.5:[10]

> Cuando no halla a su consorte,
> ni se asienta en ramo verde,
> ni bebe el agua clara ni fría,
> ni se pone debajo de la sombra,
> ni se junta con otra compañía.

The lyrical thrust is also present when San Juan turns to exclamations and outbursts of joy, as in CB 1.7, 10–12 and increasingly as the union of Lover and Beloved grows more intimate. 39.7 is the most remarkable example, and can be set out in verse lines, with rhymes and sound groups italicized:[11]

> ¡Oh almas, cri*adas*
> para estas grand*ezas*
> y para ellas llam*adas*!
> ¿qué hac*éis*?
> ¿en qué os entreten*éis*?
> Vuestras preten*siones*
> son baj*ezas*
> y vuestras pose*siones*
> *miser*ias.

[9] Ibid. 343.

[10] Ibid. 353–4.

[11] Ibid. 376–7.

> ¡Oh *miser*able ceguera
> de los ojos de vuestra alma,
> pues para *tan*ta luz est*áis* ciegos
> y para *tan gran*des voces sordos,
> no viendo que, en *tan*to que busc*áis*
> *grandezas* y glorias, os qued*áis*
> *miser*ables y bajos,
> de *tan*tos bienes hechos
> igno*ran*tes e indignos!

Among the more noteworthy features of this prose passage are the rhymes, the insistence on 'an' sounds, the parallelisms and antitheses, and the balanced number of syllables in the second half (8, 8, 10, 10, 10, 10, 7, 7, 7). The construction of the whole is as complex as the more elaborate parts of the poem. But as soon as this outburst is over, San Juan brings us down to earth again with the very prosaic: 'Síguese lo segundo que el alma dice para dar a entender *aquello*'.[12]

San Juan has recourse to rhetorical devices used in the poem at other points in the commentary. One of his favourites is *adnominatio*. CB 22.6 reads: 'Viviendo el alma aquí vida tan feliz y gloriosa como es vida de Dios, considere cada uno ... qué vida tan sabrosa será ésta que vive'; 26.13 contains a number of words from the stem 'saber' ('sabía', 'sabiduría', 'sabido'); 31.4 from 'volar' ('volaba', 'vuelos', 'vuela'); and 37.8 has: 'Gustándolo El, lo da a gustar a ella, y gustándola ella, lo vuelve a dar a gustar a El; y así, es gusto común de entrambos.' He also uses *copulatio*, above all in that unique passage in CB 36.5, where it is hard to keep hold of the thread of meaning:[13]

... lleguemos hasta vernos *en tu hermosura* en la vida eterna. Esto es, que de tal manera esté yo transformada en *tu hermosura*, que, siendo semejante en *hermosura*, nos veamos entrambos en *tu hermosura*, tiniendo ya tu misma *hermosura*; de manera que, mirando el uno al otro, vea cada uno en el otro su *hermosura*, siendo la una y la del otro *tu hermosura* sola, absorta yo en *tu hermosura*; y así, te veré yo a ti en *tu hermosura*, y tú a mí en *tu hermosura*, y yo me veré en ti en *tu hermosura*, y tú te verás en mí en *tu hermosura*; y así, parezca yo tú en *tu hermosura*, y parezcas tú yo en *tu hermosura*, y mi *hermosura* sea *tu hermosura*, y *tu hermosura* mi *hermosura*; y así, seré yo tú en *tu hermosura*, y serás tú yo en *tu hermosura*, porque *tu* misma *hermosura* será mi *hermosura*; y así, nos veremos el uno al otro en *tu hermosura*.

Finally, CB 28.4 has a good example of *conversio* (*antistrophe*), with each phrase ending in a preposition and 'Dios': 'Porque el cuerpo ya le trata según Dios ... las cuatro pasiones ... tiene ceñidas también a Dios; porque no se goza sino de Dios, ni tiene esperanza en otra cosa que en Dios, ni teme sino sólo a Dios, ni se duele sino según Dios, y también todos sus apetitos y cuidados van sólo a Dios.'[14]

---

[12] For a possible parallel, see Cuevas García, op. cit.
[13] Peers, ii. 360–1.   [14] Ibid. 325.

It is clear from these examples that San Juan was using rhetorical devices consciously and for effect. They are not the sort of figures which can be used without the author being unaware of what he is doing; and they indicate that San Juan was a skilled practitioner of the art of rhetoric in his prose as well as his poetry. A closer analysis would doubtless yield many more examples. But what of the passages which betray the influence of the *lira* rhythm? Is this a deliberate technique? Rather than setting out to write a kind of prose poetry in parts of the commentary, it is more likely that San Juan, so sensitive to sound and rhythm, wrote such passages aware that they were in a heightened form of prose but not that they were imitating the *lira*. He had an intuitive feel for the kind of language suited to these lyrical outbursts, or he had acquired it through long practice of the *lira* form. The existence of rhymes and lines of equal syllables (sometimes seven and eleven) surely reflects that sensitivity, rather than any intention to imitate the poetic form in prose.

The significance and surprising fact to emerge from this study is simply that the lyrical thrust in CB is so strongly marked. It cannot be held that CB represents a complete rejection of lyrical language in favour of analytical. Baruzi's description of the commentary as 'un extraordinaire appauvrissement du poème' is certainly not true of the passages studied above.[15] The poem's lyrical power is prolonged into the commentary, and not just in isolated parts. San Juan continues to appeal to the imagination and the emotions, through picturesque and highly charged language, in a commentary so often dismissed as an arid exercise. And this creates a very firm bond between poem and commentary. For it is at such points that they come closest to one another, and are seen to arise from the same source of lyrical inspiration in the mind of San Juan. The discovery is surprising, because lyrical inspiration is precisely the quality San Juan has been accused of lacking in his prose works.

II

But as the commentary develops its interpretative function, it begins to move away from the poem. The interpretations come at different levels. In the first place, there is what may be termed the *technique of simple expansion*, in which San Juan is content to expound the thought contained in the poem without introducing any extraneous, explanatory matter, thus remaining fairly close to the poem. Then there is the tendency towards *allegorical interpretation of the images*, in which their hidden meaning is stated. Here the poem begins to recede, and the problem of its interpretation becomes acute. It is hard to avoid the suspicion that at least some of the expositions provided have little to do

[15] Op. cit., p. 353.

with the original poetic creation, and have been influenced by external preoccupations; a suspicion confirmed when San Juan offers more than one interpretation for the same image. Finally, there is his *exegesis of Scripture*. Sometimes the texts San Juan introduces relate directly to the part of the poem under discussion; more often, they do not, and instead corroborate his teaching by their authority. At such moments San Juan has moved quite a long way from the poem, especially when he piles up Biblical texts in such a way that he seems to be writing a commentary on them rather than on his poem.

The interpretative function begins with the simple expansion of ideas and images drawn directly from the poem. 1.3, for example, amplifies the opening question of the poem: 'Y es como si dijera: Verbo, Esposo mío, muéstrame el lugar donde estás escondido.' 29.9 explains 'Que, andando enamorada': 'Conviene a saber; que, andando obrando las virtudes, enamorada de Dios.' In both cases, the commentary supplies some of the information needed to interpret the poem. True, the content is spiritualized, so that the process of interpretation has begun; but it is little more than a prose version of poetic themes which could hardly have had any other significance for San Juan and his readers. The phrase 'como si dijera' is often a clue to places where San Juan is paraphrasing the poem. It is an ambiguous expression—does it really have its subjunctive force, or is it more of a pluperfect? And what is its subject—the Bible passage or line from the poem being expounded (i.e. 'it') or the person speaking? In 13.8 just two words from the poem, 'Buéluete, paloma', are expanded into an entire paragraph:[16]

Como si dijera: *Paloma,* en el vuelo alto y ligero que llevas de contemplación y en el amor con que ardes y simplicidad con que vas porque estas [tres] propriedades tiene la paloma—vuélvete de ese vuelo alto en que pretendes llegar a poseerme de veras, que aun no es llegado ese tiempo de tan alto contemplación, y acomódate a éste más bajo que yo agora te comunico en este tu exceso.

Expansion is here accompanied by reflection on the characteristics of the dove, introduced by San Juan, no doubt, to underline the appropriate nature of the image he has selected for the poem. The predominant 'v' sound there is carried over into the prose: 'vuelo', 'llevas', 'vas', 'vuélvete', 'vuelo', 'veras'; the meaning is somewhat ambiguous, though 'contemplación' hints strongly at a spiritual interpretation; and the language has lyrical elements, like the adjectives 'alto' and 'ligero', and striking words like 'ardes'.

Sometimes expansion takes the commentary some distance from the poem. The best example occurs at CB 40.2, probably because the line under scrutiny, 'Que nadie lo miraua', is so vague:[17]

[16] Peers, ii. 244.   [17] Ibid. 382.

Lo cual es como si dijera: Mi alma está ya desnuda, desasida, sola y ajena de todas las cosas criadas de arriba y de abajo, y tan adentro entrada en el interior recogimiento contigo, que ninguna de ellas alcanza ya de vista el íntimo deleite que en ti poseo . . . a mover mi alma a gusto con suavidad, ni a disgusto y molestia con su miseria y bajeza; porque, estando mi alma tan lexos de ellas y en tan profundo deleite contigo, ninguna de ellas lo alcanza de vista.

Expansion here is already accompanied by interpretation: the soul is liberated from all created things and is deep in withdrawal. This joining of expansion and allegorical interpretation is very characteristic of San Juan, as may be seen from the following passage (CB 34.6), in which the allegorical elements are italicized:[18]

Que es tanto como decir: Ya el alma esposa se sienta en ramo verde, deleitándose en su Amado; y ya bebe el agua clara *de muy alta contemplación y sabiduría de Dios* y fría *de refrigerio y regalo que tiene en Dios*; y también se pone debajo de la sombra *de su amparo y favor* que tanto ella había deseado, donde es consolada, apacentada y refeccionada sabrosa y divinamente.

By so qualifying the images, San Juan can extract the significance he requires.

This very important aspect of the interpretative function of the commentary must be examined more closely. Sometimes it is simple, short and straightforward, sometimes longer and more complex. CB 3.3 provides a simple example, exegeting Song 3:1, 'el lecho de sus gustos y deleites'. In CB 24.1 the same image receives a different interpretation: 'El lecho no es otra cosa que su mismo Esposo, el Verbo Hijo de Dios'. Clearly, the context of the image in the poem makes all the difference to its allegorical exegesis. This is a fundamental characteristic of San Juan's interpretative methods both for his poetic text and the Bible: the significance of the image is extracted for one particular occasion only, and the same image may receive a different interpretation when it appears again. Another characteristic is the apparent arbitrariness of interpretation. CB 5.3 states: 'Passar por los sotos es criar los elementos, que aquí llama sotos'. The meaning is stated outright, with no suggestion as to why passing through the thickets should mean creating the elements—it seems a disconcerting asumption. Similarly, in CB 32.4 'ojo' is taken to mean the merciful divinity of the Beloved, though previously, in 31.9, it has referred to faith.

But sometimes allegorical interpretation is more restrained, as in CB 14.1, where San Juan relates the dove of the poem to the dove of Genesis 8:8–9.[19] If the italicized words are omitted, there is simply a retelling of the Flood narrative:

Pues, como esta palomica de el alma andaba volando por los aires *de amor* sobre las aguas del diluvio *de las fatigas y ansias suyas de amor* . . . no hallando

---

[18] Ibid. 354.   [19] Ibid. 246.

donde descansase su pie, a este último vuelo . . . extendió el piadoso padre Noé la mano *de su misericordia* y recogióla, metiéndola en el arca *de su caridad y amor.*

But by including them, San Juan not only relates the dove of the poem to a Biblical precedent, he interprets the significance of the example and applies it to his own mystical teaching about the soul's search for God.

The interpretation is sometimes rationalized. CB 18.4–5 reads:[20]

Judea llama a la parte inferior del alma, que es la sensitiva; y llámala Judea porque es flaca y carnal y de suyo ciega, como lo es la gente judaica [!] Y llama *ninfas* a todas las imaginaciones, fantasías y movimientos y afecciones desta porción inferior . . . que . . . con su afección y gracia atraen a sí los amantes, así . . . procuran atraer a sí la voluntad de la parte racional . . .

The application of 'Judea' may not be considered tasteful now, but at least its arbitrariness is somewhat tempered. The exposition of 'ninfas' makes good sense, though it is not long before San Juan reverts to his disconcerting habit of announcing that one thing means another: flowers, the virtues of the soul; rose trees, its faculties. This introduction of scholastic terminology into the exposition of images is carried to a higher degree in CB 20–21.6–7, in which lions, stags, and leaping deer are related to the irascible and concupiscible faculties of the soul. It is hard to imagine such a precise terminology being in the mind of the poet when he wrote the original line, and it is surely fair to suppose that the further he strays from the more obvious interpretation of his images (where they have any) and the more he complicates his explanations, the less likely he is to have chosen his images for the reasons suggested in the commentary. The interpretation belongs to the reflective period after the initial lyrical creation.

San Juan's allegorical technique is generally quite straightforward, such as his exegesis of images in CB 34.5:[21]

Porque con tanto amor y solicitud le conviene andar, que no asiente el pie *del apetito* en ramo verde *de algún deleite*, ni quiere beber el agua clara *de alguna honra y gloria del mundo*, ni la quiera gustar fría *de algún refrigerio o consuelo temporal*, ni se quiera poner debajo de la sombra *de algún favor y amparo de criaturas*, no queriendo reposar nada en nada.

The images are qualified by adjectival phrases which reveal the meaning locked away in them. The procedure can be summed up in algebraic shorthand, where x and y stand for images, a and b for interpretations. The basic pattern is simple: x and y mean a and b, expressed usually in the formula 'the x of a', 'the y of b'. But the applications are variable: x does not always mean a, nor y, b—and often arbitrary. Sometimes a slightly different procedure is used, like 'x signifies y', as in CB 36.6,

---

[20] Ibid. 275.   [21] Ibid. 354.

where the allegorical approach is used to delineate a fine distinction between 'monte' and 'collado', arising from a Biblical text distinguishing between 'morning' and 'evening' knowledge of God.[22] Knowledge of God through his works and creatures is 'lower' than knowledge of the divine Word. San Juan's method brings together these seemingly disparate elements and weaves them into a whole.

Already in this interpretative function of the commentary Biblical passages have been mentioned. Just as so much of the poem's imagery comes from the Bible, so many of the illustrations in the commentary stem from the same source. Some relate more or less directly to the poem, others are introduced from the outside to corroborate particular points San Juan wishes to make, and may have little or nothing to do with the poetic text. Thus the relationship of Biblical quotations to CB is not a simple one, and in this it follows what has already been established about the interpretative function in general and allegorical interpretation in particular: sometimes it is closely related to the poem, at others it is carried forward by its own momentum. There is no clear distinction drawn between mystical doctrine hidden in the words of Scripture and that hidden in the words of San Juan. Such parity is surprising, and one cannot help but feel that San Juan would have qualified it if it had been pointed out to him, by distinguishing his images and their interpretations from those of the inspired text.

But it is understandable in view of the tradition of exegesis in which he was working. He could only have undertaken the kind of exegesis of poetic imagery he did because he was already steeped in the traditional exegesis of Scripture. The method of exegesis he had learned to apply to the Bible gave him a valuable tool for the exposition of his own poetic texts. The history of Biblical exegesis is a long and venerable one, and it is not intended to raise it here except in so far as it relates to San Juan's own interpretative methods. From very early times there had been a distinction drawn between literal exegesis and other forms, various in number, but usually described as allegorical, moral, and mystical (or anagogical). Allegory had been introduced in order to wrest meaning from passages which seemed unpromising if taken only literally. Obviously, allegorical and mystical forms of exegesis allowed for a more imaginative treatment of texts than the literal, even though this might include prophecy and metaphor, explained in accordance with the sacred writer's intentions. San Juan does not often restrict himself to literal exegesis, but prefers the equally valid and authoritative allegorical and mystical ways of dealing with the sacred text; and it is this which lies behind the apparent arbitrariness of his interpretations.[23] Given this

[22] Hatzfeld relates this to an Augustinian-medieval tradition of two kinds of vision of God, op. cit., p. 76.

[23] Nieto, op. cit., argues that passages in the *Subida* show San Juan to be

training, it is understandable that he should have applied similar techniques to his own poetic texts, believing them too to be in some sense Spirit-given, as his prologue shows.

The introduction of Scripture as a source for images and a corroboration of mystical teaching is a major factor in the interpretation San Juan makes of the poem. Occasionally, as in CB 11.5, he uses the technique of simple expansion: Exodus 33:20: 'es como si dijera: Dificultosa cosa me pides, Moisés, porque es tanta la hermosura de mi cara y el deleite de la vista de mi ser, que no la podrá sufrir tu alma en esa suerte de vida tan flaca.'[24] This relates closely to the poem ('Descubre tu presencia/ y máteme tu vista y hermosura'), and is the obvious text to choose at this point, given the centuries-long debate on whether anyone had actually seen God in this life.[25]

The text may receive a fully theological application, even when its constituent elements are lyrical. Song 1:6 is interpreted in CB 1.5:[26]

. . . porque en pedir le mostrase *dónde se apacentaba* era pedir le mostrase la esencia del Verbo divino, su Hijo, porque el Padre no se apacienta en otra cosa que en su único Hijo, pues es la gloria del Padre, y en pedir le mostrase el lugar donde *se recostaba* era pedirle lo mismo, porque el Hijo sólo es el deleite del Padre, el cual no se recuesta en otro lugar ni cabe en otra cosa que en su amado Hijo, en el cual todo él se recuesta comunicándole toda su esencia *al mediodía*, que es la eternidad donde siempre le engendra y le tiene engendrado.

And all this in answer to the first line of the poem! The poem leads to a related Biblical text, allegorical exegesis of this to the relationship between Father and Son, couched in impeccable orthodox terms and using the imagery of the Biblical passage the poem originally suggested to San Juan. The extremes of the process seem very distant, and only the Biblical text enables one to see how San Juan could move so swiftly from the Beloved's absence to the relationship of the first two Persons of the Trinity.

CB 14–15.24 contains another demonstration of the process of association at work in San Juan's mind. He has been describing night 'en par de los levantes de la aurora', and is reminded of Psalm 101:8: 'Vigilavi, et factus sum sicut passer solitarius in tecto.' David, he says, was also referring to contemplation at this moment in the soul's journey; and he proceeds to enumerate the five qualities of the solitary bird, applying each to the soul in this stage of contemplation. The transition from the image of night before dawn breaks to teaching about solitude requires only one or two steps in the mind of San Juan, though to the

---

primarily a literal-historical exegete: but I cannot agree that this is characteristic of his normal procedure.

[24] Peers, ii. 230.
[25] See Butler, op. cit., pp. 55–62, 87–92, 119–20.
[26] Peers, ii. 188–9.

reader the distance from the poem, in which there is nothing about birds, souls or contemplation, seems enormous.

The allegorical method outlined above also holds true for images from the Bible. CB 20–21.2, quoting from Song 8:8–9, is explained thus:[27]

Entendiendo aquí por las *fuerzas y defensas plateadas* las virtudes fuertes y heroicas envueltas en fe, que por la plata es significada; las cuales . . . son ya las del matrimonio espiritual . . . que [el alma] aquí es significada por el *muro* . . . y entendiendo por las *tablas cedrinas* las afecciones y accidentes de alto amor . . . significado por el cedro, y éste es el amor del matrimonio espiritual.

Song 5:4 receives similar treatment in CB 25.6, though this time the formula is simply '*x = a*':[28]

El *tocamiento* del Amado es el toque de amor que aquí decimos que hace el alma. La *mano* es la merced que en ello lo hace. La *manera* por donde entró esta mano es la manera y modo y grado de perfección que tiene el alma . . . El vientre suyo que dice se estremeció es la voluntad en que se hace el dicho toque. Y el *estremecerse* es levantarse en ella los apetitos y afectos a Dios . . . que son las *emisiones de bálsamo* que de este toque redundan, según decíamos.

Again, one is struck by the arbitrary nature of these explanations. 'Vientre' and 'voluntad' are linked only by their initial letter, and it is hard to understand how San Juan so blithely assumes the one stands for the other.

Probably the most complex example of all is CB 2.6–8, which will help to delineate the interpretative process more clearly. First, San Juan relates the three verbs of the line 'Decilde que adolezco, peno y muero' to the three faculties of the soul, and states that the Beloved's absence causes the suffering the verbs describe in each of them. Then he searches for a Scriptural text to provide authority for this, and hits on Lamentations 3:19, 'Recuérdate de mi pobreza y del ajenjo y de la hiel'. He refers poverty, wormwood, and gall to each of the faculties, and finds more Scriptural support for this exegesis, thus complicating the argument considerably. Then he introduces a new threesome—the theological virtues of faith, hope, and love, which he links to understanding, will, and memory, without recourse to Scriptural proof texts. He next explains the meaning of the whole: the Bride has stated her needs so that the Beloved may supply them, as in two examples from John's Gospel (water into wine, and the raising of Lazarus). Finally, the three needs of the Bride are summarized in a passage of stylized prose quoted earlier.[29] Once the reader can follow San Juan's thought-patterns (in this case, his fascination with groups of three words and their inter-relationships), the gap between poem and commentary begins to narrow. San Juan's method may be obsolete, but at least it exists.

Three links between the commentary on images from the poem and those introduced from the Bible serve to underline the fact that San Juan uses the same method in dealing with both. First, he sometimes displays a curious punctiliousness in exegesis which is at variance with his otherwise free-handed approach. In CB 17.6 and 40.6 he goes to considerable lengths to explain why it should be 'aspira por' and not 'en' the garden, and why the cavalry descended 'a vista de las aguas', not to drink from them. He makes capital out of what seems no more than a quibble, and it is hard to believe he had such distinctions in mind when he wrote the poem. The same procedure is used in CB 30.6, exegeting Song 1:3's 'correremos' and explaining why it is in the plural. What is surely a spontaneous choice of words provides him on reflection with a chance to justify their use on doctrinal grounds.

Second, and running parallel to the tendency to introduce into the poem ideas sparked off by some association in San Juan's mind, is a tendency towards grouping together several passages of Scripture more or less relating to the same theme, as in CB 2.7, 14–15.10–11, 15, 18.21, 22.8, 23.6, 24.1,9, 29.11, 30.6, and above all 38.7–9. Here, in a desperate attempt to expound the elusive 'aquello', which began at 38.5 and continues throughout 39, San Juan turns to the seven letters to the Churches in the book of Revelation 2–3 and quotes and expounds in turn the sayings with which they conclude (based on the pattern 'el que venciere'). This section thus becomes almost an independent entity as a commentary on those chapters.

The third link between interpretation of poetic and Biblical texts is more important, because it raises the problem of alternative meanings for the same image. For example, in CB 30 the 'frescas mañanas' are first said to be youth, then acts of love by which virtues are acquired, and finally 'obras hechas en sequedad y dificultad de espíritu . . . denotadas por el fresco de las mañanas del invierno'. Not content with offering these very different interpretations, San Juan goes on to make room for other possibilities of meaning in 'las guirnaldas', which are all the holy people in the Church or particular sorts, virgins, doctors, and martyrs; and in the 'espesura' of CB 36.10–12, which is not only God's marvellous works and profound judgements, but also the many trials and tribulations desired by the soul and 'la espesura de la cruz'.[30]

But it would be wrong to suppose that this practice was confined to San Juan. It develops out of early Christian exegesis and its solution of some of the textual problems it encountered, where there might be more than one reading for a text. Beryl Smalley has pointed out that

---

[30] There may be a play on words here between 'espesura' meaning 'thicket' and 'thickness'. The latter meaning lends itself more readily to 'cruz'. Or San Juan may have had in the back of his mind a connection between 'áspero' and 'espesura': see N 1.6.6, 'camino áspero|de la cruz'; or between 'espesura' and 'peso', 'weight'.

where the version received by Origen (the Septuagint) conflicted with other versions, he did not reject them but would set them side by side and comment on both. 'The habit of making double commentaries on double texts without choosing between them will become ingrained', she writes.[31] Not only might more than one reading give rise to parallel interpretations, but one word itself might mean different things in a literal, moral, allegorical, or mystical exegesis or within any one form of these. The interpreter was concerned with the fulness of meaning, which could not necessarily be exhausted by any one interpretation. This feature of San Juan's exegesis both of his images and the Bible's must ultimately stem from this tradition.

But the alternative and often mutually exclusive interpretations nonetheless raise difficult questions. The fact of their existence implies that San Juan did not always choose his images for the reasons he gives, because he cannot possibly have had in mind in the process of composing the poem all the possible interpretations and Biblical texts introduced into the commentary. When he wrote the poem, did San Juan himself know what he intended his words to mean or why he chose them? In other words, was the whole process of interpretation an afterthought? To incline to suppose that it was neither invalidates it nor makes it less interesting. Fletcher's words need to be pondered at this point:[32]

The whole point of allegory is that it does not *need* to be read exegetically; it often has a literal level that makes good enough sense all by itself. But somehow this literal surface suggests a peculiar doubleness of intention, and while it can . . . get along without interpretation, it becomes much richer and more interesting if given interpretation.

III

There remains the third strand of the commentary to unravel: the systematic approach. It is to this element that critics have in the main referred when distinguishing between the lyrical poem and systematic treatise, though it does not account for even half of the material in CB. Few examples need be given, as it is the most obvious feature of the commentary, and is easily observed in the way San Juan structures it and adds to it passages of doctrinal significance. In the provision of structure and doctrine he moves as far as ever he does from the text of the poem.

The systematic approach is aimed at bringing into a unity all the disparate elements of the commentary. Sometimes San Juan makes brief summaries of what has been said (CB 3.4, 10, 10.8, 12.2, 22.2,

[31] *The Study of the Bible in the Middle Ages* (Indiana, 1970; originally published 1940), p. 13.
[32] Op. cit., p. 7.

24.6, 25.5, 32.2, 38.9); more frequently, he introduces what is about to happen. This is largely restricted to CB through the annotations added to each stanza in it. CB 1.2 maps out the country to be traversed:[33]

En esta primera canción, el alma, enamorada del Verbo Hijo de Dios, su Esposo, deseando unirse con él por clara y esencial visión, propone sus ansias de amor querellándose a él de la ausencia, mayormente que habiéndola él herido de su amor, por el cual ha salido de todas las cosas criadas y de sí misma, todavía haya de padecer la ausencia de su Amado, no desatándola ya de la carne mortal para poderle gozar en gloria de eternidad.

Such an introduction can only have been written with the end of the commentary in mind, since it links clearly with the last five stanzas and their theme of eternal glory to come, though much suffering has to be undergone in the meantime.

But he is also concerned to treat his subject matter systematically. Sometimes he will make generalizations, which he may or may not expand: 'El alma más vive donde ama que en el cuerpo donde anima' (CB 8.3); or 'La contemplación es un puesto alto por donde Dios en esta vida se comienza a comunicar a el alma y mostrársele, mas no acaba' (CB 13.10). He will also describe the properties of certain objects, to draw out his lesson more comprehensively, as with the solitary bird.[34] Rivers, perfect love, and lovers are treated in this way (14–15.9, 32.2, 36.1). In such small ways San Juan can be seen anxious to treat his subject matter as systematically as possible.

But this approach is most clearly manifest in his analysis of the stages of the spiritual life, often using the terminology of scholastic theology and sometimes digressing so far from the poem that he feels obliged to apologize. CB's doctrinal structure is based on the 'argumento' it places before the exposition begins and on CB 22.3's reworking of CA 27, which relates the commentary to the traditional three ways: stanzas 1–5, purgative (mortification, meditation); 6–13, illuminative (leading to the spiritual betrothal); and 14–21, unitive (leading to the spiritual marriage in 22). CB 36.2 gives the new context for the remainder of the poem—the request for eternal enjoyment of God beyond death in the beatific vision. This is the framework, imposed on the poem some time after it was written, and linked to the reorganization of the stanzas in CB, which San Juan proceeds to elaborate.

It is not hard to isolate the passages on prayer and mystical experience which are fitted into the structure of the three ways and around the symbols of betrothal and marriage. The main lines of this teaching can be followed almost independently of the poem. After the general introduction (CB 1.1–2) San Juan begins the first of the promised discussions on 'algunos puntos y efectos de oración' (1.17–18, 22). Among the

---

[33] Peers, ii. 187.   [34] See above, p. 129.

visitations God makes to the soul are 'unos encendidos toques, que, a manera de saeta de fuego, hieren y traspasan el alma y la dejan toda cauterizada con fuego de amor'.[35] 3.8 introduces another important theme, the temptations and disturbances which meet the soul as she struggles towards perfection. 7.2–5 systematizes the three manners of grieving for the Beloved into 'herida', 'llaga', and 'morir', each increasing in intensity; while 7.9 takes up another prayer experience, 'una subida noticia, en que se la da a entender o sentir alteza de Dios y grandeza'.[36] 10.1 summarizes the properties of the soul at this point: desire for the Beloved alone, loss of appetite for all things, and everything a trouble and annoyance to her. These relate quite closely to the classic signs given in S 2.13.2–4 for knowing when to leave meditation and pass to contemplation, which is not surprising, as CB is dealing with a similar transitional state.

Influenced by 'presencia' in the verse, CB 11.3 describes the three kinds of presence of God in the soul, a clear example of the poem leading directly to a theological systematization of ideas implicit in its vocabulary. The first two, 'esencial' and 'por gracia', are not relevant to San Juan's teaching here, which concerns the third, 'por afección espiritual'; but he mentions them for the sake of completeness. 13.6 describes another state of prayer, in which the soul is snatched from the body in rapture and communicates with the divine Spirit; and this is linked in 14.2 with the spiritual betrothal, a very significant moment in the soul's progress: 'En este vuelo espiritual . . . se denota un alto estado y unión de amor, en que después de mucho exercicio espiritual suele Dios poner al alma, al cual llaman desposorio espiritual con el Verbo Hijo de Dios.'[37] The commentary then describes some of the effects of this betrothal. In 14.12, for example, under the figure of 'silbo', the soul enjoys 'una subidísima y sabrosísima inteligencia de Dios y de sus virtudes, la cual redunda en el entendimiento del toque que hacen estas virtudes de Dios en la sustancia del alma; que éste es el más subido deleite que hay en todo lo demás que gusta el alma aquí.'[38] Three paragraphs later he adds that this experience also involves the revelation of truths about God and hidden secrets.

CB 16.2, 6 return to the theme of demonic disturbances in the soul, worse now because the soul has been purged of many imperfections, and the devil sometimes fights with 'temores y horrores espirituales, a veces de terrible tormento'.[39] Worse still is the absence of God which can occur during the betrothal (CB 17.1), because the soul and God have drawn so close, and this absence torments her terribly. Both these passages bear strong links with the teaching of the *Subida-Noche* on the dark night of the spirit, though the *Cántico* poem does not allow

[35] Peers, ii. 195.	[36] Ibid. 218.	[37] Ibid. 247.
[38] Ibid. 253.	[39] Ibid. 265.	

him to dwell at such length as there on the single image of the 'noche oscura'. Nonetheless, it is important to note that this characteristic part of San Juan's system is present from time to time in the *Cántico*, even when, as here, the poem makes no mention of the symbol of night.

CB 20–21.1 prepares the way for the spiritual marriage and speaks of the need to erase all imperfections from the soul. The list of images in these verses is thus made to stand for the rebellious instincts and emotions which must be purged. In 22 the soul enters the marriage, and for much of the rest of the commentary San Juan is engaged in describing its fruits. CB 23.1 says: 'En este alto estado del matrimonio espiritual con gran facilidad y frecuencia descubre el Esposo al alma sus maravillosos secretos . . . Comunícala principalmente dulces misterios de su Encarnación y los modos y maneras de la redención humana, que es una de las más altas obras de Dios, y así es más sabrosa para el alma.'[40] 25.2 describes three mercies devout souls receive from God, and 25.5 two more under the figures of the 'toque de centella' and 'adobado vino'. 26.3 introduces the traditional picture of the seven degrees of love, of which the 'interior bodega' represents the highest; and here what God communicates to the soul is inexpressible. 27.5 relates 'ciencia sabrosa' to mystical theology, 'que es ciencia secreta de Dios, que llaman los espirituales contemplación', another example of San Juan connecting the poem's terminology with the classic mystical language of the West.[41] 29.2–3 refers to an old debate, the relationship of the active and contemplative lives. San Juan comes down on the side of the latter's superiority, with an assertion that might well have worried those suspicious of illuminism: a little of this pure love towards God benefits the Church more than a whole host of external works and exercises.

In the last part of the commentary, teaching is given on two very important themes, equality of love, and transformation.[42] The theme of ineffability is also to the fore (34.1, 39.3), and there are further references to the revelation of theological mysteries (37.4) and to the identification of 'noche' with mystical theology and contemplation (39.12). Even as late as 40.1 (the five things the soul says in this verse) San Juan is still busy dividing up and analysing his subject matter, to treat it more comprehensively.

For him this was no doubt the most significant part of the enterprise. But it was not simply his own system. As promised in the prologue, he drew very heavily from scholastic theology. Its terminology, so strange to contemporary minds, crops up incessantly as the normal analytical language of San Juan. Its effect is most apparent in the following paragraphs: CB 1.10, 2.6–7, 3.5, 8.3, 10.5, 11.3–4, 12.2, 6, 14–15.14, 26, 16.10–11, 17.5, 18.5, 7, 19.4–5, 7, 20–21.4–8, 12, 26.5–9, 11,

---

[40] Ibid. 296.   [41] Ibid. 321.   [42] See pp. 162–8 below.

13–18, 27.5,7, 28.4–5, 32.8, 35.5–6, 36.1, 4–5, 9, 37.3,8, 38.1, 39.3–6, 8, 11–12, 14, 40.1, 4–6.

The influence of scholastic theology is sometimes restricted to a brief definition, like 1.10, 'Porque Dios es la sustancia de la fe y el concepto della'; or 12.2, 'Porque la fe, como dicen los teólogos, es hábito oscuro'.[43] But often it is more thoroughgoing. 14–15.14 refers to the passive or possible intellect, as does 39.12:[44]

Porque esto no se hace en el entendimiento que llaman los filósofos activo, cuya obra es en las formas y fantasías y aprehensiones de las potencias corporales, mas hácese en el entendimiento en cuanto posible y pasivo, el cual, sin recibir las tales formas . . . sólo pasivamente recibe inteligencia sustancial de imagen, la cual le es dada sin ninguna obra ni oficio suyo activo.

16.10–11 likewise contains scholastic psychology, with its division of the soul into lower and higher parts, in which the various faculties of man are located. San Juan describes these at some length, probably because his readers would have only the haziest knowledge of such technical language. Poetic images are directly related to scholastic terms: 'arrabales' of 18.7 are the interior sensual senses, like memory, fantasy, and imagination; 20–21.4–6, 8–9 expound the images in terms of digressions of fantasy and imagination, the irascible and concupiscible faculties, the three faculties of the soul, the four passions, and so on.

This language is of the greatest importance to San Juan in his commentary, because it provides him with a terminology which is precise, analytical, and accepted as authoritative, much as a modern writer might use the terminology of the accepted sciences of today in discussing spiritual matters. It enables San Juan to reduce the mysterious utterance of the poem to a language which could be grasped by those trained to think within its boundaries, and to draw important distinctions. In 26.11, for example, he tackles the question of whether the soul is in a permanent state of union after the spiritual marriage, and argues that it is with regard to its substance, but not its faculties, though often these are united too. Thus he distinguishes two levels of union, one of which always enjoys it, the other more sporadically. Today we might say that union is permanent unconsciously but not always consciously experienced. In this he no doubt reflects his own experience of a tension between the glory of union and the fact that everyday life has to go on and sometimes other activities intervene to engage the 'faculties' of the soul. In 35.5 he speaks of the soul's alienation from all creaturely affections, and his concluding remarks lay the foundation for the whole journey he has been describing: 'Porque luego que el alma desembaraza estas potencias y las vacía de todo lo inferior y de la propriedad de lo

---

[43] Peers, ii. 191, 235.   [44] Ibid. 379.

superior, dejándolas a solas sin ello, inmediatamente se las emplea Dios en lo invisible y divino'.[45] It is the nature of created faculties to be occupied with something; if they are emptied of all human activity, lofty or lowly, God, their Creator, himself raises them to the only activity left, the highest and truest, contemplation of himself.

Sometimes this systematic approach draws San Juan right away from the poem, and nowhere more clearly than when he digresses, though this is envisaged in the prologue: 'No podrá ser menos de alargarme en algunas partes donde lo pidiere la materia'.[46] Usually he is aware of the fact and feels obliged to point out when he is straying too far from the poem, showing how anxious he is to preserve some kind of relationship between it and the commentary. Good examples are 26.16—17 (the question of knowledge and acquired habits), 29.2—4 (active and contemplative lives), 11.9—10 (why the children of Israel fled of old from the sight of God), and 13.7, which introduces a digression and then does not take it up:[47]

Lugar era éste conveniente para tratar de las diferencias de raptos y éxtasis y otros arrobamientos y sutiles vuelos de espíritu que a los espirituales suelen acaecer; mas, porque mi intento no es sino declarar brevemente estas canciones, como en el prólogo prometí, quedarse han para quien mejor lo sepa tratar que yo, y porque también la bienaventurada Teresa de Jesús, nuestra madre, dejó escritas de estas cosas de espíritu admirablemente, las cuales espero en Dios saldrán presto impresas a luz.

14—15. 17—21 expounds a long passage from Job (4:12—16), which San Juan attempts to relate to the doctrine of the betrothal, because he sees in it an authority which confirms his teaching, even if it means a further detour to explore it. 25.9—11 has a rather unexpected twist suggested by the image of the 'adobado vino', when San Juan decides to summarize the difference between old and new wine, to teach those on the mystical journey who are new or old lovers.

But the strangest digression of all is in 23.6. San Juan remarks: 'Este desposorio que se hizo en la cruz no es del que agora nos vamos hablando', which in effect denies the relevance of the whole of his exposition of the stanza to the doctrine he wishes to give. For the verse can only refer to the redemption of man and the betrothal of human nature to the Son of God, whereas San Juan is speaking of the betrothal of the individual soul in a high mystical state to the risen and ascended Lord. Small wonder the verse receives such a short exposition! CB 23.6 is in fact a CB addition. He must have noticed how inappropriate the

---

[45] Ibid. 356—7. [46] Ibid. 178.

[47] Ibid. 243. Santa Teresa's works were published in 1588, edited by Luis de León. The retention of this paragraph in CB may mean that San Juan had prepared his second redaction at least as far as this point before news reached him of the event.

exposition was after he had completed CA, so he added this remark and a very long passage from Ezekiel (16:5–14) which is said to refer to the betrothal 'de que vamos hablando', without however troubling to demonstrate in what ways it does.

IV

Lyrical thrust, interpretative function, systematic approach: through analysis of these strands in CB, the relationship of poem to commentary and the way the latter itself works becomes to some extent clarified. CB is not only a systematic treatise. It continues the lyrical momentum of the poem; it expands and allegorizes the imagery, and illustrates further from the Bible; and it contains much spiritual teaching about the mystical way hidden in these images and often expounded through the analytical language of scholastic theology. Since the poem is almost entirely lyrical and does not seek to interpret itself, the commentary can be said to add elements of interpretation and systematic teaching to it, and in so doing, to prefer a functional, logical kind of language to the symbolic and creative language of the poet. The juxtaposition of these two kinds of language no doubt occasions the discomfort felt by many modern readers of the commentary. But once one begins to see how the mind of San Juan works and develops his material, the discomfort eases and one can better appreciate what he was trying to achieve. It should be added, for the sake of completeness, that in this respect there is not a lot of difference between the two redactions. The difference is of emphasis, rather than of kind. The intentions stated in the prologues are identical, and CA contains lyrical and systematic elements as well as the expected interpretations.

What has been written on this subject hitherto therefore needs some modification. While P. Eulogio was right to underline San Juan's growing concern to bring into some kind of doctrinal synthesis the disparate ideas suggested by the poem, by means of his two commentaries, that is only one part of the story. Icaza has examined the style of the *Cántico*'s prose and poetry in great detail, but her conclusions do not always do justice to the complexity of their relationship. She states her task as one of studying the relationship 'between the symbolic, ambiguous, multivalent, and thus in some ways modern poetry and the clear, didactic, aristotelian, thomist prose treatise'.[48] As has been shown, such a neat distinction between poem and commentary is not really valid, because the commentary works on several levels, not one. Our probing into poem and commentary has demonstrated how exceedingly difficult it is to capture the essence of each in exact words, because they are

---

[48] *The Stylistic Relationship between Poetry and Prose in the Cántico* (Washington, 1957), p. 8. The CA text is used throughout.

such complex works. The tendency has been to force poem and commentary so far apart that there is no meeting-ground between them. That surely is an unacceptable position. They interact constantly, and it is only on rare occasions that San Juan loses sight of the poem altogether.

Yet there remains one inescapable problem. Is the commentary necessary for understanding the poem? The answer must depend on the angle from which the question is approached, for it is really compounded of two elements: did San Juan need to write the commentary? and even if he did, does the modern reader need it?

There is nothing to suggest that San Juan intended to expound his poem before the nuns who had read the verses he brought out of prison requested him to explain their meaning. He may well have been content to let their mysterious beauty leave its own impression. But once he realized that they could be the medium for spiritual teaching the commentary was inevitable. Teaching needed a different kind of language and form. In fact, San Juan has a theory of language which forms the basis of his own distinction between the poetic outburst and the didactic treatise. Like Fray Luis, he associates poetry with divine inspiration: 'Por cuanto estas canciones . . . parecen ser escritas con algún fervor de amor de Dios' and 'Por haberse . . . estas Canciones compuesto en amor de abundante inteligencia mística'.[49] What God communicates cannot adequately be expressed in words, a theme developed more fully in N 2.17.3.[50] In the *Cántico* prologue he writes:[51]

Ésta es la causa por que con figuras, comparaciones y semejanzas, antes rebosan algo de lo que sienten y de la abundancia de el espíritu vierten secretos y misterios, que con razones lo declaran. Las cuales semejanzas no leídas con la sencillez del espíritu de amor e inteligencia que ellas llevan, antes parecen dislates que dichos puestos en razón, según es de ver en los divinos Cantares de Salomón y en otros libros de la Escritura divina, donde, no pudiendo el Espíritu Santo dar a entendèr la abundancia de su sentido por términos vulgares y usados, habla misterios en extrañas figuras y semejanzas.

The implication is that the language of mystical experience, in the Bible and in this poetry, uses the same technique of figures, comparisons and metaphors. Mysterious language therefore has a definite theological function, inside and outside the sacred text. It points towards the ineffable and is the only way in which any meaning can be communicated from it.

But the prologue does not only help to explain how San Juan envisaged the purpose of the poem and commentary. It raises questions about the kind of interpretation others may put on them. The commentary, for the reasons just given, can never be complete. Divine truths are not exhausted by words. San Juan does not rule out other

---

[49] Peers, ii. 177–8.   [50] Peers, i. 428–9.   [51] Peers, ii. 177–8.

interpretations of his poem, and himself gives only 'alguna luz general'. The exposition is thorough enough so that different people can appreciate it in their different ways, but it is not the final word:[52]

Los dichos de amor es mejor declararlos en su anchura, para que cada uno de ellos se aproveche según su modo y caudal de espíritu, que abreviarlos a un sentido a que no se acomode todo paladar; y así, aunque en alguna manera se declaran, no hay para qué atarse a la declaración, porque la abundancia mística . . . no ha menester distintamente entenderse para hacer efecto de amor y afición en el alma.

Thus San Juan, surprisingly, views his commentary, even in its second redaction, as adaptable, flexible—the exposition need not be adhered to rigidly. The possibility of alternative explanations is written into the fabric of the text, and this opens the way for an approach to the commentary in which the reader too, from his own experience, has a part to play. This might suggest that, since San Juan did not regard his own interpretations as conclusive, there is a justification for finding new ones and disregarding his. But whatever alternatives he had in mind, one thing is clear. They would all be seeking to extract the hidden core of mystical truth from the fruits the poem yields. He would not have envisaged an exegesis of the *Cántico* other than a spiritual one, and could never have accepted as valid an interpretation of his poem which viewed it primarily as a secular song of erotic love. To use his own flexible approach to justify departing from this spiritual interpretation would be a very serious misunderstanding of San Juan, though it might produce other independent points of interest.

The prologue is a valuable insight into San Juan's intentions. It sets certain features of the commentary in a clearer perspective. Not all the images or lines of the poem are expounded in the same way or at the same length. Some are obviously more significant than others. The torrent of imagery in CA 13—14 is left partially unexpounded in CB 14—15. Some lines only attract a passing mention, like 'Decid si por uosotros ha passado' (CA 4), 'Y todos más me llagan' (7), 'Por toda aquesta vega' (17), 'Que, andando enamorada' (20), 'Quando tú me mirabas' (23). CA 8, 28 and 39 in general are not expounded at great length, whereas CB 11, particularly its first two lines, receives a very full treatment. Other lengthy expositions are found in 'Adónde te escondiste' (1), 'El siluo de los ayres amorosos' (13), 'Montes, valles, riberas' (29) and 'El aspirar de el ayre' (38). The imbalance is nothing like as great as in the *Subida-Noche* between the first line and the others expounded (San Juan stopped at the first line of verse three), for out of the single image of the dark night he wove his whole doctrinal system. But when he can find little to say about a line from the *Cántico*

[52] Ibid. 178.

he does not feel obliged to pause there; instead, he passes quickly on to the next.

Then there are the different interpretations one image may receive at various points, or the way in which one reality is approached through several images. This should not be viewed as inconsistency on San Juan's part, but in the light of his remarks in the prologue about the incompleteness of his expositions. At such points he is trying to offer at least some of the alternatives, to make them fuller; and he is drawing on the common practice of Scriptural exegetes over the centuries, who found many meanings in one text. San Juan did not hesitate to apply this technique to the mysterious words he had written. Thus the 'ínsulas estrañas' refer to the Beloved in CB 14.8, but to the soul in 19.7. 'Cieruo' is not interpreted in 1, but in 13.9 refers to the Beloved and in 20–21.16 to the concupiscible faculty of the soul. 'Flores' are usually virtues of the soul (17.10, 18.5, 30.3), but also stand for its appetites (3.5) and for angels and sanctified souls (4.6). In 20–21.9 'agua' is grief, in 36.9 knowledge of God, and in 40.5 spiritual delights. Mountains are virtues in 3.4, the Beloved in 14–15.6, the harmony of man's senses and faculties in 16.10, the disordered acts of the soul in 20–21.8, and knowledge of God in 36.6. The soul is described in many images in the poem: 'uida', 'esposa', 'huerto', 'paloma, -ica', 'tortolica'; the Beloved and God by 'cieruo', 'montañas', 'valles', 'ínsulas', 'ríos', 'siluo', 'noche', 'música', 'soledad', 'cena', 'arca', 'Philomena', 'lecho', 'fuente'.

Nothing is static about the interpretations of images in the *Cántico*. There is no fixed exchange rate, by which any one image may be converted into a corresponding concept. Instead, San Juan presents a variable series of interpretations, thereby freeing himself and his readers likewise from the constraint of following a set pattern, always cashing x in return for a. His own attitude to the relationship of poem and commentary is very flexible. But is there anything in the poem which suggests that it needs some kind of explanation in order to be understood? Apart from the fact that those who first read it evidently thought so, certain passages do benefit from commentary, such as CA 17's 'En la interior bodega/ de mi Amado beuí'. The grammatical ambiguity is only cleared up when the commentary is consulted, and the fact that San Juan gives only one interpretation while in many other places offering alternatives suggests that he did not realize how ambiguous the sentence was.[53]

In the study of the mysterious atmosphere generated by the poem, it was stated that the strange and beautiful world of the *Cántico* itself contains hints of the inexpressible. This conclusion was not based on prior assumptions but drawn from the text itself, the 'allí' and 'aquello'

[53] See above, p. 89.

references, and so on. It is not surprising that San Juan returns to this theme in the commentary, and above all in CB 28. Here the poem poses a real problem of interpretation, because of its lack of definition. The objects under scrutiny are 'aquello que mi alma pretendía' and 'aquello que me diste el otro día'. It is a little disturbing to find such vagueness at what ought to be the climax of the poem. The 'something' obviously matters, but its identity is unrevealed. The reader is driven to ask what San Juan meant by writing such words; and in doing so, makes the beginnings of an apologia for the commentary.

San Juan tackles the poem in CB 38.6, 'Aquello' is what God predestined the soul for, which is not very explicit. It is also to be understood from 'lo que dijo de ello Cristo a san Juan en el Apocalipsis por muchos vocablos y comparaciones en siete veces, por no poder ser comprehendido *aquello* en un vocablo ni en una vez, porque aun en todas aquéllas se quedó por decir.' The same idea is repeated at the end of the exegesis: none of these wonderful expressions, nor all of them together, properly expounds the mystery. It might be thought that he has given enough weight to this problem, summed up in 38.9 as 'nombre que justo cuadre a *aquello* . . . no se halla'; but he returns to it immediately in 39.1, where the soul 'no quiere dejar de decir algo de aquello'. The pictures which unfold in the stanza (breeze, nightingale, thickets, flame) are meant to explain 'en cuanto le es posible, qué sea y cómo sea *aquello* que allí será' (that is, in the beatific vision).[54] In this way the whole exposition of the stanza relates to the same 'aquello'. Logical, analytical language falls far short, and even the imaginative symbolic language of poetry can only hint at the reality beyond words. San Juan uses the resources of language in different ways—poetry, analysis, allegory, symbol, vague paraphrase, Scriptural exegesis—and still 'aquello' eludes him. The poem begs the question of its meaning; the prose grapples with it bravely, but in the end the witness of both is the same: it is inexpressible.[55]

The *Cántico* demands a specifically spiritual interpretation in a number of places. The sensitive reader perhaps notices this more than one who is a stranger to San Juan's world; but even such a novice, if he reads the poem attentively, will want certain questions answered: who is this Beloved, who clothes nature with his beauty? what is the significance of the event under the apple-tree, and what does all this Biblical language indicate? why, if it is a straightforward love poem, is it so mysterious? For example, is 'christalina' simply an appropriate adjective,

[54] For quotations in this paragraph, see Peers, ii. 371–4.
[55] Zaehner, op. cit., p. 36, writes: 'Mystics of all schools insist that their experiences are not reducible to words, and few of them have had any interest in art or poetry or music as such.' San Juan must be counted an important exception to the latter remark.

or does it have associations with 'Cristo' which affect its interpretation (and provide an example of *eteroeosis*, use of a proper name as an adjective)? Thus, even without the commentaries, the poem implies the need for some interpretation. The idea that it could refer to the celebration of erotic love would have been deeply offensive in San Juan's time, and it is anachronistic to suppose that he read the Song of Songs in this way, drawing as heavily as he does on the centuries-long mystical exegesis of its text. With our popularized Freud to hand, we are inclined to take it for granted that the human sexual drive, when not fulfilled, can be sublimated and explain the intensity of divine love experienced by the mystics. We may be quite certain that as far as San Juan was concerned, and as far as the poem itself can tell us when regarded in its most natural context, its meaning is religious, and to draw out that meaning, a careful prose exposition is obviously an advantage. In undertaking this, he clearly extended his creation in ways he could not have envisaged when he began to sing the divine love in his dark prison. For here we meet San Juan the philosopher and theologian working on the material provided him by San Juan the poet. He becomes his own interpreter.

His intentions are not hard to uncover in the movement from poem to commentary. But ought this to affect a contemporary understanding and appreciation of the *Cántico*? Many recent critics would argue not, because the author's intentions are irrelevant, an approach Wimsatt has termed counter to 'the intentional fallacy' and one which it is worth examining to conclude this chapter. Wimsatt's basic premiss is 'that the design or intention of the author is neither available nor desirable as a standard for judging the success of a work of literary art.'[56] It is no doubt true that thousands of people have read San Juan's poetry and appreciate its beauty without understanding at all what the author intended them to grasp. Can other interpretations be brought to the poem, without taking note of San Juan's? I do not see how scholarship can pronounce upon such a question, because poetry is read not according to a set of literary rules but to the pleasures of an individual. A poem has two extremes: the man who wrote it and the man who reads it. It can be appreciated from both angles. If one is trying to understand it in relationship to its creator, then obviously, everything that can be discovered about its background, genesis, development and intended purpose will be of value. In the case of San Juan, this means that the commentaries cannot be disregarded, however strange they appear to the twentieth-century mind.

But evaluation of the poem as successful or not does not depend on such facts. The analysis of the poem in Chapter 5 was concerned largely

<hr>

[56] *The Verbal Icon* (New York, 1958), p. 3.

with the text itself, as a work of art, not with any presumptions about how it may relate to the biography or literary theories of its author. If the poem is to be appreciated for its inherent beauty, the commentaries are not essential, and it may speak unhindered by its author's interpretations and be received fresh by the mind. For the truth is that those who become too familiar with these interpretations lose the sense of awe and wonder which is so precious a part of the poem. The images begin to submit to the explanations given by the commentaries, so that for flowers we start to read virtues, and so on. This reduction of the poetic symbols to ciphers in a more abstract language impoverishes the poem and saps its vitality. If the expositions of San Juan are constantly in the back of the reader's mind, then he reads the poem not as it was originally written but through San Juan's long years of reflecting upon it.

One may therefore draw a distinction between understanding the poem and appreciating it, though the two are related tasks. The author's intentions are important for the first, less so for the second. But it is only when both tasks are complete that the full picture can emerge. The author's intentions should not be summarily dismissed as of no significance, especially when the poet goes to such trouble to explain exactly what he thought he meant. Poets do not generally do this, and to ignore San Juan's attempts to extract the poem's significance is to risk not only serious misinterpretation but a very one-sided evaluation of the poem. Though at the two extremes, understanding and evaluating, the question of intentionalism may be answered fairly well, there is of course a whole area in between in which it is impossible to allow any theory to dictate response. Wimsatt mentions two problems which illustrate this well and are particularly pressing in the *Cántico*: revision and allusion. Of the first he writes: 'There is a sense in which an author, by revision, may better achieve his original intention. But it is a very abstract sense. He intended to write a better work . . . and now he has done it. But it follows that his former concrete intention was not his intention.'[57] This is too extreme a theory to account for the relationship between CA and CB. San Juan's intention remained the same once he had decided to expound the verses; what changed was the detail of the method used to fulfil that intention. The literary merits of poem and commentary can be appreciated without regard for their author's intention, but once they are given an intellectual content, in this case, teaching about the mystical journey, evaluation is impossible without taking account of the thought world in which the author moved and the teaching he wished to give.

The problem of allusions is acute in twentieth-century poetry, like that of Pound and Eliot, and Wimsatt continues by remarking that 'it has

[57] Ibid. p. 5.

become a kind of commonplace to assume that we do not know what a poet means unless we have traced him in his reading—a supposition redolent with intentional implications.'[58] In the case of San Juan, one may ask how much one would miss of his poetry without realizing that he borrows freely from the Song of Songs, and not only that, from the Song already interpreted in a mystical way. It is not, perhaps, necessary to know the exact source of every borrowed passage; but it is surely impossible to understand the poem fully without being aware of this tradition, and difficult to appreciate or judge exactly what San Juan has achieved in making this borrowed language his own and welding it to material from other sources of inspiration. One has at least a term of comparison: the source, and his treatment of it. And to see a poet working in this way is surely to gain insight into the creative power of his artistic imagination, without which any evaluation of his poetry will be incomplete.

This is perhaps a case where the mean between the extremes of intentionalism and anti-intentionalism is best. To rule out, on grounds of literary theory, anything which might contribute towards a fuller understanding and appreciation of a work of art is a misuse of theory, because it prescribes artificial limits to human responses. The *Cántico* remains a mystery until San Juan's intentions are known, but even then, the task is not over, nor would he wish it to be. Through his symbolic language and richness of imagery he enables the reader to enter his world and allow his own imagination to respond to it. By stressing that even the CB commentary cannot exhaust the whole meaning of the poem, he allows the reader to approach the treatise feeling that he too has something to give in the unravelling of the mystery.

Rather than asking whether people should read the poetry apart from the commentaries, one should endeavour to discover why it is that they can appreciate its beauty when they do not understand it as San Juan did. Likewise, instead of chastising those who read only the mystical treatise and care little for the poetry which inspired it, for failing to see the link between the two, one should try to see why they can still find guidance and truth in it. The answer in both cases is the same. The language of the poem and the content of the commentaries relate to the experience of people in a way which transcends any narrow definition. We do not need to understand the world of San Juan to be moved by a poem which sings of love, mountains, trees, and flowers, of rivers, music, scents, and night. The poem offers us these pictures and our minds reach out from our own storehouse of experience to catch them and unite them to our own perceptions. And in that moment, we begin to write, in the recesses of the mind, as San Juan did so long ago, our own, personal commentary on these beautiful words.

[58] Ibid. p. 14.

7

TOWARDS AN EVALUATION OF

SAN JUAN'S THEOLOGY

I

It is a common temptation to regard San Juan as a great poet but to treat the intellectual content of his prose works as obsolete. But it is also unwise. Just as human writing is limited by the forms and themes predominant in any age, so human thinking, in which theology has always played an important part, is tied to the conceptual system of its day. Even mysticism does not escape the process of cultural conditioning. The critic's task, which in the poetry has been to offer guidance for its comprehension and evaluation, is now to look behind the sixteenth-century manner of expressing ideas, to see how they may best be interpreted and appreciated today. Modern culture can be very cruel towards intellectual systems of previous ages, and is inclined to suppose that contemporary patterns of thought cannot be bettered. A humbler, more historical approach to man's searching after truth will show that ways of expression long outmoded may still yield valuable content today. Those willing to respond to the mysterious beauty of the *Cántico* seem unwilling to consider that behind its now mysterious concepts there may lie an unsuspected profundity of thought. The words chosen may be dictated by the literary or philosophical conventions of the age, but it is what San Juan has done with them, making them carriers of beauty and bearers of a message, that should be our chief concern. Through the processes we have studied, the *Cántico* poem led him to draw from it a theology of the mystical life. Though his theological system is best seen in the *Subida-Noche*, and its overriding insistence on the experience of dark nights, the spiritual marriage celebrated in the *Cántico* is equally characteristic of his doctrine, for it is after all the end towards which the years passed in the dark nights tend. In this chapter, therefore, certain philosophical and theological issues which arise directly out of the *Cántico* will be examined, illustrated from other texts where appropriate.[1]

Mysticism is a recurrent feature in human culture. Whatever one's attitude to it, it cannot be dismissed as unworthy of serious study.

[1] There have been many studies of San Juan's theology from a sixteenth-century viewpoint, among the more important being the works already referred to by P. Crisógono de Jesús, and Trueman Dicken', *The Crucible of Love*.

William James states that 'no account of the universe in its totality can be final which leaves these other forms of consciousness quite disregarded.'[2] It is not confined to Christianity; indeed, it has been much less influential in Western Christian thought than in the Christian East or the non-Christian Orient. Islam, Buddhism, Hinduism, Judaism and the many brands of Animism all have their mystics, and so did the dead religions of Egypt, Greece and Rome. The only exception appears to be Zoroastrianism.[3] Its most characteristic feature is an intensity of personal experience of and commitment to a state or being outside and beyond the confines of the self, leading to union with this transcendent power or being or God, or absorption into it.

But the looseness of the term is such that it can describe experiences of widely differing kinds. We must therefore discover what kind of mystic San Juan was, for to call him a mystic is no more than to describe Beethoven as a composer. Today, mysticism is associated with a whole range of things with which it has little to do: it is used almost synonymously for anything mysterious or supernatural, including miracles, astrology, and the whole realm of the occult. Not only would San Juan have failed to recognize them as such, he would have condemned them as cheap and dangerous substitutes leading men towards the demonic, not the divine. This debased modern usage ought to be discarded, and can have no place in this study.

While a study of the phenomenon of mysticism itself may produce valuable insights, the proper critical approach to the subject as an element in Christian religious thinking lies in systematic theology, for mysticism is then set alongside all other elements and evaluated according to its place in the whole theological system, rather than as an independent issue. The systematic theologian must establish the criteria by which the mystic's claims are tested and evaluated. He must, for example, weigh the claims of private revelation through mystical experience against those of objective historical revelation, and discover how far it represents an authentic Christian insight into the relationship between God and man.

The subject has received considerable attention from modern theologians. San Juan's theology will thus be probed through the keen eyes of two giants of twentieth-century systematic theology, Paul Tillich (1886–1965) and Karl Barth (1886–1968), both, as it happens, Protestants, yet each pursuing a distinctive theological attitude towards mysticism and representing in many ways opposite viewpoints.[4] Our

[2]   *Varieties of Religious Experience* (Gifford Lectures, 1901–2; London and Glasgow), p. 363.
[3]   See Zaehner, op. cit., p. xii.
[4]   Their major works, on which this study is based, are Tillich, *Systematic Theology*, 3 vols. (1951–63), combined volume (Welwyn, 1968); Barth, *Church Dogmatics*, 13 vols. (Edinburgh, 1939–69).

present concern, rather than being an examination of San Juan from within his neo-scholastic framework, is to penetrate beneath his sixteenth-century terminology and bring his thought to life for today. This method has the further advantage of viewing San Juan with some objectivity. Tillich and Barth bring their contrasting opinions to bear upon mysticism from a world historically, culturally, and theologically detached from that of San Juan, so that evaluation of his theology will be the more firmly based for it.

First, the place of mysticism itself within Christian theology must be clarified. James has proposed 'four marks which, when an experience has them, may justify us in calling it mystical'.[5] The first is ineffability: 'The subject of it immediately says that it defies expression, that no adequate report of its content can be given in words', something that we have already encountered in San Juan. The second is 'noetic quality'. Though they appear to be states of feeling, mystical experiences also communicate knowledge, 'states of insight into depths of truth un-plumbed by the discursive intellect'. CB 23.1 and 37.4 both describe knowledge of God beyond the ordinary powers of the intellect. The other marks, according to James, are common but less sharply defined. The third is transiency: the experience lasts but a short while. Here we may recall San Juan's teaching that even though the spiritual marriage once reached is in some sense permanent, it is also transient: the potential is there, but the union is not always consciously experienced (CB 26.11). Lower states are consistently short-lived, like the 'centella' of CB 25.5, a sudden flaring up of love. The final mark is passivity: 'the mystic feels as if his own will were in abeyance, and indeed some-times as if he were grasped and held by a superior power'. The fact that San Juan divides the dark nights into active and passive aspects suggests he knew this only too well. But passivity goes further. True contempla-tion can only be 'given' by God, and cannot be achieved through human effort—a theological distinction of considerable significance.

San Juan well exemplifies the marks James indicates as proper to mystical experience. As with any mystic, it is experience that counts first. Ideas, concepts, follow later. Each of these marks refers to experi-ence: the inability to communicate it, knowledge beyond the reach of thought, experience which is short-lived, and one which is given rather than sought. And the fundamental problem mysticism sets Christian theology lies in the relationship between the revelation which comes to the individual in such mystical states and the revelation handed down in Scripture and interpreted through the tradition of the Church. This partly explains the discomfort felt by ecclesiastical authorities in the presence of mystical movements, for these threaten the Church with a

---

[5]   Op. cit., pp. 366–8.

new revelation (often of a private, possibly esoteric kind) which may be at variance with the public testimony it gives of God's revelation to mankind. The early Church felt this keenly in the long struggle against the Gnostics, who set against the received tradition all sorts of private revelations, often of a fantastic nature, into which they called people to be intiated.[6] Through this struggle, the concept of the Church as the repository of revelation emerged. The Church was the guardian of Christ's teaching and the interpreter of Scripture, and any individual who claimed a revelation other than that which was open for all men to believe through the Church was judged to stand outside the faith once delivered to the saints. The struggle has never been absent in Christian history, and its results have been positive, since the Church has managed to free itself from extravagant and esoteric teachings.[7]

The tension between revelation through individual experience and that through tradition is peculiarly evident in mysticism, and, it may be added, in any mystical or allegorical exegesis of Scripture which owes more to individual fantasy than to textual interpretation, since this too tends towards subjectivism. Barth attacks mysticism because it cuts the ground away from the objectivity of historical revelation by proposing an alternative way of salvation in which men no longer need the historical witness of Scripture and tradition to the acts of God. Time after time in the *Church Dogmatics* he returns to the attack: 'In those who are called mystics, mysticism includes a technique and craft in virtue of which man thinks he can bring about union with God quite apart from the biblical history of salvation and the end'; and refers to 'the liturgico-sacramental, or privately cultivated mysticism which so quickly made its way as an alien body into Christianity'. He takes a classical mystical experience like that of Augustine and Monica at Ostia, and claims that 'however it may be with the reality and contents of this experience, it is certain that God is not reached by way of the image of such a timeless and non-objective seeing and hearing', for this means 'abandoning . . . the place where God encounters man in His revelation and where He gives himself to be heard and seen by man'.[8]

God has revealed himself, says Barth, through his historical acts, coming from outside man's situation to bring liberation. The mystic prefers to ignore history because he reaches out into the timeless, and the world where God has acted because he looks beyond creation to the Creator. The mystic moreover looks within himself, to his experience, as a bearer of revelation, which threatens the objectivity of God's acts and also his transcendence, his standing outside man. It is an insidious

[6]   The *Contra haereses* of Irenaeus is a good example of the struggle.

[7]   See Ozment, op. cit.; Nieto, 'Two Spanish mystics as submissive rebels', *BHR* 33 (1971), 63–77.

[8]   iii. 4, 59; iv. 4, 11; ii. 1, 11.

threat because mysticism does not appear anti-religious:[9]

The mystic insists upon interpreting everything that is taught and practised in any particular religion according to its inward and spiritual and vital meaning . . . The mystic will give prominence to the fact . . . that everything external is only a form and picture, that the transitory is only a parable, that its truth is only in relation to the inexpressible . . . The mystic will say the most dangerous things, e.g. about the secret identity of the within and the without, of the ego and God. But he will say them quite piously and always in connexion with a religious tradition which apparently asserts the opposite . . . He will claim freedom only for this interpretation of tradition, not freedom to supersede tradition . . . In his own way, he has a sincere affection for the whole system of external religion . . . because he needs it. It is the text for his interpretations. It is the material for his spiritualising. It is the external of which he has to show the inward meaning.

Tillich, on the other hand, stresses the positive function of mysticism, in conscious opposition to Barth. He does not regard it as the summit of Christian discipleship, but endows it with a distinctive theological function, as that which prevents man from elevating into his ultimate concern anything other than God. Authority and tradition in the Church can be so distorted that men focus their worship on them, not God. Mysticism conserves the essential mystery, and by pointing always to the infinite prevents men from identifying the finite with the transcendental. True, it runs the risk of making revelation irrelevant to the actual human situation and of removing its concrete character; but in spite of these recognized limitations, it does have a clear historical and theological function. Tillich also describes what he calls 'baptised mysticism', in which the mystic submits his experience to a Christian interpretation:[10]

If theologians paid more attention to the limits seen by the mystics themselves, they would have to give a more positive evaluation of this great tradition. One would then understand that there is something one could call 'baptised mysticism', in which the mystical experience depends on the appearance of the new reality and does not attempt to produce it.

Even Barth grudgingly admits that mysticism may not be wholly alien to Christian thinking, provided it is grounded in the person of Christ, as in Paul (Galatians 2:20): 'it is no longer I who live, but Christ who lives in me'. He writes: 'This will always be the language of a mysticism . . . which has a proper sense of proportion. The Christian does not claim the fulness of the union of God with man for his own experience and self-consciousness, but professes the other, the Mediator, in which it has taken place for him.'[11]

How does the theology of San Juan stand up to such criticism? When he refers to 'mystical theology' he has in mind not a systematic science like scholastic theology, but an experience. He addresses these revealing words to M. Ana de Jesús in the *Cántico* prologue: 'aunque a

V.R. le falte el ejercicio de teología escolástica con que se entienden las verdades divinas, no le falta el de la mística, que se sabe por amor en que, no solamente se saben, mas juntamente se gustan.'[12] Experiential theology here seems elevated above systematic, since it unites knowledge with feeling. In CB 39.12 mystical theology is defined as 'sabiduría de Dios secreta o escondida, en la cual ... a oscuras de todo lo sensitivo y natural, enseña Dios ocultísima y secretísimamente al alma sin ella saber cómo'.[13] In 37.4 he implies that scholastic and mystical theology are on a par since learned men discover the mysteries which holy men understand, which fits in with the teaching of many mystics that certain theological truths may be revealed in mystical states, even though afterwards they cannot be described.[14]

San Juan's insistence on solitude in his exposition of CB 35 might suggest that in mystical union the normal practices of the religious life can be bypassed, because the soul rises from the visible and inferior to the invisible and lofty:[15]

Y también es cosa conveniente que, pues el alma lo ha dejado todo y pasado por todos los medios, subiéndose sobre todo a Dios, que el mismo Dios sea la guía y el medio para sí mismo. Y habiéndose el alma ya subido en soledad de todo sobre todo, ya todo no le aproveche, ni sirve para más subir otra cosa que el mismo Verbo Esposo.

A thoroughgoing Barthian might wince at such words, since they seem to imply that a soul which has reached individual union with God no longer requires those aids needed by the less advanced on the road to salvation. If the Church possesses the true way to God, when the ultimate goal of union with him has been reached, the means it establishes to help reach this goal cease to be of value to the mystic. One can see why ecclesiastical authorities have sometimes taken such stern measures against cults of private spirituality: they threaten the institution. They claim to have reached the goal, while the rest must struggle along on the lower level aided through the normal channels of grace. The Church is bound to respond that all such experience, because of its extreme subjectivity, must be tested against the norms of historical revelation, which, in San Juan's terms, would mean the witness of Scripture and tradition preserved by the Church. Any mystical claim which failed this test must be judged heterodox.

Does the mystical way taught by San Juan bypass the objective historical revelation? Not according to him. He was a loyal son of the Church, obeying his superiors even when it hurt, as in the tribulations suffered at their hands towards the end of his life.[16] He took full part

---

[12] Peers, ii. 179.   [13] Ibid. 379.
[14] CB 23.1; Santa Teresa, *Las moradas*, vii. 7.
[15] Peers, ii. 357.
[16] See P. Crisógono's *Vida*, ch. 19 (BAC *Obras*, pp. 304–25).

in the monastic offices and was ardent in his attendance at and celebration of Mass. He submitted all his writings to the judgement of the Church, as he invariably states in his prologues (though one remembers Barth's word about the mystic protesting his orthodoxy while asserting a doctrine incompatible with it). Moreover, in S 2.27, dealing with the kinds of revelations the Church might well have feared, he declares that the truths of the faith have already been given, and that the mystic is enabled to appreciate them, rather than being inspired with new beliefs:[17]

Y aun acerca de los misterios de nuestra fe, suele Dios descubrir y declarar al espíritu las verdades dellos; anque esto no se llama propriamente revelación, por cuanto ya está revelado, antes es manifestación o declaración de lo ya revelado . . . si . . . en cuanto a lo que toca a nuestra fe se nos revelase algo de nuevo o cosa diferente, en ninguna manera habemos de dar el consentimiento . . . De donde, por cuanto no hay más artículos que revelar acerca de la sustancia de nuestra fe que los que ya están revelados a la Iglesia, no sólo no se ha de admitir lo que de nuevo se revelare al alma . . . sino que, cerrando el entendimiento a ellas, sencillamente se arrime a la doctrina de la Iglesia y su fe.

San Juan would have countered Barth's attack by pointing to such passages. He did not teach withdrawal from public acts of worship or from any of the obligations the Church lays on men. His spirituality was a complement—an intensely personal one—to the faith proclaimed from the pulpit and celebrated in the Mass. But the tension is implicit in his writing, for the solitude of mystical theology and active participation in community life do not easily coexist. If he had been forced to choose, would San Juan in the end have opted for the solitary road to God? So the dangers which Barth perceives lie in the implications of what San Juan teaches. But he never pursued them relentlessly, and would surely have shrunk back very quickly from making any remarks which compromised the Catholic faith he held so firmly. This is typical. He says things which appear to pull him in the direction of quietism or nihilism, but always stops in time. So we ought not to conclude that his mysticism is essentially alien to the objective historical revelation on which Christianity is grounded. He belongs rather to Tillich's company of baptised mystics. To condemn him for not always holding the two sides in balance—the expression of his mystical fervour and the corresponding need to retain the objective element—is not very fruitful. That is a peril all theologians face, since emphasizing one set of ideas will be interpreted by other theologians as undervaluing other sets. At least San Juan's mysticism, arising from his participation in a worshipping community, avoids the temptation of discounting the institutional, organized side of religion. The most serious accusation against him is that if some of his statements, taken in isolation, are stretched to their logical conclusion, they come perilously close to implying an individual

[17]   Peers, i. 192.

way to God which does not need at its higher levels the normal forms
of organized religion.

II

It is now time to look at particular areas of San Juan's theology, to
see how far this provisional conclusion is justified. At the heart of
philosophy lies the quest for truth through reason. Theology is concerned with the truth about God through reason and revelation. When
the claims of the mystic are examined, the two disciplines meet, and
questions arise like how the mystic knows his experiences to be true,
and how they can meaningfully be expressed. James draws three
important conclusions about the truth of mystical claims:[18]

(1) Mystical states, when well developed, usually are, and have the right to be,
absolutely authoritative over the individuals to whom they come.

(2) No authority emanates from them which should make it a duty for those
who stand outside of them to accept their revelations uncritically.

(3) They break down the authority of the non-mystical or rationalistic consciousness, based upon the understanding and the senses alone. They show it to be only
one kind of consciouness. They open out the possibility of other orders of truth,
in which, so far as anything in us vitally responds to them, we may freely continue
to have faith.

The first applies to San Juan only after he has analysed the mystical
states. 'Esto creo no lo acabará bien de entender el que no lo hubiere
experimentado', he writes in CB 7.10.[19] Such assertions are common in
mystical literature. But not every experience is self-authenticating for
San Juan. He devotes many chapters of the *Subida-Noche* to various
kinds of revelations, many of which come from the devil, and very few
of which carry the certainty that they are of God. So while there is no
doubting that such experiences occur, as a theologian San Juan grapples
with their interpretation and only then pronounces upon their validity.
Unless they come from God, they carry no authority at all, and are to
be shunned.

James's second conclusion introduces the problem of validating
mystical experiences—how do we know they are true? San Juan's
epistemology derives from his Thomist training. Knowledge is not innate,
but conveyed through the senses to the mind, which can then form
concepts. But this works only for natural knowledge, and it is supernatural knowledge the mystic claims to possess. This can only be given
from its source, God, given, not already innate, as a Platonist might
have held. The individual cannot save himself by turning within himself
to discover what he knows naturally but is too blinded by the body's
passions to see. He has to be saved from beyond himself, by the gift of

---

[18] Op. cit., p. 407.   [19] Peers, ii. 218.

God. This squares with mainstream Christian thinking throughout the centuries, that the initiative in salvation lies with God, and helps us to appreciate that San Juan does not fall into the trap of an entirely subjective religion.

By what criteria, then, can we judge claims to possess supernatural knowledge, given that it cannot be tested through normal objective means, empirically? The temptation is to say that we cannot, that such claims ought not to be admitted. San Juan does not try to skate around the problem, but tackles it from another direction. No created thing can do justice to the being of God or serve as a means of reaching union with him (S 2.12.4, CB 26.4, 30.1, 39.2 ff.). The soul must therefore be purged of all knowledge naturally acquired which might hinder union; and the new knowledge she gains from God as she does so is so pure that it cannot be expressed:[20]

Cuando ésta sabiduría de amor purga el alma, es secreta para no saber decir de ella el alma nada ... que, demás de que ninguna gana le dé al alma de decirla, no halla modo ni manera ni símil que le cuadre para poder significar inteligencia tan subida y sentimiento espiritual tan delicado; y ansí, aunque más gana tuviese de decirlo y más significaciones truxese, siempre se quedaría secreto y por decir, porque, como aquella sabiduría interior es tan sencilla y tan general y espiritual, que no entró al entendimiento envuelta ni paliada [con] alguna especie o imagen sujeta al sentido, de aquí es que el sentido e imaginativa, como no entró por ellas ni sintieron su traje y color, no saben dar razón ni imaginarla para decir algo della; aunque claramente ve que entiende y gusta aquella sabrosa y peregrina sabiduría ... Porque esto tiene el lenguaje de Dios, que, por ser muy íntimo al alma y espiritual, en que excede todo sentido, luego hace cesar y enmudecer toda la armonía y habilidad de los sentidos exteriores y interiores.

This important passage shows San Juan at work trying to understand why language breaks down as a communicator of the truth of mystical experience. The philosophical problem remains, in that no objective solution to verifying claims is found; but it is at least tempered by the fact that San Juan gives a careful account of why this is not possible.

Tillich has remarked that 'the subject-object cleavage underlies language ... no language is possible without the subject-object cleavage and that language is continuously brought to self-defeat by this very cleavage'. The experience of mystical union is precisely the one in which this distinction is obliterated, because the subject, the soul, is one with its object, God. Tillich goes on 'Language, under such impact, is beyond poverty and abundance. A few words become great words! This is the ever repeated experience ... with ... holy literature.'[21] The *Cántico* celebrates that union of subject and object of which Tillich speaks, but in a language which has to be different from the logical or analytical kind, which is too firmly wedded to the differentiation of

[20] N 2.17.3; Peers, i. 428–9.   [21] iii. 269–70.

subject and object. Perhaps this point needs to be appreciated more in the study of literature inspired by the experience of the holy. San Juan's 'Esto tiene el lenguaje de Dios' and Tillich's 'A few words become great words' witness, remarkably, across centuries of great cultural change, to the same conclusion about language when its content is greater than words can tell.

We seem to have reached an impasse. San Juan has explained why supernatural knowledge creates a problem of communication, and why words are inadequate to express truth about God as one might about things. Convincing or not, his claim to know the truth through mystical experience cannot simply be accepted. It cannot be judged—that much is evident—as natural experience is judged. Is there any other criterion?

The only one which can test the worth of the claim is the empirical criterion of its fruits. This is not a philosophical solution, for knowing the effects of something and not its cause does not mean that its cause thereby can be verified. But at least it has a practical bearing; and it is a test frequently used by San Juan. You know whether a mystical experience comes from God by its effects on your subsequent behaviour. If it is from him, your life will more closely follow his will. If not, then it will leave no good effects in the soul, cause no spiritual growth, but rather lead to disturbance and sin. The kind of distinction drawn in S 2.11.6, referring to corporeal visions, is valid throughout the spiritual life:[22]

También las que son de parte del demonio (sin que el alma las quiera) causan en ella alboroto o sequedad, o vanidad o presunción en el espíritu; aunque éstas no son de tanta eficacia en el alma como las de Dios en el bien; porque las del demonio sólo pueden poner primeros movimientos en la voluntad—y no moverla a más si ella no quiere—y alguna inquietud, que no dura mucho si el poco ánimo y recato del alma no da causa que dure; mas las que son de Dios penetran el alma y mueven la voluntad a amar, y dejan su efecto, al cual no puede el alma resistir.

San Juan thus chooses a very practical test for mystical experience, and proves thoroughgoing in applying it. There is no question of indulging in such experiences for their own sake. James comments that the fruits of such experiences may be bad in those with naturally passive spirits and feeble intellects, 'but in natively strong minds and characters we find quite opposite results. The great Spanish mystics, who carried the habit of ecstasy as far as it has often been carried, appear . . . to have showed indomitable spirit and energy, and all the more so for the trances in which they indulged.'[23] Santa Teresa is the prime example; but San Juan is not far behind.

There is however an important rider to add to this question of determining the truth of such experiences. It is that none of the

attributes of the mystical life popularly believed to be of its essence—
trances, locutions, visions, raptures, ecstasies—are either sought or
recommended by San Juan. There is an intense purity about his teaching
here. His watchword is 'siempre negarlas' (S 2.16.10), always negate
them. Though some may be given by God, it is safer to ignore them
because the devil practises so much deception in such states, and they
can hinder union:[24]

De todas estas aprehensiones y visiones imaginarias y otras cualesquiera formas o
especies . . . ahora sean falsas de parte del demonio, ahora se conozcan ser
verdaderas de parte de Dios—el entendimiento no se ha de embarazar ni cebar en
ellas, ni las ha el alma de querer admitir ni tener, para poder estar desasida,
desnuda, pura, sencilla, sin algún modo y manera, como se requiere para la unión.

No such visions (here is the theological reasoning) can be a means
towards union, because they are other than God, and God alone is the
ground of union. This is a far cry from modern notions of what con-
situtes mysticism, yet it is a vital part of San Juan's teaching and a
notable contribution to the theology of mysticism. It may have been
said before, but never so forcefully, so comprehensively. He allays the
fears of those who align mysticism with magic, and suggests that such
experiences occur only because human flesh is too frail to bear the
naked reality of God's truth and reacts in this way (S 2.21.2). God
permits this to happen because it is all part of the process of purgation,
by which the faculties of men are perfected (2.17). These chapters
(10–32) of the second book of the *Subida* work out in great detail for
every aspect of the spiritual life the principles enunciated by San Juan,
and no one who has not read them can appreicate how acute his theological penetration is here. Had he been writing in the twentieth
century, he might have wanted to say that many of the supernatural
experiences men claim belong more properly to the realm of psychoso-
matics than to mystical theology. In the last resort, most of them may
be discounted, because they are potentially dangerous. They occur, but
do not need to be verified, because they are to be negated. All that
counts is the ultimate mystery, God. That is where the problem of
knowledge in San Juan really leads us: to the question of the reality of
God. If it is denied, then San Juan's whole system is undermined. If it is
accepted, then the bounds of philosophical reasoning, though the truths
this establishes will have been gratefully received, have already been
passed.

In the spiritual marriage, however, there can be no deception caused
by human weakness or demonic interference, so the problem of knowledge reasserts itself at the end of the journey. Again, one can only point
to the fruits. The achievement of men and women like San Juan and

[24] S 2.16.6; Peers, i. 124–5.

Santa Teresa, considered simply as shapers of history, was enormous. They did not withdraw from human commerce but involved themselves in it and, with others they inspired, sought to improve man's lot. They avoided the excesses of extreme asceticism or an unbalanced attitude to the problems of life. And perhaps in this contribution to the spiritual lives of people then and ever since, and in the literature they produced which continues to delight, the quest for ascertaining the truth of what they experienced and taught finds a partial (though not a philosophical) answer.

III

The next problem is properly theological, and may be described as the question of negation and affirmation, involving San Juan's attitudes towards creation and the relationship of body and soul in man. The idea that God cannot be known positively through his attributes but only by negating them reveals a theology intensely aware of the transcendence of God, of a metaphysical gulf between God and his world so great that no human language can capture his being in definitions. Although San Juan is influenced by pseudo-Dionysius, this part of his teaching is not greatly to the fore. San Juan gives little attention to the problem of how if at all we may know God through his attributes, and when we speak of negation in San Juan's system, it means the negation of all created things as man rises towards the uncreated God.

According to Christian theology, there is a metaphysical gulf between God the Creator and everything he has made. God is other than that which he has created, and there is no comparison possible between them. He is utterly transcendent, above, beyond creation. But while God and the creatures are completely distinct in essence, there is nonetheless a relationship between them, since God created them and without him they could not exist, an ontological dependence best brought out in S 2.5.3: 'Y esta manera de unión siempre está hecha entre Dios y las criaturas todas, en la cual les está conservando el ser que tienen; de manera que, si . . . desta manera faltase, luego se aniquilarían y dejarían der ser.'[25]

Christian theology also affirms the essential goodness of God's creation. But there exists another gulf between God and man here—a moral one. For this relationship has been distorted by human sin, and man is estranged from God. Creation, once the paradise where he walked in harmony with God (Genesis 2:5—25), has rebelled, become a harsh wilderness for him (3:16—19). Sin has permeated mankind and creation has suffered its consequences. With San Juan, the emphasis on both the metaphysical and moral gulfs between God and man could be interpreted

[25] Peers, i. 75.

as too negative an outlook on man and creation. The *Cántico* commentary begins with a sombre warning of the brevity of life, the uncertainty of the times, the ease of perdition, the difficulty of salvation, the vanity of human existence.

Underlying his attitude to fallen man is his account of the relationship between body and soul. We should note that 'alma' has a wider meaning for him than that conveyed by our 'soul': he means by it something like 'the whole inner life of man'. And he confuses us even more when he refers to 'el fondo' or 'la sustancia del alma'. This indicates the locus of union, and raises the question of what this centre is supposed to be, for it does not normally appear in the anatomy of the human soul. San Juan seems to be moving into metaphorical language, rather than analytical, trying to suggest that union has been experienced in the innermost depths of his being. Certain medieval mystics use similar expressions, notably Eckhart with his 'Fünklein' or 'Grund' of the soul, Ruysbroeck's 'inmost part of his spirit' and Tauler's 'fundus animae'; and it is interesting to note it reappearing, via San Juan, in William Law's *The Spirit of Prayer.*[26]

In spite of his predominant Thomism, San Juan tends towards the popular Platonic view of a soul sharply distinguished from the body and as if imprisoned by it: 'ella está en el cuerpo como un gran señor en la cárcel, sujeto a mil miserias'.[27] She belongs, moreover, more to the object of her love—God—than to the body in which she is imprisoned (CB 8.3). It is remarks like these which raise the problem of negation and affirmation. Does San Juan adequately affirm the goodness of creation? And if so, why is the soul encouraged to purge herself of all created things, as if they were a hindrance? Ought he to draw so sharp a distinction between body and soul, as if to imply that the flesh is incurably weak? What account does he give of the doctrine of the Incarnation, in which the Word was made flesh? Are there grounds for believing that his negation of all created things 'would, if rigorously carried out, sweep away, not only the grosser business of the flesh, but all art and music and literature, all the expansions of grace and beauty'?[28]

It must be admitted that San Juan's view of negation is out of line with contemporary views of the problem. As part of creation, man, body and soul, is made good, in the image of God, though this is obscured by the Fall. His desires are not to be thought of as incurably sinful, though often they are so misdirected that he abandons the will of God. As a matter of fact San Juan does not teach that the body itself and its natural appetites are in themselves sinful. It is the will which

---

[26]   In *Select Mystical Writings of William Law,* ed. Hobhouse (London, 1948), p. 81. Law possessed a copy of the *Subida.*

[27]   CB 18.1; Peers, ii. 273. Contrast Aquinas, *Summa* la.12, 84.5.

[28]   More, *Christian Mysticism* (London, 1932), p. 62.

sins and perverts these desires to wrong ends. Sin is therefore spiritual in origin, and it should not be thought that San Juan taught that matter itself is evil. By and large, however, modern theologians find it hard to accept that the right road to God is one which negates so much of what it means to be a human being. God has revealed himself, become incarnate, in the material world, where men can see and touch him. The message of the Incarnation is unequivocal: involvement in the life of the world, not withdrawal from its temptations, is the way of Christ and the calling of the Christian. Modern theology rightly disputes the notion that men were given bodies only to deny them, for they have to make sense of the given material of time and history. In San Juan's teaching, divine union takes place only in the depths of the soul and does not engage the rest of a man's being, which must, by implication, be cast away.

Barth attacks the whole idea of negation on the grounds that it is an advanced form of self-centredness:[29]

Before God man is not nothing, but something, someone. God is far from finding pleasure in the nothingness of men as such . . . We do not have here a directive to mystical self-emptying, to entrance into the night of quiescence, of silence, of an artificial anticipation of death . . . There is nothing, nothing at all, to justify the belief that God has created us for the practice of this self-emptying, or that it has to be recognised and adopted as the way to reconciliation with God . . . Christian faith is the day whose dawning means the end of the mystical night.

Such statements as 'todo el ser de las criaturas, comparado con el infinito ser de Dios, nada es . . . el alma . . . es nada y menos que nada' would hardly endear San Juan to Barth.[30] That he is thinking of San Juan becomes evident in another passage:[31]

In a purely formal sense no one, not even a Spanish mystic, has ever really looked away from himself and beyond himself, let alone transcended himself in a purely formal negation. If we try to do this . . . we are really looking quite cheerfully at ourselves again, however solemnly we may pretend that it is otherwise. What we see is only our own frontier, and we see this only from within. The look away and beyond ourselves can take place from and beyond ourselves can take place only when it has an object which irresistibly draws it; when it is a look which has a definite content; when this beyond is not nothing but something or someone.

These quotations give eloquent testimony to the Christian view of the dignity of man before God. But Barth's insistence that negation is trapped within the self is more questionable. There is a sense in which we are never free of self, nor ought we to be, since it is given us by God. Our quest for him moves within this limitation. What changes, in the Christian ethic, is that energy is redirected, away from the self towards others and the Other. There is a strong prima-facie case for regarding San Juan as true to this principle. The purging of the self is not an end

[29] iv. 1, 628–9.   [30] S 1.4.4.; Peers, i. 25.   [31] iv. 2, 284.

in itself, but the means to freedom from whatever constrains us to be selfish. Although San Juan may use symbols of darkness and nothing to describe where that freedom lies, he is always looking towards God, and if he chooses to use such language it must not be pressed too literally, but taken as the paradox it is: an elaborate way of asserting that God is other than us, that our words about him, however fine, only gaze through a glass darkly. The 'beyond' for San Juan is not nothing, but someone, mysterious, compelling, the true end of created man.

Barth has made the mistake of treating 'nothing' literally. There is a long tradition against which its meaning should be measured, as in the doctrine that God created the world *ex nihilo*. As Copleston points out, this is an ambiguous expression.[32] It might mean 'not created at all', but Aquinas says that this is not the customary meaning. Its intention is to affirm, not to deny creation, and its true meaning is 'not out of anything', not out of any pre-existent material. San Juan's 'nada' is a hyperbolic expression intended to drive home the metaphysical gulf between God and his creation. It does not mean the absence of a 'definite content', 'something or someone', but the presence of one whose being is such that it dwarfs all others.

Certain facts, then, begin to mitigate too severe a judgement on San Juan's theology of negation. It is couched in the language of ambiguity and paradox which tradition handed down to him. Moreover, it is not creation itself which man must negate, but the distortion introduced into it by the Fall and human sin. San Juan does not have a pessimistic view of created being in itself and cannot be considered a dualist. He may more justly be criticized for his pessimistic view of man and creation under sin. But though his is a very radical view of sin, it is still derived from Christian tradition, in this case Augustinian rather than Thomist; and if it is to be criticized, then this has to be borne in mind.

San Juan does not teach the negation of the body alone, either. The soul must also be purged, the night of the senses completed by that of the spirit. In fact, temptations on the spiritual level are far more insidious than those which affect the body, because man thinks he is progressing upward. San Juan devotes a large part of the *Subida-Noche* to the night of the spirit, in which each aspect of man's spiritual life is ruthlessly examined, its temptations and imperfections exposed, reformed. Prayer and high mystical experiences are not exempt, because the higher one goes, the further there is to fall. The tremendous purity of San Juan's doctrine again confronts us: nothing less than God, no visions, no ecstasies, can be worthy of worship.

Above all, the end of San Juan's teaching involves a revaluation, not a negation, of creation. The soul which reaches the spiritual marriage

---

[32] *Aquinas* (Harmondsworth, 1955), pp. 141–2.

looks out with new eyes on the created world. This is most beautifully expressed in L 4.4–7, and some of this must be quoted, to redress
the balance:[33]

Le parece al alma que todos los bálsamos y especias odoríferas y flores del mundo
se trabucan y menean, revolviéndose para dar su suavidad, y que todos los reinos y
señoríos del mundo y todas las potestades y virtudes del cielo se mueven; y no sólo
eso, sino que también todas las virtudes y sustancias y perfecciones y gracias de
todas las cosas criadas relucen y hacen el mismo movimiento, todo a una y en uno
. . . Acá no sólo parecen moverse, sino que también todos descubren las bellezas
de su ser, virtud y hermosura y gracias, y la raíz de su duración y vida; porque
echa allí der ver el alma como todas las criaturas de abajo tienen su vida y duración
y fuerza en él . . . Y, aunque es verdad que echa allí de ver el alma que estas cosas
son distintas de Dios en cuanto tienen ser criado, y las ve en El con su fuerza, raíz
y vigor, es tanto lo que conoce ser Dios en su ser con infinita inminencia todas
estas cosas, que las conoce mejor en su ser que en ellas mismas. Y éste es el deleite
grande de este recuerdo: conocer por Dios las criaturas, y no por las criaturas a
Dios; que es conocer los efectos por su causa y no la causa por los efectos.

Maritain, commenting on the mystics' 'contempt for the creatures', has
described this as 'a rehabilitation of the creatures in God':[34]

It is a loving contempt of all things other than the beloved. And the more he
despises creatures in the degree to which they might be rivals of God, or objects
of a possible choice to the exclusion of God, the more he cherishes them as loved
by God, and made by Him as fair and worthy of our love. For to love a being in
and for God is not to treat them as a mere means or a mere occasion for loving
God, but to love and cherish their being as an end, because it *merits* love, in the
degree to which that merit and their dignity spring from the sovereign love and
the sovereign loving-kindness of God.

In an unexpected way, this is borne out by the poetry. A man who
truly despised all creation could hardly have written the *Cántico*, in
which created beauty plays so important a part. And this theological
movement towards a revaluation of the creatures also illuminates the
poem. In CA 3–5 the Lover hastens across creation, but the Beloved
has already passed that way: the poetic equivalent of 'conocer por las
criaturas a Dios', a limited knowledge, passed over swiftly. In 13–14
natural beauty is a symbol of all the Beloved is: San Juan is not identifying him in a pantheistic way with creation, but singing in poetry the
sheer beauty of God. 35–6 reaches knowledge of the creatures through
God: 'vámonos a uer *en tu hermosura*'. He does not recapitulate all the
images used before to show how they are now seen through the eyes of
one who has first experienced the beauty of God; he takes a few and
adds some more, to suggest through that wonderful poetic sensibility of
his the revaluation of the created order:

---

[33] Peers, iii. 188–9.
[34] *True Humanism,* trans. Adamson, pp. 65–6; but taken from his earlier *The
Degrees of Knowledge* (London, 1937).

> Gocémonos, Amado,
> y vámonos a uer en tu hermosura
> al monte u al collado,
> do mana el agua pura;
> entremos más adentro en la espesura.

Here, with the 'subidas cauernas de la piedra' and the mosto de granadas' of the following stanza, poetry and theology are indissolubly joined.

IV

A further theological problem concerns the relationship of the self and God. Mystics speak of union between them; Christian theology maintains an eternal distinction. Does San Juan compromise this doctrine? Some Eastern religions teach the dissolution of the self in divine union, monism as opposed to theism. Passages in San Juan could be taken to imply this, and we need to determine whether or not he strays from the orthodox view.

The commentary on the last few stanzas of the *Cántico* often refers to transformation or participation in God, and it is the meaning attached to such statements which lies at the heart of this problem. The eternal distinction between God and the creatures is maintained by San Juan, as we have seen.[35] But there is another important principle enunciated, concerning love, which also regulates the theology of union, that love brings about a likeness between the lover and the loved (as in S 1.4.3). The tension between these two principles, the first creating a separation, the second a joining together, is not hard to see.

The following passages contain the important statements of the theme of participation and transformation in the *Cántico*, and they must be set together in this way because they would be misleading in isolation:

CB 26.4: El mismo Dios es el que se le comunica con admirable gloria [de] transformación de ella en El, estando ambos en uno, como si dijéramos ahora: la vidriera con el rayo del sol o el carbón con el fuego, o la luz de las estrellas con la del sol; no, empero, tan esencial y acabadamente como en la otra vida.

31.1: Con tanta fuerza ase a los dos, es a saber, a Dios y al alma, este hilo de amor, que los junta y los transforma y hace uno por amor, de manera que, aunque en sustancia son diferentes, en gloria y parecer el alma parece Dios, y Dios el alma.

31.2: Que con la omnipotencia de su abisal amor absorbe al alma en sí con más eficacia y fuerza que un torrente de fuego a una gota de rocío de la mañana.

39.3: Porque no sería verdadera y total transformación si no se transformase el alma en las tres Personas de la Santísima Trinidad en revelado y manifiesto grado.

39.4: En que el alma se hace deiforme y Dios por participación.

39.6: De donde las almas esos mismos bienes poseen por participación que El por

---

[35] See above, pp. 157–9.

naturaleza; por lo cual verdaderamente son dioses por participación, iguales y compañeros suyos de Dios.

39.9: En esta unión el alma jubila y alaba a Dios con el mismo Dios.

39.14: La llama . . . que consume y transforme el alma en Dios . . . Lo cual no puede ser sino en el estado beatífico . . . porque en la transformación de el alma en ella hay conformidad y satisfacción beatífica de ambas partes . . . lo cual acaece en el alma que en esta vida está transformada con perfección de amor, que aunque hay conformidad, todavía padece alguna manera de pena y detrimento.[36]

This evidence suggests four conclusions:

(i) San Juan is not afraid to use terms like transformation, absorption and participation. Some of his expressions seem very bold, with possible pantheistic interpretations, and the soul exalted to divinity.

(ii) Whatever union is achieved in this life, it is but an imperfect shadow of the beatific vision, where it is experienced fully.

(iii) Traditional images are used to describe the union: the sun's ray shining through glass, coal and fire, starlight and sunlight, dew burned up by fire. If pressed too literally they have dangerous implications: More attacks them because they suggest annihilation of the soul.[37] Dew, for example, is burned away; yet it represents the soul.

(iv) San Juan distinguishes the soul's substance from God's, and places likeness or oneness at another level. But he does not always state this explicitly, and when he does not, his remarks could be given a pantheistic construction.

But to draw heterodox conclusions would be unwise. In the first place, since union is experienced in all its glory only after death, it is the doctrine of union in the beatific vision which presents the greatest theological difficulty—a union which San Juan does not attempt to describe. Some of the terms, moreover, properly understood, are acceptable: transformation and participation need not imply loss of identity, but a sharing of the divine glory as realization of the created potential of the soul. Others, more poetic, can be appreciated as long as no attempt is made to interpret bold figures of speech literally. The statement that God and the soul are different in substance is an important safeguard against which San Juan's less qualified remarks may be tested. But it cannot be denied that statements which in effect call the soul God ('el alma se hace deiforme y Dios por participación', 'dioses por participación, iguales y compañeros suyos de Dios') tread dangerous ground for the Christian theologian. They introduce the suspicion of pantheism, and one may fairly conclude that he would have been wiser to qualify them; though those who appreciate his full theological

---

[36] Peers, ii. 313; 339; 374–6; 378; 380–1.
[37] Op. cit., pp. 53–5.

system and the tradition from which it sprang can argue strongly that such statements must always be interpreted in the light of the fundamental distinction in substance between Creator and creature.

Certain clues confirm this view. The *Subida-Noche* is much more cautious in its language; the *Llama* contains remarks as potentially hazardous as those in the *Cántico*. The reason is that the former is a systematic theology of the whole of the spiritual life, and almost free of the constraint of expounding poetic images, so that its system develops according to the demands of theology, not imagery, and it is more guarded. The latter are works which reach out to the highest point of union a man can reach in this life, which foreshadows the glory to come, and in which language is strained to its limits. Moreover, San Juan was not writing for publication, but for uneducated nuns. These clues support the view that the theology of the *Cántico* and *Llama* ought, where necessary, to be interpreted in the light of the systematic principles laid down in the *Subida-Noche*. To latch on to apparently dangerous statements and see veiled heresy in them is not to give due respect to San Juan the theologian. They must be measured by what we know of his theology as a whole.

Further, rather than criticizing such statements, we should ask what drove San Juan to make them. We have seen how his apparent devaluation of the created order needs to be understood through his intense awareness of the holy and transcendent God. Likewise, these apparent assertions of the soul's oneness with God stem from another focus of mystical experience, of equal intensity: that of the intimate relationship between them in union. This is sound Christian orthodoxy. Though transcendent, God is also personal, and has established the possibility of a deep relationship of love between himself and the individual. Such an experience drives the mystic who attempts to express it into a bold language in which love raises and binds him into union with God. He is driven to proclaim this even though it is in tension with the infinite distance between God and his creation, because he has experienced both moments of insight, celebrating in one breath the unreachable mystery of God, and in the next the closest sharing of the divine love. There is no reconciliation possible or necessary: these are the two extremes of the Christian experience of God, transcendence and immanence, and the mystic is profoundly aware of both.

V

The experience of a union of love needs further elucidation. Is the love behind the mystical drive of San Juan a love for reward, and thus in the end selfish and grasping (*eros*), or is it pure and disinterested self-giving (*agape*)? An absolute distinction between the two kinds of love is maintained by Barth and by Nygren, who according to D'Arcy 'wished to sweep away all vestiges of Greek and Scholastic thought on love from the Christian idea of Agape. He maintained that self-centred love had crept into Christian thinking, been baptized by St. Augustine and as a result had contaminated medieval thought'.[38] Barth makes a very powerful statement of this distinction, and aims his remarks once more at mysticism. *Agape* gives itself away to the other person, joyfully; *eros* 'may even reach out to the Godhead in its purest form and thus be a most wonderful love of God. But in all its forms it will always be a grasping, taking, possessive love—self-love—and . . . it will always betray itself as such'.[39]

Tillich's view, simply, is that *agape* involves not only the love of God for his creatures but also the love of the creature towards God, which is bound to involve some element of desire, even self-interest. Love must at least include the will to unite, or there could be no piercing of the wall of separation between man and God. *Agape*, as Paul teaches in 1 Corinthians 13, is greater than all, because it unites the various kinds of love, overcomes their shortcomings, and transforms them. Man's love for God is therefore bound to contain elements of *eros* and cannot be entirely without hope of reward. This does not however invalidate it. D'Arcy's conclusion, considering San Juan's 'equality of love' teaching, is: 'In this Agape all that Nygren demanded is present. God is all in all, and there is no trace of that kind of self-love which interferes with perfect love. But self is there, the self and the intellect, for it is God who loves them and gives them both increase.'[40] CB 38.5 illustrates this: the soul is not looking to the glory God will give her, 'sino darse ella a El [en] entrega de verdadero amor sin algún respeto de su provecho'.[41]

Clearly the soul desires God in San Juan's teaching. The poem itself bears witness to this in lines like 'Acaba de entregarte ya de vero', 'Apaga mis enojos . . . véante mis ojos', 'Si formases de repente', and all the aspirations of the last five stanzas. But is this as selfish as Barth and Nygren maintain? The one theological point they neglect is that if man is made in the image of God, it ought to be natural for him to desire God, his true end. And how can a man give his self to God, when that self, compared with God's infinite glory, is so poor and blind? At this point Christian doctrine has always proclaimed the worth and dignity of man in the sight of God. If that were not so, God would not have troubled to enter the created order as the Incarnate Son, to restore and liberate it. Man is therefore something, not nothing, to God, and no mystical encounter would be possible if he were not precious in God's sight. Therefore man has something to give God in response to his gift of

---

[38] *The Mind and Heart of Love* (London, 1954), p. 11; referring to Nygren's *Agape and Eros*, trans. Watson (London, 1953).
[39] iv. 2, 734–5.   [40] Op. cit., p. 344.   [41] Peers, ii. 371.

salvation: a man can give himself, his love. In one sense this love is not needed by God, who is All in and to himself; but in another sense, he wants it, for man is his creature, made to love God, not to be in rebellion against him. If there is desire to possess and enjoy God, it is because man has been made for that purpose. San Juan avoids the trap of glorifying self-love as mystical love by his teaching on 'igualdad de amor'.[42]

As usual, he has a principle in mind: 'la propriedad del amor es igualar al que ama con la cosa amada'.[43] 'Igualar' will mislead us if we think of it as meaning 'making equal in being with'; we should rather understand it as 'removing the distance between'. The teaching, outlined in CB 32.6, states that God loves with Love itself, nothing less. He cannot love anything less than he loves himself, so that what he loves, he loves as himself. He loves the soul in grace not only for himself, but for itself too, and this love grows as the soul grows in beauty. CB 38.3 provides the greatest statement of this theme:[44]

> Esta pretensión del alma es la igualdad de amor con Dios . . . porque el amante no puede estar satisfecho si no siente que ama cuanto es amado; y como el alma ve que con la transformación que tiene en Dios en esta vida, aunque es inmenso el amor, no puede llegar a igualar con la perfección de amor con que de Dios es amada, desea la clara transformación de gloria, en que llegará a igualar con el dicho amor . . . así entonces le amará también como es amada de Dios . . . que le ama tan fuerte y perfectamente como de El es amada, estando las dos voluntades unidas en una sola voluntad y un solo amor de Dios.

'Igualdad de amor', therefore, is not possible in this life, and was experienced only in foretaste by San Juan, so that it belongs to speculative rather than dogmatic theology. It does not suggest equality of being, and cannot be taken to support the idea that San Juan, like so many Eastern mystics, imagined that the soul merged into the being of the One after death. He is talking about equality of love. Whether beings who are not equal can share an equal love is not a question he asks, though More, discussing Ruysbroeck's union in love, doubts whether the distinction made between union of love and of essence 'is anything more than a verbal precaution and has any practical validity'.[45] Yet equality of love is only possible because the love experienced by the soul is the Holy Spirit dwelling there (Romans 5:5), the bond of love in the Trinity, and it is the sharing of this love which leads to 'igualdad', as San Juan makes plain in CB 39.3–4, 14. Thus, when the mystic's will matches God's, he is sharing in the very love of the Godhead, willing only what God wills and returning to him the love which God has given to indwell within him.

---

[42] See Juan de Jesús María, ' "Le amará tanto como es amada" . . .', EC 6 (1955), 3–103; and Miguel Angel de Santa Teresa, 'La "reentrega" de amor así en la tierra como en el cielo', EC 13 (1962), 299–352.

[43] CB 28.1; Peers, ii. 323.   [44] Peers, ii. 369–70.   [45] Op. cit., p. 50.

A possible danger in such teaching is that it might imply that God is obliged to love the soul as he loves himself. Barth strongly attacked Angelus Silesius, the seventeenth-century mystical poet, for reducing God in this way, by teaching that God cannot be without the soul who loves him, and that he owes it as much as it owes him. Barth protests that this is to make God into our debtor; and he further claims that there must be no hint of impatience, 'either on the part of God or the soul, to possess the desired object'.[46] Images suggesting such impatience are common enough in mystical writers: Meister Eckhart pictures God as lying in wait for us with love as the fisherman hooks the fish.[47] San Juan's *Canciones a lo divino* 'Tras de un amoroso lance', with its refrain 'Que le di a la caza alcance', use the image of hunting to describe the soul's quest for God; and in CB 33.7 God is depicted as falling in love with the soul more and more, as if anything were lacking in his love from the outset. Once more, perhaps, poetic hyperbole wrests control from theological caution.

In spite of this, the doctrine of 'igualdad de amor', for all its short-comings and for all the boldness of speech which lays it open to mis-interpretation, helps to resolve the dilemma of Christian love in its mystical outreaching. If San Juan is to be believed, there is no difference in kind between the soul's love for God and his for it, because the wills are united in the shared love of the Holy Spirit. Therefore, the love experienced by the soul must be the fullest and most perfect *agape*, the very love of God. It may be that on the journey, the love of the mystic contains elements of grasping and desiring to possess; but this does not necessarily mean self-love. The real question is whether or not God is the end desired (which would fulfil man's created destiny), or simply the rediscovery of the self. If the element of desire in man's love for God is to be abandoned, the result is a God who is not to be desired and enjoyed; and to possess God for the sake of delivering the self from the bonds of self-centredness is, after all, to be faithful to the call of the Gospel (Mark 8: 36). If considerations of self are withdrawn, love will be operating in a vacuum. It is always a matter of giving and receiving; if only of giving, then whoever receives it is put in the awkward position of having obtained, however unreluctantly, a commodity which ought not to tarnish Christian love! Even if the Barthian position were accepted, it would still be unjust to accuse San Juan of teaching a grasping and possessive self-love as the culmination of the mystical quest.

Once more, the question why San Juan wrote in such terms needs to be asked. The answer is the same as with his language of transformation and absorption. The intensity of his mystical experience led him to boldness of language, to poetic and imaginative statements rather than

[46] ii. 1, 281.   [47] Petry, op. cit., p. 191.

trapping the experience in exact words, which would have been impossible. Such passages should not be treated as statements of formal theology; they suggest as much as they state. To treat them as though San Juan were consiously teaching man's absorption into God or his equality of being with the divine is to treat the language he uses as if it were part of a *Summa* rather than an approach to the ultimate mystery.

The problem of love issues in one practical consequence: the choice between the active and contemplative lives. San Juan, with the bulk of the tradition, asserts the superiority of the latter, the danger being that if this life is preferred, the soul will concentrate on the solitary road to God and fail in the love and service of others. San Juan, like Santa Teresa, spent much of his time and energy in the active service of his fellows, so that the problem is primarily of theoretical interest, and his views should be set alongside his example.

There are undercurrents of polemic in this question, which come to the fore in CB 29.2–3 (and the much longer discussion in L 3.46–61). San Juan explains that when the soul reaches this state of union it must abandon exterior works and exercises and concentrate on loving God alone, 'porque es más precioso delante de Dios y del alma un poquito de este puro amor y más provecho hace a la Iglesia, aunque parece que no hace nada, que todas estas obras juntas'.[48] Damage is done if such a soul has to busy itself about outward concerns, and it pleases God far more than those who spend all their time in such activities, by remaining alone with God. He is really addressing spiritual directors here, and one can understand why they would feel unhappy if one of their charges withdrew into solitary contemplation, which might degenerate into extreme self-indulgence, disguised as religious fervour. But the opposite danger, as observed by San Juan, was to interfere with genuine spiritual communications from God and prevent the soul from following the path God was indicating.

Barth criticizes the whole idea of contemplation as a Christian vocation, though when he refers to it as 'the first step on the mystic way' it is clear that he cannot be thinking of writers like San Juan.[49] Contemplation begins when God gives it, after meditation, and is certainly not the first step. Barth states that contemplation is not specifically Christian because it is found in the mystical techniques of other religions; but his main objection is theological: 'God withdraws from every kind of contemplation. For God acts. He acts through his Word'.[50] As God has been active in seeking out lost mankind, so man's proper response is actively to seek God: this is his theological justification for the supremacy of the active life. What he fails to recognize is that the contemplative life, as generally understood, ought to be just as

---

[48] Peers, ii. 328.   [49] iii. 4, 560.   [50] Ibid. 563.

much man's 'active' response to God. To speak of passivity and doing nothing, of the whole negative side of mystical teaching, is to tell only one part of the story. San Juan, after all, shared in a reform of his Order which made exceptional demands upon him. His life is not that of an escapist who merely wanted to placate his spiritual desires in his own way and on his own.

VI

It is time now to attempt an evaluation of San Juan's contribution to the theology of mysticism. His major achievement was surely to have classified, systematized, and subjected to rigorous theological analysis a whole range of mystical experiences which had often been described before, but never in so thoroughgoing a manner or with such keen intellectual penetration. His scholastic model of the human personality helps him to make this analysis: he can explain what happens to what part of a man, why certain phenomena are caused, and what their value is. All this can still be understood and appreciated in its broad outline, even though the terminology is strange to us. The substance of thought and the depth of insight remain an impressive testimony to a creative mind.

But his theological achievements are greater. First, he holds out the possibility of growth and progress in the Christian life, rescuing the religious instinct in man from bondage to imposed forms. He is a theology of human experience, however rarified; not of abstractions. He holds out this possibility of growth to the uneducated, poor, and simple. For them he describes a growth towards union with God through love rather than intellectual probing. He takes them beyond the normal institutional practices of religion, though he remains loyal to these. And he stresses the dignity of man, by claiming as his ultimate goal nothing less than union with the Creator, to be enjoyed eternally. Here he comes close to the Eastern Church's teaching on the deification of man: Christ has become man, so that man may rise with him to become God. The price he pays for this is a potentially dualistic approach to the relationship of soul and body and an apparently negative approach to the world of matter and the flesh, redeemed however by his vision of the creatures contemplated through God.

Moreover, there is a tremendous purity about his teaching. Suspicion of mysticism runs deep in certain quarters. Though San Juan teaches the use of certain aids to devotion which the Reformers would have condemned, these are only aids, and must be abandoned when union approaches, because to cling to them will hinder progress. He thus attacks all forms of real idolatry in a way the Reformers might have appreciated, had they been able to penetrate the thick shell of polemic to see the kernel of his teaching. God remains the ultimate mystery, beyond every human attempt to capture and confine him. But he is known in the love which he gives.

Nor is there any question of self-salvation. The higher reaches of prayer cannot be achieved. God may grant them, he may withhold them: that is up to him. In this way, San Juan is saying the same kind of thing as the Reformers, with their emphasis on justification by faith. Men cannot be saved by what they do: there has to be another way. Luther saw it as faith; San Juan, in his own way, agrees. Men are brought to God by what God has done and by their response to that action. If he calls them to enter the dark nights, they must respond and persevere, waiting for the dawn of his promise: 'Que no todos los que se exercitan de propósito en el camino del espíritu lleva Dios a contemplación, ni aun a la mitad (el porqué El se lo sabe)'.[51] Of course, Luther and San Juan *are* very different; but in their different ways they are both, perhaps, trying to feel after the same kind of balance between human effort and the divine initiative in salvation.

There are areas of San Juan's teaching which raise serious theological problems, notably the problem of authenticating mystical knowledge, the conflict between subjective religion and the objective historical revelation, the negation of the created order and the sharp distinction between body and soul. But he avoids the major pitfalls and does not teach self-salvation, withdrawal from the community's religious life, the dissolution of the self, or the identity of the ego and the One. There are reasons for his inadequacy in such areas, and they are to be found among the inevitable tensions of theology. And San Juan's importance as a theologian is best seen precisely here. He does not run away from the difficulties, by ignoring them or providing naïve answers. Ineffability preoccupies him, but he does not maintain that mystical experience is self-authenticating. In a remarkable way, he reflects the tension between the holy and transcendent God and the personal Father of each individual human. His teaching on creation finds him at one extreme; that on participation and equality of love, at the other. He does not try to build artificial bridges between these extremes, but moves freely from one to the other, depending on the experience he is describing. For they are the extremes of the Christian experience of God, and have to be held alongside one another. Sometimes man is stunned into awe and wonder before the majesty of God; sometimes he is swept up into an intimate communion with him. San Juan's is an eloquent witness to such a God. Merciless in his exposure of all that is not such a God, he provides an answer to the spiritual hunger of men couched not so much in the language of philosophy as of love.

Finally, a warning to emphasize what has been said about the danger

[51] N 1.9.9.; Peers, i. 356.

of treating San Juan as if he were a dogmatic theologian. In his 'After-thoughts', Butler observes:[52]

I hope it may not be deemed over venturesome for one not pledged by profession to any particular Catholic theological school to wonder if the rigid methods of speculative theology . . . really are helpful towards explaining the nature and the facts of mystical theology and of contemplation . . . There are no doubt minds to whom such schematizations . . . may appeal; but there are others to whom they do not. I confess myself one of the latter; and I have a feeling that many of the difficulties that have arisen . . . are occasioned by an undue pressing of theological theories.

The suggestion warrants thought. How can 'mystical theology', deliberately distinguished by San Juan and many others from scholastic theology, be treated as though it were another branch of that subject? Theological perception is required to see that it squares with Christian doctrine, but there is no need to divide mystical experience up into neat parcels. A middle way is needed, between uncritical acceptance of all mystical claims, and an over-rigid systematization of them.

Perhaps the time has come to qualify the term 'system', so often used in the course of this study. San Juan makes many divisions in his teaching, and they do not all fit one another. Their unity lies in the material they are analyzing, the mystical encounter itself. This is what the dark nights, the three ways, and the seven or ten degrees of love are pointing to: the same substance, but classified from a different angle. Purgation, illumination, and union go on throughout. One is not followed chronologically by the next. In that sense, perhaps, CA is a better guide to the ups and downs of experience than the more systematic CB, which puts everything in its proper place. Even CB warns us that this is so:[53]

Pero no se ha de entender que a todas las que llegan a este estado se les comunica todo lo que en estas dos canciones se declara, ni en una misma manera y medida de conocimiento y sentimiento; porque, a unas almas se les da más y otras menos, y a unas en una manera y a las otras en otra, aunque lo uno y lo otro puede ser en este estado del desposorio espiritual. Mas pónese aquí lo más que puede ser, porque en ello se comprehende todo.

And there San Juan tells us what he means by 'system': including all that can be included, so that everything is covered. It is a comprehensive survey of the subject, but not everyone will experience every element in it.

After all, a system does not reflect experience as it happens, haphazardly: it seeks to set all the possible experiences alongside one another, and to evaluate them in relation to each other, so that you know where you are. San Juan's is a reflective analysis of the questions which have arisen from his own experience, and should be treated like a map, on which he traces the best way between two points. From it you can discover where you are in relation to other places, whether you have made progress in the right direction, where the path should take you next. But not everyone will stick exactly to the path: there are many others, less clearly defined. And though the map illustrates in symbols the reality to be encountered, there are aspects of that reality it can never adequately communicate. So with the way of the mystic. San Juan's map is fuller than most, because he has reached sight of the destination and has brought a keen intellect and an outpouring of intense love to illuminate the way for other travellers.

It may be that San Juan has hit upon something of great and lasting significance. History has been deeply scarred by the violence and destruction men have worked on one another, and the healing of their alienation continues to escape them. One way is to pass laws to make people do what they ought to do. But it may be that a better way of attracting men to live in peace and for love is the way San Juan first used when he wanted to express the wonder and glory of the mystical union between man and God. Instead of spelling out in detail how the world may be set to right, it may be that the better way is to show them images of haunting beauty, which can play upon their minds and feelings, and draw them to the good not reluctantly, but gladly. Then, when they begin to understand and feel the call of love and become committed to its increase, then the details may follow as the beauty once glimpsed takes root and bears its reconciling fruit.

APPENDIX

An English Version of the *Cántico*

This version attempts to convey as faithfully as possible the sense of the original CA poem (with CB 11) without reducing it to plain prose or altering it to fit the English into the tight structure of the *lira* form.

BRIDE
1. Where is it that you hid,
Beloved, and left me to lament?
Like the stag you fled,
having wounded me,
calling, I came out after you, and you were gone.

2. Shepherds, who might go
there through the sheepfold to the hill,
if you should chance to see
him whom most I love,
tell him that I suffer, grieve, and die.

3. Searching for my loves
I'll go over these mountains and riversides;
I shall not pick the flowers,
nor shall I fear the wild beasts,
and I shall pass fortresses and frontiers.

QUESTION TO THE CREATURES
4. Oh woods and thickets
planted by the hand of the Beloved!
Oh meadow all of green
enamelled with flowers,
say if he has passed through you!

REPLY OF THE CREATURES
5. Showering down a thousand graces
he passed through these thickets swiftly
and, looking on them as he went by,
with his countenance alone
he left them in beauty clothed.

BRIDE
6. Alas! and who can heal me?
Yield yourself at last, and truly.
Do not send me
from this day on another messenger;
for they cannot tell me what I desire.

7. And all who wander
come telling me a thousand of your graces,
and all wound me the more,
and there leaves me dying
I know not what that they are stammering.

8. But how do you persevere,
Oh life, not living where you live?
and treating so that you die
the arrows you receive
from what of the Beloved within you you conceive?

9. Why, since you have wounded
this heart, did you not heal it?
And since you stole it from me,
why did you leave it thus
and fail to take the plunder you have stolen?

10. Extinguish my complaints,
since none is sufficient to undo them,
and let my eyes see you,
since you are their light,
and for you alone do I desire to have them.

(CB 11) Reveal your presence,
and let your sight and beauty kill me;
consider the sickness
of love, which is not cured
save by presence and the countenance.

11. Oh crystalline fountain!
If in these your silvered features
you should suddenly form
the eyes I long for
which in my inmost self I have portrayed!

12. Withdraw them, Beloved,
for I go flying!

BRIDEGROOM
Return, dove,
for the wounded stag
appears on the hill
in the breeze of your flight, and takes refreshment.

BRIDE
13. My Beloved, the mountains,
the solitary, wooded valleys,
the strange islands,
the resounding rivers,
the whistling of the loving breezes,

14. the peaceful night
before the rising of the dawn,
the hushed music,
the resonant solitude,
the supper which recreates and causes love.

15. Our flowering bed,
entwined with lions' dens,
decked out in purple,
built of peace,
crowned with a thousand shields of gold.

16. In pursuit of your track
the maidens run along to the road
to the touch of the spark,
to the spiced wine,
outpourings of divine balsam.

17. In the inner cellar
of my Beloved I drank, and when I came forth
along all this riverside
I knew not a thing,
and I lost the flock which formerly I followed.

18. There he gave me his breast,
there he taught me very appetizing knowledge,
and I gave to him indeed
myself, leaving not a thing;
there I promised him to be his bride.

19. My soul has been taken up
and all my treasure in his service.
No longer do I keep a flock,
nor have I any other office now,
for now alone in love is my employment.

20. So now, if on the common pasture
from this day forth I be not seen or met,
you'll say I've gone astray;
for, being in love,
I was lost, and now am found.

21. From flowers and emeralds
On fresh mornings chosen,
we shall make garlands,
flowering in your love,
and woven into one strand of my hair.

22. In that strand alone
which you looked at flying on my neck,
you looked at it on my neck,
and on it you were caught,
and in one of my eyes you were wounded.

23. When you used to look at me,
their grace your eyes upon me would imprint;
for that reason you loved me well,
and for it mine deserved
to adore what they saw in you.

24. Do not despise me,
for, if you found dark colouring on me,
well may you look upon me
after you looked upon me,
for on me you left grace and beauty.

25. Catch for us the vixen,
for already our vine is flowering,
while from roses
we make a bouquet,
and let no one appear upon the mountain.

26. Cease, you dead north wind;
come, you south wind, reawakening love;
blow through my garden,
and let its scents run free,
and the Beloved will feed among the flowers.

BRIDEGROOM

27. Entered has the bride
into the delightful garden she desired,
and at her pleasure rests,
her neck reclining
upon the sweet arms of the Beloved.

28. Underneath the apple-tree,
there you were betrothed to me,
there I gave you my hand,
and you were restored
where your mother had been violated.

29. You light birds,
lions, stags, leaping deer,
mountains, valleys, riversides,
waters, breezes, ardours,
and watchful fears of nights:

30. By pleasant lyres
and sirens' song, I call upon you
to cease from your anger
and not to touch the wall
so that the bride can sleep more safely.

BRIDE

31. Oh nymphs of Judaea!
while among the flowers and rose-trees
the amber gives off perfume,
stay in the outskirts,
and do not touch our portals.

32. Hide, my sweet darling,
and look upon the mountains with your visage,
and do not say it;
but look at the companies
of her who goes among strange islands.

BRIDEGROOM

33. The white dove
to the ark with the branch has returned;
and already the turtle-dove
her desired mate
by the green riversides has found.

34. In solitude she lived,
and in solitude already she has built her nest,
and in solitude her beloved
guides her all alone,
likewise by love in solitude wounded.

BRIDE

35. Let us rejoice, Beloved,
and let us go to see in your beauty
the mount and the hill
where the pure water flows;
let us enter further into the thicket.

36. And then to the lofty
caverns of stone we shall go,
which are well hidden,
and there we shall enter,
and we shall taste the juice of pomegranates.

37. There you would show me
what my soul was claiming,
and there you would give me,
you, there, my life,
what you gave to me before:

38. The blowing of the breeze,
the song of sweet Philomel,
the thicket and its loveliness
in the calm night,
with a flame which consumes and gives no pain.

39. For nobody was looking . . .
Nor did Aminadab appear;
and the siege was subsiding,
and the cavalry
in sight of the waters was descending.

BIBLIOGRAPHY

I. TEXT

1. *Manuscripts*

Jaén, Carmelite Convent, MS. Arch.n.531.
Sanlúcar de Barrameda, Discalced Carmelite Convent (photographed edition, ed. P. Silverio de Santa Teresa, 2 vols., Burgos, 1928).
Segovia, Carmelite Fathers.

2. *Early editions and translations*
(arranged chronologically)

Obras espirituales que encaminan a una alma a la perfecta unión con Dios (Alcalá, 1618).
Obras espirituales . . . Con una resunta de la vida del Autor y unos discursos (Barcelona, 1619).
Cantique d'amour divin entre Iésvs-Christ et l'âme dévote composé en espagnol par le B. Père Jean de la Croix . . . Traduit par M. René Gaultier, Conseiller d'Estat. (Paris, 1622).
Declaración de las Canciones que tratan del exercicio de amor entre el alma y el esposo Cristo en la cual se tocan, y declaran algunos puntos, y efectos de oración (Brussels, 1627).
Opere spirituali che conducono l'anima alla perfetta unione con Dio (Rome, 1627).
Cantico Espiritual entre el alma y Cristo su Esposo en que se declaran varios y tiernos afectos de Oración y Contemplación, en la interior comunicación con Dios (Madrid, 1630).
Opera Mystica V. ac Mystici Doctoris F. Joannis a Cruce . . . ex Hispanico idiomate in Latinum nunc primum translata per . . . Andream a Jesu (Cologne, 1639).
Obras espirituales que encaminan a una alma a la más perfecta unión con Dios, en transformacion de amor (Seville, 1703).

3. *Modern editions*
(arranged chronologically)

Gerardo de San Juan de la Cruz, *Obras del místico doctor San Juan de la Cruz*, 3 vols. (Toledo, 1912–14).
Chevallier, Philippe, *Le "Cantique spirituel" de saint Jean de la Croix* (Desclée, Paris, 1930).
Silverio de Santa Teresa, *Obras de San Juan de la Cruz, doctor de la Iglesia*, 5 vols. (Biblioteca Mística Carmelitana 10–14, Burgos, 1930).
Peers, E. Allison, *The Complete Works of Saint John of the Cross*, translated from the edition of Silverio de Santa Teresa, 3 vols. (Burns Oates, London, 1935; revised edition, 1953).
Chevallier, Philippe, *Le texte définitif du "Cantique spirituel"* (Abbaye Saint Pierre de Solesmes, 1950).
Simeón de la Sagrada Familia, *San Juan de la Cruz: Obras completas* (El Monte Carmelo, Burgos, 1959).
Crisógono de Jesús, Matías del Niño, Lucinio Ruano, *Vida y obras de San Juan de la Cruz*, 6th edn. (Biblioteca de autores cristianos, Madrid, 1972).

II. OTHER TEXTS

Aquinas, St. Thomas, *Summa Theologiae*, ed. Gilby and O'Brien, 60 vols. (Eyre & Spottiswode, London/New York, 1964–).

Augustine, St., *De Trinitate*, in Library of Christian Classics VIII, 38–181. (S.C.M., London, 1955).

Bernard of Clairvaux, St., *St. Bernard on the Love of God*, ed. E. Gardner (London etc., 1915).

–– *On the Song of Songs*, trans. K. Walsh (I.U.P., Shannon, 1971).

Bernardino de Laredo, *Subida del Monte Sión*, in *Místicos franciscanos* ii. 25–442 (Biblioteca de autores cristianos, Madred, 1948).

Biblia Vulgata iuxta Vulgatam Clementinam, ed. Colunga and Turrado, 4th edn. (Biblioteca de autores cristianos, Madrid, 1965).

'Book of the Institution of the First Monks', translated B. Edwards (Boars Hill, Oxford, 1969).

Cloud of Unknowing, The, translated and ed. C. Wolters (Penguin, Harmondsworth, 1961).

Córdoba, Sebastián de, *Las obras de Boscán y Garcilasso trasladadas en materias Christianas y religiosas* (Granada, 1575 and Zaragoza, 1577).

–– *Garcilaso a lo divino*, ed. G. Gale (Castalia, Madrid, 1971).

Dionysius the Areopagite, *Oeuvres complètes du Pseudo-Denys l'Aréapagite*, translated and ed. M. de Gandillac (Paris, 1943).

Eliot, T. S., *Four Quartets* (Faber, London, 1959).

Erasmus, Desiderius, *Colloquios de Erasmo*, in Nueva biblioteca de autores españoles, *Orígenes de la novela* iv. 149–249 (Madrid, 1915).

–– *El Enquiridión o manual del cavallero cristiano*, ed. D. Alonso, in *RFE*, Anejo 16 (Madrid, 1932).

Garcilaso de la Vega, *Obras completas*, ed. E. Rivers (Columbus, 1964).

Góngora, Luis de, *Góngora y el "Polifemo"*, ed. D. Alonso, 2 vols., 4th edn. (Gredos, Madrid, 1961).

Herrera, Fernando de, *Poesías* (Clásicos Castellanos, Madrid, 1914).

Hilton, Walter, *The Scale of Perfection*, translated by G. Sitwell (London, 1953).

Irenaeus, St., *Selections from the Work against Heresies*, in Library of Christian Classics I. 343–97 (S.C.M., London, 1953).

Jewish Poets of Spain, The, ed. D. Goldstein, 2nd edn. (Penguin, Harmondsworth, 1965).

Kempis, Thomas à, *The Imitation of Christ*, translated and ed. L. Sherley-Price (Penguin, Harmondsworth, 1952).

Late Medieval Mysticism, ed. R. Petry, in Library of Christian Classics XIII (S.C.M., London, 1957).

Law, William, *Select Mystical Writings of William Law*, ed. S. Hobhouse, 2nd edn. (London, 1948).

Lazarillo de Tormes, La vida de, ed. R. O. Jones (M.U.P., Manchester, 1963).

Luis de León, *Obras completas castellanas*, ed. F. García, 2 vols. (Biblioteca de autores cristianos, Madrid, 1957).

Marvell, Andrew, *The Poems and Letters of Andrew Marvell*, ed. H. M. Margoliouth, 2 vols., 3rd edn. (Oxford, 1971).

Menéndez Pidal, Ramón, *Flor nueva de romances viejos* (Espasa-Calpe, Buenos Aires, 1938).

Milton, John, *Milton: Poetical Works*, ed. D. Bush (London/Oxford, 1969).

Origen, *The Song of Songs: Commentary and Homilies*, ed. R. Lawson, in Ancient Christian Writers xxvi (Longmans Green, London. 1957).

Osuna, Francisco de, *Tercer abecedario espiritual*, ed. M. Andes (Biblioteca de autores cristianos, Madrid, 1972).

Oxford Book of Portuguese Verse, The, ed. B. Vidigal, 2nd ed. (Oxford, 1952).
Rolle, Richard, *The Fire of Love*, translated and ed. C. Wolters (Penguin, Harmondsworth, 1972).
Teresa de Jesús, Santa, *Obras completas*, ed. E. de la Madre de Dios and O. Steggink, 2nd edn. (Biblioteca de autores cristianos, Madrid, 1967).
Valdés, Alfonso de, *Diálogo de las cosas ocurridas en Roma*, ed. J. Montesinos (Clásicos Castellanos, Madrid, 1956).
— — *Diálogo de Mercurio y Carón*, ed. J. Montesinos (Clásicos Castellanos, Madrid, 1965).
Valdés, Juan de, *Diálogo de doctrina christiana*, ed. D. Ricart (Mexico, 1964).
Villalón, Cristóbal de, *El Crotalón*, in Nueva biblioteca de autores españoles, *Orígenes de la novela* ii, 119–250 (Madrid, 1907).
— — *Viaje de Turquía*, ed. A. Solalinde, 4th edn. (Espasa-Calpe, Madrid, 1965).

III. CRITICISM

1. *General Studies*

Baruzi, Jean, *Saint Jean de la Croix et le problème de l'expérience mystique*, 2nd edn. (Paris, 1931).
Bouterwek, Frederick, *History of Spanish and Portuguese Literature*, 2 vols. (London, 1823).
Brenan, Gerald, *St. John of the Cross: His Life and Poetry* (C.U.P., Cambridge, 1973).
Cilveti, Angel L., *Introducción a la mística española* (Cátedra, Madrid, 1974).
Crisógono de Jesús, *San Juan de la Cruz, su obra científica y su obra literaria*, 2 vols. (Ávila, 1929).
Eulogio de la Virgen del Carmen, *San Juan de la Cruz y sus escritos* (Madrid, 1969).
Luis de San José, *Concordancias de las obras y escritos* (Burgos, 1948).
Morel, Georges, *Le sens de l'existence selon saint Jean de la Croix*, 3 vols. (Paris, 1960–1).
Ottonello, Pier Paolo, *Bibliografia di S. Juan de la Cruz* (Teresianum, Rome, 1967).
Peers, E. Allison, *Studies of the Spanish Mystics*, 3 vols. (London etc. 1927–60).
— — *St. John of the Cross and Other Lectures and Addresses* (London, 1946).
— — *Handbook to the Life and Times of Saint Teresa and Saint John of the Cross* (London, 1954).
Ruano, Nazario, *Desnudez: lo místico y lo literario en San Juan de la Cruz* (Mexico, 1961).
Ruiz Salvador, Federico, *Introducción a San Juan de la Cruz* (Biblioteca de autores cristianos, Madrid, 1968).
Sismondi, Simonde de, *De la littérature du midi de l'Europe*, 3rd edn., 4 vols. (Paris, 1829).
Ticknor, George, *History of Spanish Literature*, 3 vols. (London, 1863).

2. *Textual Criticism*

Baruzi, Jean, 'Le problème des citations scriptuaires en langue latine dans l'œuvre de saint Jean de la Croix', *BH* 24 (1922), 18–40.
Bataillon, Marcel, Review of Dom Chevallier's critical edition (Paris, 1930), *BH* 33 (1931), 164–70.
— — Review of Krynen, *BH*, 51 (1949), 188–94.
Carlo, Agustín Millares, and José Ignacio Mantecón, *Album de paleografía hispano-americana de los siglos XVI y XVII*, 3 vols. (Mexico, 1955).
Chandebois, Henri, 'Lexique, grammaire et style chez St Jean de la Croix', *EC* 3 (1949), 543–7, and 4 (1950), 361–8.

Chevallier, Philippe, 'Le "Cantique spirituel" de saint Jean de la Croix a-t-il été interpolé?', *BH* 24 (1922), 307–42.

— — 'Le "Cantique spirituel" interpolé', a series of seven articles, *VS* supplements (1926–31).

Duvivier, Roger, *La Genèse de "Cantique spirituel" de saint Jean de la Croix* (Paris, 1971).

— — *Le Dynamisme existentiel dans la poésie de Jean de la Croix* (Paris, 1973).

Eulogio de la Virgen del Carmen, 'La Sagrada Escritura y la cuestión de la segunda redacción del "Cántico espiritual" de San Juan de la Cruz', *EC* 5 (1951–4), 249–475.

— — 'Un manuscrito famoso del "Cántico espiritual": las notas del códice de Sanlúcar de Barrameda y su valor crítica', *MC* 62 (1954), 155–203.

— — *El "Cántico espiritual"–trayectoria histórica del texto* (Teresianum, Rome, 1967).

— — 'Primeras ediciones del "Cántico espiritual" ', *EC* 18 (1967), 3–48.

Gerardo de San Juan de la Cruz, *Los autógrafos que se conservan del Místico Doctor San Juan de la Cruz* (Toledo, 1913).

Juan de Jesús María, '¿Las anotaciones del códice de Sanlúcar, son de S. Juan de la Cruz?', *EC* 1 (1947), 154–62.

— — 'El valor crítico del texto escrito por la primera mano en el códice de Sanlúcar de Barrameda', *EC* 1 (1947), 313–66.

— — 'La segunda redacción del "Cántico espiritual" y el comentario al mismo de Agustín Antolínez, O.S.A.', *MC* 53 (1949), 13–37.

— — 'El *Cántico espiritual* de San Juan de la Cruz y *Amores de Dios y el Alma* de A. Antolínez, O.S.A.', *EC* 3 (1949), 443–542, and 4 (1950), 3–70.

— — 'La última palabra de dom Chevallier sobre el "Cántico espiritual" ', *MC* 60 (1952), 309–402.

Krynen, Jean, 'Un Aspect nouveau des annotations marginales du "borrador" du "Cantique spirituel" de saint Jean de la Croix', *BH* 49 (1947), 400–21, and 53 (1951), 393–412.

— — *Le "Cantique spirituel" de saint Jean de la Croix commenté et réfondu au xviie siècle: un regard sur l'histoire de l'exégèse du Cantique de Jaén* (Salamanca, 1948).

— — 'Du nouveau sur Thomas de Jésus', *BH* 64 bis (1962), 113–35.

Ledrus, M., 'Sur quelques pages inédites de saint Jean de la Croix', *Gregorianum,* 30 (1949), 347–92, and 32 (1951), 247–80.

— — 'Les "Singularités" de second *Cantique*', *Gregorianum,* 33 (1952), 438–50.

Simeón de la Sagrada Familia, 'Un neuevo códice manuscrito de las obras de San Juan de la Cruz usado y anotado por el P. Tomás de Jesús', *EC* 4 (1950), 95–148.

— — 'Tomás de Jesús y San Juan de la Cruz', *EC* 5 (1951–4), 91–159.

— — 'Nueva copia manuscrita de las obras completas de San Juan de la Cruz', *Archivum Bibliographicum Carmelitanum,* 3 (1958), 247–50.

— — 'Tríptico sanjuanista', *EC* 11 (1960), 197–233.

Vilnet, Jean, *Bible et mystique chez saint Jean de la Croix* (Desclée, Paris, 1949).

3. *Literary Criticism*

Alonso, Dámaso, *Poesía española* (Gredos, Madrid, 1950).

— — 'La poesía de San Juan de la Cruz', *Boletín del Instituto Caro y Cuervo,* 4 (1948), 492–515.

— — *La poesía de San Juan de la Cruz,* 4th edn. (Aguilar, Madrid, 1966).

Bataillon, Marcel, 'La tortolica de "Fontefrida" y del "Cántico espiritual" ', *NRFE* 7 (1953), 291–306.

Blecua, José M., 'Los antecedentes del poema del "Pastorcico" de San Juan de la Cruz', *RFE* 33 (1949), 378–80.

Cossío, José M. de, 'Rasgos renacentiastas y populares en el "Cántico espiritual" ', *Escorial* 25 (1942), 205–28.

Crosbie, John, 'Amoral "a lo divino" poetry in the Golden Age', *MLR* 66 (1971), 599–607.

Cuevas García, Cristóbal, 'La prosa métrica en Fray Bernardino de Laredo', *RL* 35 (1969), 5–51.

Curtius, Ernst, *European Literature and the Latin Middle Ages*, translated by W. Task (London, 1953).

Emeterio de Jesús María, *Las raíces de la poesía sanjuanista y Dámaso Alonso* (Burgos, 1950).

Eulogio de la Virgen del Carmen, 'El "Prólogo" y la hermenéutica del "Cántico espiritual" ', *MC* 66 (1958), 3–108.

—— 'La clave exegética del "Cántico espiritual" ', *EC* 9 (1958), 307–37, and 11 (1960), 312–51.

—— 'Estructura literal del "Cántico espiritual" ', *MC* 68 (1960), 383–414.

Fletcher, Angus, *Allegory: The Theory of a Symbolic Mode* (Ithaca/London, 1970).

García Lorca, Francisco, *De Fray Luis a San Juan: La escondida senda* (Madrid, 1972).

Glaser, Edward, ' "El cobre convertido en oro"—Christian 'rifacimentos' of Garcilaso's poetry in the sixteenth and seventeenth centuries', *HR* 37 (1969), 61–76.

Guillén, Jorge, *Language and Poetry: Some Poets of Spain* (Cambridge, Mass., 1961).

Hatzfeld, Helmut, *Estudios literarios sobre mística española* (Gredos, Madrid, 1955).

Honig, Edwin, *Dark Conceit: The Making of Allegory* (New York, 1966).

Icaza, Rosa María, *The Stylistic Relationship between Poetry and Prose in the "Cántico espiritual" of San Juan de la Cruz* (Catholic University of America, Washington DC, 1957).

Lida, María Rosa, 'La poesía de San Juan de la Cruz', *RFH* 5 (1943), 377–95.

Martí, Antonio, 'La retórica sacra en el siglo de oro', *HR* 38 (1970), 264–98.

—— *La preceptiva retórica española en el siglo de oro* (Madrid, 1972).

Morales, José L., *El "Cántico espiritual" de San Juan de la Cruz: su relación con el Cantar de los Cantares y otras fuentes escrituristicas y literarias* (Madrid, 1971).

Orozco, Emilio, *Poesía y mística* (Madrid, 1959).

Peers, E. Allison, 'The alleged debts of San Juan de la Cruz to Boscán and Garcilaso de la Vega', *HR* 21 (1953), 1–19, 93–106.

Pérez Embid, Florentino, 'El tema del aire en la poesía de San Juan de la Cruz', *Arbor* 5 (1946), 93–8.

Ricard, Robert, ' "La Fonte" de saint Jean de la Croix et un chapître de Laredo', *BH* 58 (1956), 265–74.

Sonnino, Lee, *A Handbook to Sixteenth-Century Rhetoric* (Routledge & Kegan Paul, London, 1968).

Tillmans, W. G., *De aanwezigheid van het bijbels hooglied in het "Cántico espiritual" van San Juan de la Cruz* (Brussels, 1967).

Vega, Angel C., *Cumbres místicas* (Aguilar, Madrid, 1963).

Wardropper, Bruce W., *Historia de la poesía lírica a lo divino en la cristiandad occidental* (Madrid, 1958).

Wimsatt, W.K., *The Verbal Icon* (New York, 1958).

Yndurain, Francisco, 'Mística y poesía en San Juan de la Cruz', *RL* 3 (1953), 9–15.

4. *History and Theology*

Allgeier, Arthur, 'Erasmus und Kardinal Ximenes in den Verhandlungen des Konzils von Trient', *Spanische Forschungen der Görresgesellschaft*, 4 (1933), 193–205.

Barth, Karl, *Church Dogmatics*, 13 vols. (Edinburgh, 1936–69).

Bataillon, Marcel, *Erasmo y España*, 2nd ed. (Mexico, 1966).

Benedictine of Stanbrook Abbey, A, *Mediaeval Mystical Tradition and Saint John of the Cross* (Burns Oates, London, 1954).

Bord, André, *Mémoire et espérance chez Jean de la Croix* (Paris, 1971).

Bruno de Jésus-Marie, *L'Espagne mystique au 16e siècle* (Paris, 1946).

Bruno de San José, 'El senequismo y San Juan de la Cruz', *MC* 46 (1942), 381–424.

Butler, Cuthbert, *Western Mysticism*, 3rd edn., with *Afterthoughts* (Constable, London, 1967).

Chevallier, Philippe, 'La Doctrine ascétique de saint Jean de la Croix', *VS* 16 (1927), 175–96.

Copleston, F. C., *Aquinas* (Penguin, Harmondsworth, 1955).

Crisógono de Jesús, 'Introducción al estudio de la filosofía en el misticismo de San Juan de la Cruz', *RE* 1 (1941–2), 231–40.

Daniélou, Jean, *Origen*, translated W. Mitchell (London/New York, 1955).

D'Arcy, M.C., *The Mind and Heart of Love*, 2nd edn. (London, 1954).

Dictionnaire de théologie catholique, ed. A. Vacant, E. Mangenot, E. Amann, 15 vols. (Paris, 1925–50).

Efrén de la Madre de Dios, 'La esperanza según San Juan de la Cruz', *RE* 1 (1941–2), 255–81.

Gabriel de Santa María Magdalena, 'L'Union transformante', *VS* 16 (1927), 223–54.

Garrigou-Lagrange, Réginald, 'La Nuit de l'esprit selon saint Jean de la Croix', *VS* 16 (1927), 197–222.

–– 'Saint Thomas et saint Jean de la Croix', *VS* (supplement), 25 (1930), 16–37.

Grant, Robert M., *The Bible in the Church* (New York, 1960).

Hanson, R. P. C., *Allegory and Event* (S.C.M., London, 1959).

Hardman, Sister Anne, *Life of the Venerable Anne of Jesus* (London, 1932).

Hügel, Friedrich von, *The Mystical Element of Religion as studied in Saint Catherine of Genoa and Her Friends*, 2 vols. (London/New York, 1908).

Huizinga, Johan, *The Waning of the Middle Ages*, translated F. Hopman (London, 1937).

Inge, W. R., *Christian Mysticism* (The Bampton Lectures, London, 1899).

James, William, *The Varieties of Religious Experience* (The Gifford Lectures, 1901–2; The Fontana Library, 1960).

Jedin, Hubert, *A History of the Council of Trent*, translated E. Graf. 2 vols. (Nelson, London etc., 1957–).

Kenny, Anthony, ed., *Aquinas: A Collection of Critical Essays* (New York, 1969).

Knowles, David, *The English Mystical Tradition* (London, 1961).

Lenferink, Pancratius, 'Bibliography of the Printed Carmelite Breviaries and Missals', (Teresianum, Rome, 1955).

Lewis, C. S., *The Allegory of Love*, with corrections (Oxford/London, 1938).

Longhurst, J.E., *Erasmus and the Spanish Inquisition: The Case of Juan de Valdés* (Albuquerque, 1950).

McConica, J. K., *English Humanists and Reformation Politics* (Oxford, 1965).

Maritain, J., *The Degrees of Knowledge*, translated B. Wall and M. Adamson (London, 1937).

–– *True Humanism*, translated M. Adamson (London, 1938).

Márquez, A., *Los alumbrados: orígenes y filosofía 1525–1559*, (Taurus, Madrid, 1972).

Menéndez Pelayo, Marcelino, *Historia de los heterodoxos españoles*, first published 1882 (Biblioteca de autores cristianos, 2 vols., 2nd ed., Madrid, 1965–7).

Miguel Angel Diez de Santa Teresa, 'La "reentrega" de amor así en la tierra como en el cielo', *EC* 13 (1962), 299–352.

More, P. E., *Christian Mysticism: A Critique* (London, 1932).

Nieto, José C., 'Two Spanish Mystics as Submissive Rebels', *BHR* 33 (1971), 63–77.

— — 'Mystical Theology and "Salvation-History" in John of the Cross: Two Conflicting Methods of Biblical Interpretation', *BHR* 36 (1974), 17–32.

Nygren, Anders, *Agape and Eros*, translated P. Watson (London, 1953).

Olmedo, Félix G., *Juan Bonifacio* (Santander, 1938).

Ozment, Steven E., *Mysticism and Dissent* (New Haven/London, 1973).

Payne, Robert, *The Holy Fire* (London, 1958).

Ricard, Robert, 'Notes et matériaux por l'étude du "socratisme chrétien" chez sainte Thérése et les spirituels espagnols', *BH* 49 (1947), 15–37, 170–204.

Román de la Inmaculada, 'El fenómeno de los alumbrados y su interpretación', *EC* 9 (1958), 49–80.

Selke de Sánchez, Angela, 'El caso del bachiller Antonio de Medrano, iluminado epicúreo del siglo xvi', *BH* 58 (1956), 393–420.

Smalley, Beryl, *The Study of the Bible in the Middle Ages*, originally published 1940 (Indiana, 1970).

Stace, W. T., *Mysticism and Philosophy* (Macmillan, London, 1961).

Tillich, Paul, *Systematic Theology*, 3 vols. (combined volume, Nisbet, Welwyn, 1968).

Trevor Roper, H. R., *Historical Essays* (London, 1957).

Trueman Dicken, E. W., *The Crucible of Love* (London, 1963).

— — 'The Imagery of the Interior Castle and its Implications', *EC* 21 (1970), 198–218.

Underhill, Evelyn, *Mysticism* (London, 1911).

— — *The Mystic Way* (London/Toronto, 1913).

Zaehner, R. C., *Mysticism Sacred and Profane* (Oxford etc., 1961).

INDEX